ALSO BY DOUGLAS WHYNOTT

Giant Bluefin

Following the Bloom

A Unit of Water, a Unit of Time

A Country Practice

A
COUNTRY
PRACTICE

Scenes from the
VETERINARY LIFE

DOUGLAS WHYNOTT

North Point Press

A DIVISION OF FARRAR, STRAUS AND GIROUX

NEW YORK

North Point Press
A division of Farrar, Straus and Giroux
19 Union Square West, New York 10003

Copyright © 2004 by Douglas Whynott
All rights reserved
Distributed in Canada by Douglas & McIntyre Ltd.
Printed in the United States of America
First edition, 2004

Library of Congress Cataloging-in-Publication Data
Whynott, Douglas, 1950–
    A country practice : scenes from the veterinary life / Douglas Whynott.— 1st ed.
      p.   cm.
    ISBN-13: 978-0-86547-647-9
    ISBN-10: 0-86547-647-0
    1. Shaw, Chuck.   2. Veterinarians—New Hampshire—Walpole—Biography.
  3. Veterinary medicine—New Hampshire—Walpole.   I. Title.

SF613.S43W58 2004
636.089'092—dc22

                                                      2004006201

Designed by Abby Kagan

www.fsgbooks.com

1   3   5   7   9   10   8   6   4   2

This is a work of nonfiction. The events depicted in this book are true, but the names of
some people and their animals have been changed for the sake of privacy.

For Kathy Olsen

That is what caring really is, a feeling of identification with what one's doing. When one has this feeling then he also sees the inverse side of caring, Quality itself.

—Robert Pirsig,
Zen and the Art of Motorcycle Maintenance

CONTENTS

1 The Surgeon   3

2 The Associate   27

3 Old Home Days   50

4 Death Week at the Clinic   75

5 Teaching Points   98

6 The Third Vet   121

7 What You Do Well   144

8 A Horse Rescue   167

9 Feeling Bovine   186

10 The Line of Separation   209

11 Spring Arrivals   231

12 The Review   254

Epilogue   276

Acknowledgments   287

A Country Practice

1

THE SURGEON

1.

On New Year's Eve of Chuck Shaw's first year in Walpole, New Hampshire, a few months after he had bought his veterinary practice, he got a call from a policeman in Bellows Falls, Vermont, across the Connecticut River. A dog had been found in a snowbank after he had been hit by a car—an HBC, as it is called—and the police wanted to bring him in to be euthanized.

They met at the clinic, and Chuck took custody of the dog, but he didn't put him down. Maybe an owner would show up, he said. As a new vet with a small practice, Chuck held his patients dear. He was one to take an animal home and put it in a box in his bedroom at night if he thought it needed watching over. Chuck stabilized the dog, sewed up his cuts, and put him in a cage for the night.

A dog heals quickly, and soon this one was up and walking around. Chuck named him Duffer. He was a mongrel, likely a Lab and setter cross, with a feathered tail and a happy-to-see-you personality. With no word coming from Bellows Falls about an owner, Chuck began to search for a home for Duffer. Of course the possibility existed that if no one adopted him within a few months, Chuck might euthanize him. Such was the nature of the business. Until then, Duffer could serve as a blood donor if Chuck needed one. Veterinarians often keep a big dog around for that purpose, or they know of a farm dog who can serve as a candidate.

Duffer soon revealed a special talent—that of an escape artist. Each night when Chuck went home, he locked Duffer in one of the cages, and each morning Duffer was out and waiting. He didn't do any damage, just flipped the latch or undid the cord. Chuck was alternately amused and annoyed. He didn't want animals getting out of his cages.

March came, and Duffer still had not been placed in a home. Then came the fateful day, late that month, when Chuck got a call about another dog who had been hit by a car. The owner was one of Chuck's clients, and it was clear that the animal would need extensive surgery and a lot of blood. Chuck looked at Duffer and said, "Your time has come." He began the surgery, and when he had taken the blood he needed, he gave Duffer the fatal injection. Chuck set Duffer out in the garage and made a mental note to dispose of him later, but with the rush of cases soon forgot Duffer was there. He finished the surgery, made a farm call, and went home for the night.

The next morning at the clinic, Chuck was looking at his appointment schedule when he heard a scratching at the door. He wondered if an animal had gotten out. He opened the door, and in stumbled Duffer. He looked as if he had had a very bad night, as if he was wondering what had happened. He shook himself off, cold and bewildered, but happy to be in the warm treatment room again, and happy to see Chuck. Chuck was amazed that he could have survived the loss of blood, not to mention the injection. He said, "This dog is going to live. This dog is a survivor." He adopted Duffer then and there, and took him home that night.

Later, Chuck established a policy that no healthy animal would be euthanized at his clinic. In the meantime Duffer became the first in a long line of clinic pets. It was a good idea to have a pet at the clinic. A healthy animal could be a reassuring sight to a worried client, or an anxious pet, or a staff member who had seen a bit too much real life on a particular day.

Chuck brought Duffer to the clinic for four more years, until one day Duffer wandered off. Chuck searched in the brush and the woods around the clinic throughout the day, until he concluded that Duffer had gone off to die. An escape artist to the end.

Two decades later, at Chuck's new clinic on Route 12, a door opened from the treatment area into the reception room and a light shone through, but no person came out. Instead, out walked a cat, stubby-legged and rotund, with short gray hair, a white shirtfront, and little white bootlets. His name was Hobbs, and he was the current clinic pet.

Hobbs was a survivor too. He had once been a feral cat, scarred and infected from fights, living on a diet of whatever he could catch or scavenge. But his feral days were long behind him, and the lean scavenger had become an overweight fourteen-pound pussycat. His obesity was one reason Hobbs was not supposed to be in the reception room; he did not send a good message about nutrition and weight control. Hobbs also got into trouble out front. He walked on the computer keyboard and froze the system. He used the rubber plant as a litter box. And sometimes, being a former feral cat, he could get aggressive.

But Hobbs was a great clinic cat. He could give comfort. One day a client named Chase Romano brought her cat in for treatment. Chase owned a bookstore, and her handsome black cat, Bookcat—or Bookie—had developed a kidney problem. He had become dehydrated and needed daily subcutaneous injections of fluids that Chase was learning to give. She would also soon decide to take him on all of her book-buying trips, outfitting her van with a litter box. While they waited in the reception room, the door opened and a light shone through, but no person came out. Then Hobbs jumped up on the table in front of Chase, startling her. She later said, "I saw the fattest cat I've ever seen in my life. I don't know how he launched himself up on the table. Poor skinny little Bookie, and there was this huge fat gray cat, just looking at him. Staring at him, nose to nose. I had to laugh."

Now Hobbs squinted his green eyes with pleasure at the hand reaching down, and he walked back into the treatment room through the door I held open for him.

2.

In twenty-one years Chuck had treated thousands of animals. His patients consisted of several thousand cats and dogs, three thousand dairy cows, and, through his associate Roger Osinchuk, several hundred horses. His was a true mixed practice. Scattered around Walpole and other nearby towns were sheep, llamas, pigs, donkeys, birds, ferrets, goats, and guinea pigs that came under the umbrella of their care.

Many of his clients had stories about him. The dairy farmer who at first didn't trust the young doctor to work on his cows but put them under his care after Chuck saved his dog's life. The penniless client whose cat had a fishhook caught in her stomach. The woman who remembered that even though he disapproved, Chuck had put her dog down after her husband died. Over the years she had become grateful for his humane treatment.

Chuck was on call this weekend, which meant handling office appointments, overseeing treatments and feedings of boarders, and responding to emergency calls. Still doing it after all these years, Roger had said of Chuck and his dutiful approach to being on call. Roger meant to praise Chuck, but there was a touch of sarcasm. In this two-vet country practice, the on-call schedule could be brutal, as Roger well knew—and he had thought of leaving because of it. Chuck alternated with Roger, one of them on call every other weekend or every other weeknight. Being on call, with its demands on time and body, was possibly the most contentious issue among veterinarians. It was *the* issue, Chuck had said, because young vets were increasingly less willing to be on call.

Chuck's weekend had been typically busy. Friday night began with a long session with a client who had a seizuring border collie. After doing some research, Chuck told her that border collies are among the breeds susceptible to neurological problems. He decided to wait to see what developed. Then a call came in from a woman whose elderly dog had spinal problems and couldn't move. She brought the dog to the clinic, and Chuck examined her in the backseat of the woman's car. The dog's spine was making crunching sounds, and Chuck said that it didn't look good. He explained the treatments they could try and the injections he might give. He told her she could take the dog home, leave her for observation, or euthanize her. She decided to have a family discussion and then told Chuck they wanted to put the dog to sleep. She asked if he made house calls. He said he did, and followed them home.

He performed the euthanasia in their backyard, and just as he finished, his beeper went off. About a mile away, a Rottweiler had gotten a cross section of bone lodged over his lower jaw. Chuck said he would come right over. He wondered what he had in the car to sedate the dog, and rummaging through the boxes, he found a drug that he thought would work. When the arrived, he gave the Rottie a partial dose, and the dog became unconscious. Chuck tried to pull the bone off, but it was lodged too tightly. The owner said he had a hacksaw in the basement, and left to get it, but Chuck feared they would mangle the Rottie. He ran to his car, found some obstetrical wire, and cut the bone off before the owner came back with his saw.

Home again and preparing for dinner, Chuck got beeped for an HBC—a Lab that had run in front of a pickup truck. He met the owners at the clinic, and from 9:30 to 11:00 p.m. he got the dog stabilized for the corrective surgery he would do on Saturday. Then he went home and had dinner with his wife, Ellie.

On Saturday morning he went to a dairy farm and treated several sick cows, then returned to the clinic for office appointments. He gave an enema, the third, to a twenty-four-pound cat named Crunchy. He spent most of the afternoon mending the broken bones of the HBC Lab, using steel pins and wires.

At seven that night he got a call from someone whose parakeet had a bloody wing. "Wait and observe," Chuck told her. At midnight he got a call from a woman boarding three kittens for the Humane Society because of overcrowding. Two were healthy, but the third was vomiting. Chuck asked how long it had been vomiting, but the call struck him as rude. He finally asked the woman why she had waited so long and called him in the middle of the night.

An earlier call had not struck him as rude at all. It came from a woman named Sally Buttermore who lived in Charlestown, just north of Walpole on the Connecticut River. Chuck had known Sally for many years. She and her family lived in a mobile home with a large kennel attached. Sally bred terriers, and even though she didn't have a lot of money, she tried hard to take care of her animals. She said that someone had shot her cat with a .22 rifle and the bullet had gone through a hind leg. The cat was nursing four kittens.

Sally asked what it would cost to amputate the leg. Chuck didn't answer. He wanted to see where she was headed. He said only that he could amputate the leg.

"How much will it cost me to put her to sleep?" she asked.

"Two thousand dollars," Chuck said. Then, "You're not going to put that cat to sleep." One injustice had already been committed against the cat. He wasn't going to kill her for getting shot.

"How much can you pay for an amputation?" he asked.

After a moment Sally said, "We can pay a hundred dollars." That was about half of what Chuck would normally charge, but he knew a hundred dollars didn't come easily to this client. He made a deal with her. He would do the surgery on Sunday morning, and she would take the cat home on Sunday night. There would be no boarding.

Now the little cat was laid out on the table in the surgery. She was a calico, brown and gold and black, small and slender, her tiny nipples raised on her belly. She had a bloody crater on her rear leg.

Chuck bent over her, examining the leg. He was tall and lean, though he could easily turn gaunt and thin after long stretches of being on call. He had brown hair, gray above the ears, soft blue eyes, and thick eyebrows. He had been a navy pilot during the Vietnam War, flying an attack plane from a carrier. At times his rugged singularity seemed to suggest this experience. Though he could be charming and friendly—as he put it, a real schmoozer when he wanted to be—Chuck was a thoughtful sort of person who tended toward quietness, especially when puzzling over cases.

Chuck usually had several high school kids working at the clinic. They fed the animals, took the dogs into the runs, and did various other jobs as needed. Two girls were with him now. One was a senior named Andrea, who had been accepted into a marine biology program at a good college and was working at the clinic to gain experience. Tony, a sophomore, stood next to Chuck and held the gas mask over the cat's nose while Chuck made the first incision. She was exceptionally slender and wore a lot of makeup, but she was wiry and tough. Tony had worked at a dairy farm for three years, helping out after school and on weekends, when her mother got her out of bed and drove her to the farm for the 3 a.m. milking.

While Chuck peeled back the layers of muscle on the cat's leg, he talked to the girls about what had happened the night before. When he told them about the woman who called at midnight about the vomiting cat, he tapped his bloody scalpel at them for emphasis, saying, "Don't you ever do that to a vet. You got that? Don't ever do that to a vet." Tony smirked and popped her gum. Andrea was looking a little pale.

Chuck pulled another strand of leg muscle out of the way and pointed to a white strand running through it. "The sciatic nerve," he said. "This is the one where if you stress it, you can have sciatica and get all laid up." Then he cut through the nerve.

Andrea had seen enough. She told Chuck she was feeling light-headed and had to kneel down.

"Good," Chuck said. "Good that you said so. Kneel down before you fall down." He laid bare the bone while Andrea crouched down and put her arms around her knees. A minute later she said she needed a drink of water and left the surgery.

"One time three eighth-graders from Charlestown came to visit the clinic," Chuck recalled. "I was doing an autopsy on a cat that day, and I gave them an anatomy lesson. The three of them were standing side by side, two girls and a boy. I was naming the organs when all of a sudden the girl in the middle passed out and went straight backwards. The two other kids just watched her, so I yelled, 'Catch her!' but they were too late, and down she went. I thought she'd be hurt by the way she landed, but she wasn't."

Andrea came in and said she thought she'd go home if Chuck didn't mind. He told her he hoped she felt better soon.

The femur on the little cat was so small that Chuck decided not to saw through it, but to use the razor-sharp obstetrical wire. He pulled the wire back and forth a few times and then pulled away the leg and held it up. It was good that Andrea didn't have to see this part.

"I would have been a great Civil War surgeon," Chuck said. "Civil War surgeon and a World War II bomber pilot."

He finished up by folding muscle over muscle, skin over skin, just like a napkin, and tied a neat line of sutures. Chuck placed great importance in sutures. He said they were the first thing the client saw, and all they had to judge the work by.

"She'll be fine on three legs," Chuck said, pulling off the latex gloves. He carried the little cat to a cage and set her on a heating pad. After lunch he went on a call to a dairy farm, performed surgery on a cow, and returned to the clinic at five-thirty for the second round of feedings and treatments of the boarding animals. Sally Buttermore picked up her cat, and by the next morning that cat was nursing her kittens again.

It was the kind of case that meant something—service for a long-term client, a fair exchange, a life saved, an injustice indirectly addressed.

3.

Chuck—Dr. Charles Park Shaw—made the decision to become a veterinarian before going to Vietnam. He was attending flight school in Virginia Beach. By the end of 1969 he would be one of a squadron of twenty pilots based on the aircraft carrier *Constellation*—at twenty-three, the youngest member.

He figured he should decide what he was going to do when he returned home. He knew he didn't want to become a commercial pilot. He had been a math major in college, at the University of Kansas, and he tended to be methodical. He wrote a list of priorities for the job he wanted.

Number one, he wanted to work outdoors. Two, he wanted to be in a profession. Being an officer in the navy had shown him the value of being a professional, with its prospects for achievement. Third, he wanted some kind of profession with physical activity. He knew that he wasn't someone who would stick to a disciplined exercise program. Fourth, he wanted to work with people and help others if he could, as that seemed important for the well-lived life. Fifth, but perhaps most important, he wanted to be independent, to be self-employed and have his own business.

It was a list with narrow options. Forestry perhaps, but that lacked the people component. Doctor, lawyer, and teacher were all indoor jobs without the physical component. The only profession he could come up with that covered all the categories was veterinarian. Later, when he applied to vet school, he was asked whether he loved animals. He said he did but wasn't actually sure. He didn't have much experience with animals other than family pets. It wasn't until many years later that he thought about it again and realized that the answer had become yes.

If the making of the list was methodical, the purpose was also emotional. This was the kind of decision often made before going to war, the kind of decision that states, I will be this certain something, and therefore I will *be*—I will have survived.

Chuck flew eighty-eight missions in Vietnam, bombing passes and supply routes in Laos. He had wanted to fly since he was a boy, from the time his older cousin attended Annapolis. Flying symbolized independence to Chuck. But as he put it, there happened to be a war there. After his first bombing run, his navigator had said to him, "Congratulations, you've just made a little girl fatherless," and Chuck hadn't forgotten it. He had thought about his role in the war a thousand times, but he also thought he had done the right thing by taking part when others less privileged had no choice to do otherwise. He had loved flying in formation and landing and taking off from the carrier. Nothing since had been so exciting. But he had also seen antiaircraft fire fly up by the wingtips. His homecoming had been typical for that time. When the *Constellation* arrived in San Diego harbor in the spring of 1970, no one had been there to greet them. "No one at all," Chuck said. "I'm not talking about a parade. There was no one."

Chuck had grown up in Cheshire, Connecticut, but his father had grown up in Kansas, and Chuck decided to attend veterinary school at Kansas State University. He was married then, another thing he had done before going off to war. KSU had a strong agricultural component to its curriculum, and eventually Chuck began to think he would enjoy working with dairy animals. Farm work would provide variety to a practice, he figured. It had the people component, and the treatment of a dairy herd could be a steady income. After receiving his D.V.M. degree, he stayed at Kansas State for another year and got a master's degree in veterinary pathology while his wife finished her doctorate in toxicology.

They returned to Cheshire, Connecticut, and for a few months Chuck worked in a high-volume small-animal clinic, spending most of his time in appointments, minor surgeries, and on call, making $250 a week. It wasn't quite what he wanted, so when his wife was accepted to law school, they moved with their two sons to a town near Concord, New Hampshire. Chuck had a brief tenure at a mixed animal practice, mostly pets and horses, and another at a strictly small-animal practice. They weren't quite right either. He had set a goal in veterinary school of owning his own practice within two years. When Chuck asked the state veterinarian if he knew of any practices for sale, he was directed to Walpole, a small town on the Connecticut River, which is the western border of New Hampshire.

There were more than twenty dairy farms in and around Walpole when Chuck arrived in 1979. When he drove down the main street of Walpole and saw the stately columned houses, he wondered where the wealth came from. It wasn't what he expected of the rural practice that had been described to him. Chuck stopped at what he thought might be the right place, an ornate colonial with a carriage barn in the back that might be the vet hospital, but he was told to keep going. Farther down the road he came to a small building made of cinder blocks—not much more than a two-car garage with an adjoining room. A sign read WALPOLE VETERINARY HOSPITAL, and Chuck thought, Okay, I can deal with this. I'll be out of here in three years. He was there for sixteen.

The practice had been started in 1954 by a veterinarian named Tucker Burr. Burr had built up a large-animal practice along with a healthy clientele of small-animal owners, most of whom Chuck inherited. In those days he would return from a farm call or dinner and see the cars lined up along the road, sometimes a dozen or more, and people sitting on the stone wall, waiting. Hardly anyone had complained about having to wait too long back then.

In those first years, sometimes working with an associate and sometimes going solo, Chuck routinely worked eighty to a hundred hours a week. He held office hours five days a week, every day except Wednesday and Sunday, and had night hours on Monday and Friday. He made farm calls and house calls on Saturday and was available for on-call duty around the clock.

Chuck thought he had practiced a lot of good medicine in that concrete building. "We worked hard to keep the place somewhat decent," he said. An X-ray machine hung from a broomstick laid across the rafters in the garage, and they laid the animals on a sheet on the concrete floor to take the X-rays. The exam room doubled as the surgery, and with the office close by, the receptionist could lean in and see what was going on. The anesthesia unit had a peanut butter jar on top as a replacement for the original vaporizer, and the unit was rolled behind a door during office appointments. There was no toilet in the place, though Tucker Burr had made his available, a short walk up the pathway to his house. Chuck put a portable toilet in the unheated garage after a female associate said she wouldn't join the practice if he didn't provide proper accommodations.

Chuck bought the practice when he was only eighteen months out of vet school. Now, as he looked back, he thought he probably should have waited, and worked longer as an associate under a more experienced veterinarian. But he said, "I was like most of my classmates in vet school. There were a lot of Vietnam veterans, and we just wanted to go out and get into it. Compared to the war, running a practice didn't seem all that intimidating. I learned a lot of stuff the hard way. I'm sort of stubbornly independent and feel I have to learn things on my own."

There wasn't much of a life outside of the practice. To make matters worse, Chuck got divorced soon after moving to Walpole, and his sons remained in Concord. Chuck saw them on weekends, leaving to get them after Friday office hours. He hired sitters to stay overnight in the event of emergency calls, and took his boys with him during the day. His schedule was often wearing, and he had to hide his edginess and exhaustion from his clients. "I thought it could have been a case of post-traumatic stress syndrome from the war, but that didn't hold up. I was just under a lot of stress at that time." Still, he remembers with fondness those days when the boys played with barn kittens while he treated dairy cows.

After a couple of years in Walpole, Chuck started dating Ellie Ewaskio, who was also divorced and also from Cheshire, Connecticut, and now living in Vermont. They had dated briefly in college, and their fathers, who were in the same church choir, had discovered that the two were living close by. On their first date, just before Christmas, Chuck cleaned the veterinary tools and supply boxes out of the back of his station wagon and tossed in a wreath to mask the smell.

Soon he took to leaving Duffer with Ellie and her two girls—a promise of things to come, a bonding dog. They married two summers later and had their first family gathering the following Christmas, the first time in seven years that Chuck hadn't been on call on the holidays. They had just sat down to dinner when a knock came at the door. A farmer had tried to call Chuck's associate at the clinic, but the telephones were out. One of his cows was having a difficult calving—could Chuck come? He went and pulled the biggest bull calf he had ever seen, and the cow was so good, standing the whole time. Then he returned home, and they had a family dinner after all.

By the time he bought land for a new clinic in 1995, Chuck knew exactly what he wanted. The land was on Route 12 below Walpole village, part of a pasture on the bank overlooking the Connecticut River. The new building was large, 5,500 square feet, shaped somewhat like a barn, but the architect had broken the rooflines and added telescoping dormers that suggested a house as well as a clinic. There was even a reference to Walpole's classic architecture in the columns at each door. At one end of the building were the dog runs, and at another end was a garage entryway with a stock pen for large animals. The building was painted beige, but the doors were pink—a dash of color that also made it easier to give directions. Chuck planted the flower gardens and did most of the landscaping. He had found gardening the ideal hobby for a veterinarian, because it could be easily interrupted when a call came in.

Chuck and the architect took the flow of people and animals into consideration. There would be two doors—one for entering and another for leaving—on opposing sides of the reception room. There was an office just off the reception area, and down that hallway were the grooming room and a bathing room. The exam rooms would form a buffer zone between the reception room and the treatment area—where only the vets and the animals were allowed. The treatment area was the most spacious room of all, off of which were a surgery, an X-ray room, hospital rooms (one each for cats and dogs), boarding areas, and a laundry room. The surgery had a picture window that faced the Connecticut River, with views to the Vermont side. The X-ray room had a modern machine instead of one hanging from the rafters. There were good-quality blood analyzers, microscopes, centrifuges, and ultrasound, plenty of tables and sinks, a full stock of drugs and antibiotics, reference books, refrigerators, and lots of light. In the center of the building was the staff room.

Chuck gave prime consideration to airflow. At the old clinic, moisture had condensed on the concrete walls, making the air thick with the smell of animals. After years of working in that environment, Chuck claimed that his sense of smell had become distorted. He said he could smell dog shit a mile away and pick up the scent of a tomcat the moment he walked in the door. At the new clinic, air would move from the reception area through the treatment rooms to the boarding areas, and then be shunted outdoors. There would be no animal smells lingering in the reception area or exam rooms.

It was the kind of setup a young veterinarian dreamed of. Chuck said that because of the new clinic, he had been able to hire someone of Roger's caliber. Possibly the same would be true for the next associate, yet to come.

4.

After he had amputated the leg of the Buttermores' cat, Chuck went to Windyhurst, a dairy farm in Westmoreland.

Chuck played a variety of roles at the dairies. The most important was that of reproduction specialist, which consisted primarily of uterine palpation during regularly scheduled herd checks. The vet reached inside the cow's rectum and, by feeling the uterus through the rectal wall, determined whether the cow was pregnant and, if not, what condition her ovaries and uterus were in. The purpose of his gynecological work was to get the cows pregnant as soon as possible after calving, to minimize the period of no milk production between calvings.

Chuck also played obstetrician when calvings were not proceeding smoothly. The method of pulling calves depended on the reason for the problem. In one method he reached into the cow, repositioned the calf, got hold of the hoofs, and drew the calf out. In a more difficult calving, he put chains on the hoofs, fastened a light winch to the chains, and cranked the calf out; the mother usually made it through this procedure, but not the calf. As a last resort, he might do a cesarean section, but that was to be avoided if possible because it posed greater risk to the cow's health and milk production, and was more expensive. Chuck had long arms, and he had developed his delivery skills as highly as his palpation techniques. When the calves did survive, he served as pediatrician for the heifers, giving them vaccinations and treating them if they became ill. He didn't treat the male calves, usually. They were sold into the veal market.

He served as bovine podiatrist too, since a cow lasts only as long as her feet do. And he served as general practitioner, treating such problems as cut milk veins caused by slivers in the cow's bedding or by one cow stepping on another's udder. He treated for milk fever, a condition that came as a result of a cow giving up her calcium to milk and then collapsing from exhaustion. The cure for this usually was a boost from a concentrated infusion of bottled calcium. Chuck treated for pneumonia and other lung ailments brought on by the stuffy conditions inside barns; to prevent this, farmers sometimes tore off parts of the walls of their barns and put up screens to let the air flow through, even in winter. He treated for various infections, pulled retained placentas, and did procedures to correct a "windsucker." This happened when a cow tore her vulva at birth and then—to beat the boredom, Chuck claimed—somehow sucked in air and made a sound like a tuba. Or maybe it was a trombone.

Chuck attended conferences and meetings to learn more about dairy farming and herd medicine, and he talked to farmers about nutrition, cow comfort, bedding space, and breeding practices and genetics. Though he wasn't actually on the staff at any of the dairy farms he serviced, he came close to it. One dairyman had calculated that for the $14 per hundredweight he was getting for his milk (milk prices are determined by pounds), he was paying Chuck 60 cents in veterinary services.

Today Chuck was doing a DA, an operation to correct a displaced abomasum. The abomasum is the "fourth stomach" of the cow, though cows actually have only one stomach, called the rumen, and three modified esophagi. The abomasum can become problematic after a cow gives birth. It can twist, fill up with gas, and move into the vacated space left by the calf. There were lots of reasons why this happened, and it had always happened on dairy farms, but modern feeding practices had resulted in a higher incidence of DAs. Chuck and Roger did about 120 of them a year, as many as cat spays.

Before the surgery had been developed and had become more commonly practiced, farmers tried to correct the condition by rolling the cow over on her back, running her around in a field, or taking her on a bumpy ride in a truck. One of Chuck's clients, a farmer named Peter Barrett, remembered that during his father's time, when a cow got a DA and her milk production crashed, they would simply "ship her," or send her to market for beef. They didn't really know what a DA was then, he said. The Barretts had hired Chuck to do their DAs because he was the only vet in the area who would do them on the farms rather than in the clinic.

DAs had been less frequent in the past, because farmers put their cows out to pasture between milkings. Most of the dairy cows Chuck treated nowadays never saw a pasture or ate green grass. They stayed in the barn and ate a mixture of silage (chopped and fermented corn or grass), grain, and additives such as brewer's grain, a by-product of the beer industry. One farmer even added stale candy bars, discount priced, to give them more calories. This high-energy, high-fat diet, or "hot feed," as Chuck called it, resulted in higher milk production, but it could also put cows into a state of metabolic upset, which complicated their health conditions after calving and made them susceptible to DAs.

"It was when farmers started feeding grain that production went up," Chuck said. "The problem is, they can burn a cow out. If you push a cow nutritionally, you can cross over a line." Experienced farmers got close to the line but didn't cross over. If they did it successfully, the results in milk production could be astounding. Some of the highest-producing cows among Chuck's patients were making 160 pounds—almost 18 gallons—of milk a day, or, in Chuck's words, "ten percent of their body weight in milk, every day." The dairy cows of old, eating grass, would make, as Peter Barrett said, "thirty-five to forty pounds a day if they were lucky." A farmer now aimed to get 30,000 pounds of milk, nearly 3,500 gallons, during a cow's entire lactation period, from calving to calving.

Chuck's rate for a DA surgery was about $200, so it took a cow, depending on her productivity, about ten to twenty days to pay off the cost of it. He thought the cow was less stressed and had a better chance of surviving if she stayed on the farm. Chuck claimed that he had a 90 percent success rate with his DAs, that nine out of ten cows survived and were back in the milk parlor soon after the surgery—or, often, the very same day of the surgery.

Windyhurst was run by Roger Adams, who was close to sixty, and his son Stuart, who was in his thirties. Stuart had taken the farm further into the commercial realm, but it still looked about as idyllic as any New England farm. If you were traveling north along Route 12 from Keene, you came to a point where the woods were left behind and the Connecticut River valley opened up with long views into Vermont—the true farm country of New Hampshire, you might think. There was Windyhurst, sitting on a rise—the usual white colonial farmhouse, the foursquare chimneys, and a capacious barn painted red—with that grandeur and the river as a backdrop. If you had to be a dairy cow, this would be the place to be one. Chuck would agree. Roger Adams, he said, was willing to take the treatment further than anyone, in a system that would only go so far with treatment of dairy cows.

It was a windy and bright March day, with ice floes drifting on the Connecticut. Chuck parked his Volvo wagon by the barn. He grabbed his surgery kit, a battered metal picnic cooler, and made his way through the office, past the bulk milk storage tank, and through the milking parlor, which was clean and silent now. He kicked open a swinging door and walked into the barn. Beyond a row of pens were the open areas where the Holsteins milled about. In the pens were two cows. One had just calved, and her calf was sitting near her. The other was the DA cow, and she was standing listlessly, with glazed eyes and sunken ribs.

Stuart Adams, a peaceable-looking man with the fresh-faced air of gentleness and determination that dairy farmers often seem to have, came up to greet Chuck. As Chuck got to work, they had a conversation that seemed to illustrate the dif-

ference between Stuart and his dad, as well as between older
generation and new. Chuck said he had read that if a farmer
couldn't get a cow bred for 250 days after calving, he should
give up and ship her for beef. Stuart said he agreed, but that
his dad liked to go further than 250 days, often well beyond a
year. "He remembers the days when farmers had just thirty-
five cows." Stuart had built the herd to 150 milking cows, but
Roger still made most of the decisions.

Stuart put a halter on the DA cow and tied her by the head
into the corner of the pen. Chuck gave her an injection of
sedative, enough to calm her but not enough to make her lie
down. She had to remain standing throughout the surgery. He
plugged in his barber's clippers and shaved a patch along her
side, behind her ribs. He doused the shaved area with Betadine, scrubbed it with a brush, doused, and scrubbed again.
When a puff of air blew through an open doorway, Chuck
asked Stuart to close the door to keep out the dust that could
infect the cow. "Time is trauma," Chuck said. "In this environment we've got to get in and out as quickly as possible."

Before Stuart could close the door, Roger Adams walked
in. He and Stuart were certainly apples from the same tree,
though Roger was the bigger apple, with his generous belly
and greater blush to his cheeks. Roger rested his arms on the
stall and looked at the cow Chuck was preparing for surgery.
"You can tell she's a DA by looking in her eyes," he said. "You
can tell a lot by a cow's eyes. They should be bright and shiny.
With older farmers, looking at cows, used to be wet eyes.
That's what they looked for. It was eyes with them."

Chuck took an oversized syringe and needle from his box
and used its cutting edge to trace a line through the patch he'd
shaved. The cow didn't like this, and tried to kick Chuck with
her back leg, but Stuart lifted her tail, which got her to lower
the leg, as if a crank had been turned. Chuck made several in-

jections of lidocaine, a local anesthetic, along the line he'd scribed in her side.

He took a scalpel from his kit and began cutting into the layers of skin and fascia. The cow didn't like this either, though she probably couldn't feel much by then. When the incision was about eight inches long, Chuck set the scalpel down and lathered his arms with Betadine. He put a plastic sleeve over his left arm and pulled it to his shoulder. He had cut the fingertips off the sleeve so that his fingers would have a better grip.

Chuck put both hands into the incision, and as if he were opening a curtain, he tore the muscle wall and enlarged the incision to twice its length. Tearing, he said, resulted in less bleeding. Then he reached in with his gloved hand, right across the cow's body, until he found the displaced abomasum, which felt like a warm and slippery basketball, he said. Using a needle he had cupped in his hand, he punctured the inflated stomach. He stood there, shoulder-deep in the cow and leaning into her side, while the gas slowly leaked out. She tried to kick again, but Stuart pushed up on her tail and she put her hoof down.

There was time for conversation while the abomasum slowly shrunk to size. They talked about maple syrup—Roger said he would be making pancakes on "Sah-day" at the restaurant they ran in conjunction with the farm. They talked about fishing on the Connecticut and the trout fishing opening soon elsewhere. Chuck said he hadn't done any trout fishing in a while, though he'd like to.

Roger Adams said he had been to church that morning. Chuck hadn't. He was an every-other-week churchgoer, depending on the call schedule. Something spurred Roger to say, "We see evidence of God, we all do, every day in the barn. It's impossible to be around here and not believe in God. These people who believe in evolution are missing the point. Isn't that true, Stuart?"

"Yeah," Stuart said, but not with much enthusiasm.

Chuck smiled. It was possible to see it both ways. You could see evidence of God or the miracles of nature in these mysterious, even majestic animals, with their striking coats, their wet and curious eyes, their astounding abilities. If you looked back through history, many others had seen it—bovine worship had been prevalent throughout the world's great cultures, among the Sumerians, the Egyptians, the Romans, the Hindus, the Masai, and countless others. Some have said that early Christians counteracted the influence of bovine worship by converting the divine cow into the horned devil. Yet why wouldn't these animals be seen as aspects of God, with the sustenance they give, the peace about them, and the power in their counterpart, the bull?

As for evolution, how could you ignore its workings in this queen of mammals, whose lineage had passed through the great wild cattle that roamed Europe and western Asia and extended to the first Holsteins brought to America from Holland in the 1850s. These cows had made commercial dairying a viable and profitable pursuit. Their genes were now available by way of the Internet. The hand of man was now pushing the edges, touching the womb, making them super-mammary in the effort to extract fifteen to twenty gallons of milk per day from each of them. Here, in this barn, was the course of evolution as well as the presence of God, if Roger Adams had it right.

And this had to be one of the strangest surgeries in the world.

Chuck repositioned the now shrunken abomasum and tacked it to a lobe of fat called the omentum. When the tacking was done, he let go, like a fisherman tossing a sinker and line into the water, and the organs dropped back into the cow.

Milking time had come, and the herdsman began leading the cows into the milking parlor. Small groups stopped by the pen on their way. They wanted a close look, and they raised their big wet noses as if they were feelers. One cow reached her head through the bars and examined Chuck's clippers with her nose. Chuck had hoped to finish before the cows came by and stirred up more dust, and he sutured quickly as they nosed about. Soon the milk-room vacuum pump began making a sucking beat that pulsed through the barn.

The DA cow was not yet done. Chuck stabbed an IV needle into the vein in her neck and fed in a liter of dextrose solution to give her some energy. Stuart held the bottle up while the sugar drained in. Finally, in a last assault, Stuart held the cow's head while Chuck pushed a tube down her throat and siphoned in ten gallons of water mixed with powdered feed, to fill the rumen and hold the abomasum in place.

Wonder of wonders—when Chuck gathered up his tools and carried them out through the parlor, Stuart Adams threw some fresh hay into the stall, and the DA cow, curious now, nosed at it and started eating.

"We'll milk her at the end of this cycle," Stuart said.

It was important to remember that as gruesome as the DA surgery could seem, the cow's life had been saved. She would have become beef otherwise.

Chuck wasn't impervious to the wonder or the demands. On the way back to the clinic he said, "It's amazing what we ask of the cow. We ask so much of them. We ask that they give us a hundred and twenty pounds of milk a day. The farmer knows how much he expects of the cow. And he knows that if he takes care of the animal, it all works out in the end. The farmer who doesn't take care of his animals doesn't make it. That's why when people say cows are mistreated, they don't understand."

2

THE ASSOCIATE

1.

Veterinary practices are organized along the standard range of business forms, including the corporation, the partnership, and the sole proprietorship. Any of those types of practices are capable of employing associate veterinarians, who are essentially full-time employees without a share in ownership. Chuck Shaw's practice took the relatively rare form of a sole proprietorship mixed practice with a single associate.

The relationship between a practice owner and an associate carries a set of responsibilities on both sides. Since it is less common for a veterinarian to do an internship, as in the medical profession, the majority of veterinarians pass from school straight into a private practice. The relationship therefore has overtones of a mentorship, yet the practice owner expects the new veterinarian to be capable of doing a good portion of the work and to bring in enough income to cover at least part of his salary. A fair exchange is expected by both parties—a contribution to the business on the part of the practice owner, a salary and beneficial experience on the part of the associate veterinarian.

The majority of veterinary clinics limit their treatment to cats and dogs. According to statistics published by the American Veterinary Medical Association, of the 22,000 private veterinary practices in the United States, 16,000 treat small animals exclusively or predominantly. Nearly 33,000 of the 45,000 veterinarians in private practice work in small-animal clinics. Another 7,000 veterinarians work in practices devoted solely to bovine or equine treatment, or a combination of both.

Only 1,262 practices in the United States are true mixed animal practices, parceling care somewhat equally between large and small animals, commercial and domestic species, companion animal medicine and production medicine. Approximately 3,608 veterinarians work in these mixed practices, which have an average number of three vets per practice. Only about 25 percent of mixed animal practices follow the two-vet owner-and-associate model that Chuck's does. And with its equal share of the workload—in the clinic, on the farm, and on call—being a new associate in such a practice can be quite a challenge.

The people willing, let alone eager, to fall into that category form a very small pool, and Chuck had an increasingly difficult time finding graduates who could handle the demands of his practice. The kind of work his practice offered wasn't for the timid or the frail, or for those needing a great deal of training or supervision. Chuck expected his associates to be independent, like he was, and to be self-starters.

His first associate had stayed only a few months before leaving to start his own practice in Vermont. His next associate was a Minnesota woman interested in large-animal work. It was relatively rare for women to go into mixed practice, but Chuck admired her knowledge and her cheerful nature, and he felt lucky to have hired her, because he had been told he'd go through six or seven associates before he found a compatible one who would stay. But after Chuck bought the land to build a new clinic, she told him she would be leaving; she was happy, but her husband, a forester, was not.

His third associate stayed two years before buying a small-animal practice in Keene. The fourth had an interest in exotic animals, and though he was capable, Chuck encouraged him to think about other opportunities. The last he'd heard, this associate was working in a game preserve in Kenya. The fifth, another woman, wanted to work with cows, but she stayed only five months before moving to a predominantly bovine practice in eastern New York. Following her departure, Chuck worked alone for a year. He hired a retired mixed-practice vet to do relief work, including during a time one summer when he and Ellie and the four kids made a cross-country road trip.

His sixth associate was what Chuck called a "money guy" —someone good at generating income for the practice and willing to be on call. He left after fifteen months for a small-animal practice, where there was more money to be made. Chuck spent another year alone before hiring a veterinarian from Canada. She stayed a year before marrying another vet and moving to his practice in Ontario.

The eighth associate stayed four years. She was small, but prided herself on doing all the work, large animal and small. At the dairy farms during calvings, she had called Chuck for assistance only on those few times when her arm was not quite long enough to reach the calf. She held her own taking calls too, but in the fourth year the schedule began to wear her down. It got to the point where, each morning, she sat outside the clinic in her truck, gathering herself together to go in. When she got a call from a small-animal practice in Keene, she left.

Four months later Roger Osinchuk arrived, and he hit the ground running. Chuck claimed that Roger was one of those 2 or 3 percent of associates who made money for the practice in their first year.

2.

Roger was of medium height ("five feet nine if I can get away with it"), stocky and solid, with light skin and dark curly hair. He wore wire-rimmed glasses that gave him a doctorly look, and his friendly, down-home personality helped him get along with the farmers among Chuck's clientele. That he communicated well and enjoyed spending time with farmers and horse owners wasn't surprising, since Roger had grown up on a cattle ranch in western Canada and still had a lot of the cowboy in him. He liked to say, "There's only one thing I wanted to do since I was a kid, and I'm doing it."

Roger had made the decision to become a vet when he was five years old, after watching a veterinarian do a cesarean section on a cow in the middle of a subzero Alberta winter. It appeared to him that the veterinarian was an important person in the community, and he still felt that way.

Another person he perceived as important was a rancher named Georgie Butz, who had the valuable skill of knowing how to castrate a horse. Watching, Roger felt the excitement, and hoped someday to be able to do the procedure himself. Before leaving to attend Atlantic Veterinary College on Prince Edward Island, Roger took lessons in castration from Butz and from the vet who had first inspired him, Gary Etherington. When Roger graduated from vet school, his parents gave him an $800 tool called an emasculator, a complex set of pliers that could crimp and cut at the same time. During graduation weekend Roger entered an informal competition you would find only at a vet school, a timed contest in horse castration. Roger won, even beating one of his professors, and at the graduation ceremony received an award for proficiency in large-animal work.

Because Roger grew up working with horses on a ranch that depended upon them, he had also become an expert trainer, seeking out and learning from the old-time trainers. He had a pony of his own at six, paid to have a mare bred to get his first foal at age ten, and trained horses for money during his teens. Since coming to Walpole, he had built a sizable equine component into Chuck's practice.

For the time being, he had decided not to return to Alberta to practice veterinary medicine. He loved that country ranch, but he wanted to do mixed practice. Where Roger came from, a veterinarian basically did two things, pregnancy checks on beef cows in the fall and calvings in the spring. Mixed practice was more interesting, Roger thought, and a mixed-practice vet reached further into the community. Roger enjoyed having people wave at him on the roads around Walpole or stop to talk to him at the post office. In a few months he seemed to know just about everyone in town.

One spring day when the snow was gone from all but the shady spots in the woods, Roger drove to Putney, Vermont, on the west bank of the Connecticut River, to do some work at a stable of Belgian draft horses. The client would be taking his horses to pulling contests at fairs that summer, and he needed certificates for blood tests and inoculations. He had also asked Roger to do some dentistry work on the Belgians.

Roger had handled the office appointments that morning while Chuck was on a herd check. Among other things, he had given a round of steroids to a cat to suppress an immune system problem causing inflammation of the gums. He had also given an injection of subcutaneous fluids to Chase Romano's Bookcat. Roger had been worried that Bookie might not make it, but his kidney condition had markedly improved, and Roger was feeling pleased about it.

His dog, Dexter, was beside him in the truck. A chubby mutt with curly graying hair, Dexter was cautious until he got to know you. His caution was justified. For four years Dexter had served as a blood donor at Atlantic Veterinary College, where he'd been kept in a pen and walked once or twice a day by veterinary students. Roger was one of those students. Two or three times a month Dexter had given his pint of blood, sitting patiently while it drained through a tap in his neck, and getting a treat, usually a donut, afterward. This hard life—not only the confinement and the work but also the variation in his handlers—finally drove him crazy. Dexter was a one-person dog, Roger said. Eventually Dexter refused to come out of his pen, and when he was walked, he pulled at his leash and tried to break away. Roger adopted him and walked him four times a day through a raw Prince Edward Island winter. Gradually Dexter came around. He could still stand for a pint if needed, but Roger felt he'd done enough, and Dexter's chief job now was to be Roger's companion, riding in the truck on calls and sleeping on his bed at night.

Roger turned up a rutted pasture road that rose to a bluff, passing by junked cars and defunct logging equipment. He parked by a swaybacked barn. A barefoot girl of about thirteen came out of a mobile home and told Roger that her father wasn't home, but he'd told her to stay home from school that day to help with the horses. She introduced herself as Melissa and ducked inside to get her boots.

Roger mulled the situation over. He was concerned both about the girl and the fact that the owner wasn't there to pay him. "Horse owners are notorious for not paying their bills," he said. When the girl came out, she told him she had some cash, though not enough to pay for everything. Roger said he would do the dental work and take blood for tests but withhold the paperwork until the girl's father came to the clinic to pay the bill.

They walked down a path and through a canvas door into the old barn, the girl leading the way and Roger carrying a bucket of tools. Inside were a row of stalls and an alleyway. A potbellied pig was sleeping on a bed of hay. He groaned when Roger walked near him, but didn't open his eyes or try to move. One of the draft horses was out of his stall and eating from a bag of corn nearby.

The horse's name was Jon. Melissa said he was a new arrival to the stable, that he had come from Kentucky through a dealer in draft horses. He was a typical Belgian giant. She said he could be very nervous, that he wasn't used to this barn or to his new handlers. "We'll work on him last," Roger said, and she put him back in his stall.

There were three other horses in the barn and another four outside in a paddock. All but one were Belgians, immense and powerful, with tawny coats and blond manes, some long and curly, some in a Mohawk brush cut, all with broad, muscular rumps tapering down to slender legs and booted fetlocks. Belgians were usually the star performers at the fairs, their pulling contests getting top billing on Saturday nights. Melissa's father had worked with draft horses in the woods, logging with his own father, and the two of them had been training draft horses for competition for five years. They had taken twelve horses to the fairs last year, and they would take eight, in four paired teams, this year.

These competitions had begun years ago as the culmination of the agricultural season, the farmers competing with the animals they worked with. Things had changed. A top-performing draft horse could now bring as much as $30,000 at auction, and because of this, many of the old-time horse-men claimed that the sport had become corrupt and had lost its sense of fun. There was truth to what they said; Chuck had gotten a call about a man who was using electric shocks to get his horses fired up for the pulls. The horses at this Vermont barn weren't top-dollar animals, but they had seen their share of competition. They seemed like a group of old athletes past their prime.

Melissa said they'd start with Doc.

"Can you handle him?" Roger asked. She said she could, and brought him from the stall. He lumbered beside her, his big feet shaking the ground.

"You hold him while I float his teeth," Roger said. She took Doc's halter in one hand and rubbed him with the other.

"Floating" is akin to filing. Floating and other horse den-tistry is done by veterinarians, but it falls within the farrier's trade too, and in this countryside there were even "tooth fairies" who made a business of it. Chewing wears down a horse's molar teeth and leaves sharp edges that need to be trimmed.

Roger's tools consisted of a bucket of water, a hand pump for squirting water into the mouth, a pair of long steel files with wooden handles, and a set of ominous long-handled nip-pers that looked like bolt cutters. While Melissa talked sweetly to the horse, Roger reached into his mouth and grabbed his tongue, pulling it out of the side of his mouth like a sausage. Apparently this triggered some kind of compliancy, and was analogous to the dentist's command to "open wide." With Doc's tongue in his left hand, Roger took a file in his right and began to scrape.

The filing sound had a musical and mesmerizing effect, and it was accompanied by the cooing of the girl. To this duet was added the bobbing, jazzlike head beat of the horse with his wide-open mouth. When Doc stomped his feet or stepped too close to the pig, the pig joined in, letting out a groan and a grumble—*hoobla-hoobla-hoobla*—ending with a snort. The whole ensemble had a shish-boom-bah sort of effect. Amazingly, Doc stood still while Roger picked up those long-handled nippers and cut off the tips of his canines with a sound like the pruning of a tree branch.

Melissa brought out another Belgian, named Joe. He was an old sailor, gray around the eyes, and he knew the routine. He knew it so well, in fact, that Roger soon discovered he didn't even have to hold Joe's tongue. This meant he could file with both hands. Joe's tongue darted in and out, and his eyes kept the forbearing expression of any dental patient, fixed in the distance, waiting for it to be over. Roger was the one grimacing as he scraped upward, trying to stay on the tooth.

Prince was third in line for floating. A white Belgian and Percheron cross with black eyes and long white eyelashes, Prince wasn't quite as tall as the Belgians, but he was broader and more muscular. He too was an old fellow, well into his teens, and this would be his last year in competition, Melissa said.

Roger asked, "Is this the one that can be a bit of an orangutan?"

"Not this one," she said. "That's Jon."

Roger filled the hand pump and squirted water into Prince's mouth to wash out the hay scraps, then fell to scraping with a fury, grimacing and squinting as before. Prince was as cooperative as Joe or Doc, but he had more lively feet. While his head bobbed to Roger's scraping, Prince raised and stomped those feet, moving forward and back, a bit at a time. He did that because he could, Roger said. "You've got to be more patient than they are. There's no point in trying to overpower him, because you'd never win." So Prince did his little dance, with the vet and girl moving with him, the pig occasionally adding a groan. Prince also let Roger use the nippers without protest.

"Okay, next horse," Roger said. "The next one's the bad one, right?"

"Yes," Melissa said. She went to get Jon from the last stall.

"How old is he?"

"Nine," she said.

Jon had worried eyes, high-arched and rimmed with white. His white-blond mane shook, and he held his head high; he seemed a good seven feet tall.

Melissa said, "Easy now, Jonnie, okay, easy now, good boy."

Jon pulled his head high as Roger approached him. Maybe Jon had experienced bad dental work or some errant tooth fairy, because when Roger opened Jon's mouth and grabbed his tongue, Jon stiffened. Roger looked left, right, with Jon's pink tongue firmly in hand. Clearly they were at a crossroads, the place where vets have those moments of decision that come to be a routine part of the work. He thought he could have gone further and wrestled with Jon, but he didn't want to take a chance that the girl would get hurt.

"Okay," Roger said. "Only one is a little pointy. There's no use getting into a big fight over it." Jon pulled back when Roger released his tongue. They went outside to gather the rest of the Belgians, and a few minutes later all eight horses were in the eight stalls, massive and quivering and stepping, shaking and breathing their heavy, grassy breaths.

The last four didn't need floating, so Roger moved to the task of getting blood samples to test for a disease called equine infectious anemia. Certificates were required for competitions and interstate travel. After taking the samples, Roger would give rabies shots, also required by law.

To get the samples, he used a device called a Vacutainer, which worked by a two-step process. First Roger inserted a double-ended needle into the jugular vein on the horse's neck. The horse usually flinched then, and Roger rode with that flinch. On the recoil he pushed a test tube with a vacuum onto the other end of the needle. The tube rapidly filled with blood. Roger was exceptionally quick at the Vacutainer process. He moved down the row of stalls getting his samples and filling out the paperwork, and Melissa again played the calming influence, standing beside him and talking to the horses.

While Melissa was occupied with one of the horses, Roger slipped alone into Jon's stall. He ran his hands over Jon's neck and talked to him. As he talked, he pinched a fold of skin at Jon's neck and pushed in the needle. Jon flinched with such power that the rope tying him into the stall snapped taut as a bowstring. On the recoil, the Vacutainer cuff came loose. When Roger reached for it, he didn't see the blur of a hoof, though he felt it. He backed out of the stall, turned, and leaned against a post. His face was drained and white. A mud streak ran down his shoulder and over his stomach. On the way down, the hoof had caught hold of his trousers.

"I almost got the wind knocked out of me in there," Roger said. A shredded piece of pant leg hung from his knee. He turned to Melissa. "Let's wait till your dad gets home to do this one." He then continued on, getting the rest of the samples. Melissa paid for the floating and said she'd tell her father to come to the clinic for the test results. Roger said he'd return to get that sample from Jon—which he did two weeks later.

Earlier that day, on the way to this stable, Roger had talked to me about his experiences as a horse trainer on his family's ranch in Alberta. Now, on the ride back to Walpole, his eyes lively behind the wire-rimmed lenses, he said, "That's the first time I ever got struck. And I've had horses since I was six. That's what I get for bragging that I knew something about horses."

The accident was the news of the day at the clinic. A veterinary technician, Laurel Gibbs, joked that Roger had gotten the pants scared off him. He changed into a clean pair and began the afternoon's office appointments.

To make a point, Chuck called it an attempted murder. "You never know how unpredictable horses can be," he said. He told a story about a guy he'd gone to school with who became a horse specialist in Oklahoma. He went out alone one day to work on a horse and didn't come back. The horse had kicked him, and he died.

"Horses are fleers, not fighters," Chuck said. "But if it were me, I would have told the owner that I'd do it when he was there. That way if anyone gets hurt, it's the owner."

3.

Veterinarians come out of school with a thorough grounding in the principles of the profession and with knowledge developed well beyond the basic level. They have spent thousands of hours studying animal medicine, and have learned how to think in diagnostic ways and how to make decisions along ethical lines. But there are gaps in a veterinary education, primarily because there is far too much to cover in too short a time—only four years. Well-prepared veterinarians know where to go to get information about conditions they may not have encountered, but there are many conditions or procedures they haven't seen or done.

For example, during Roger's fourth year of vet school, in his required course in small-animal surgery, amputations were not covered. Partly this was because the class worked on whatever cases were available, and an animal in need of an amputation did not happen to appear that semester. But even if one had appeared, the leg would not have been amputated, because amputations were considered to be failures. Instead they would have repaired the leg.

One weekend when Chuck was away, Roger was on call when a pit bull came in after being hit by a car. Clearly the pit bull needed to have its leg amputated, and Roger realized that he had to do it. If Chuck had been in Walpole that weekend, he would have come to help, and probably led Roger through the surgery, but as Roger put it, "I looked around, and there were no other vets there." He took the big *Small Animal Surgery* off the shelf, read the section on femoral amputations, and proceeded with the surgery. The experience was nerve-wracking but successful.

Now, on this Monday morning, Roger was faced with his second amputation, on a twelve-year-old gray-bearded Irish setter named Clyde. During the past weekend, at a meeting of Irish setter owners in New Jersey, a veterinarian had taken a brief look at Clyde and said he should be put down immediately. Lynn Hayes, a veterinary technician who worked for Chuck, happened to be at that meeting. Lynn bred Irish setters, and she thought Clyde was a great dog. Clyde had a sister named Bonnie, and the pair had been living in New Jersey with the director of the Irish Setter Rescue League. They would be adopted together if Clyde could be saved. Lynn had called Chuck from New Jersey and asked if he would work on Clyde if the rescue league paid for it. Chuck said he couldn't, because he had a scheduled dairy herd check, but he said Roger was attending a seminar on ultrasonography that weekend in downstate New York, and if Roger agreed, and the dog could be delivered to him, Clyde could come to Walpole. Chuck saw it as a way for Roger to gain experience.

They found a meeting point in Connecticut, and Clyde rode in the passenger seat of Roger's truck. Lynn hadn't known what exactly was wrong with Clyde. He and Bonnie had first been given up two years ago, when their elderly owners died—it took being around a clinic to appreciate how often animals became orphaned this way. The rescue league placed them with someone who lived in a second-floor apartment— not the best situation for a pair of energetic setters, Lynn said, but it wasn't easy to place a pair of ten-year-old dogs. Unfortunately, they didn't get proper care. When the new owner decided to return them to the rescue network, a volunteer came to get them and saw that Clyde was limping. She was told that he had taken a fall down the stairs and had developed arthritis. But the moment Roger touched the dog's leg, he knew it was broken.

Back in the clinic in Walpole, Roger had *Small Animal Surgery* out on the table again and was rereading the section on femoral amputations. Lynn crouched down nearby in front of an open cage and gave Clyde a preparatory shot of sedative in his foreleg. When he felt the needle, Clyde wailed and tried to sit up.

"Come on, Clyde," Lynn said. "You're such a big baby."

Lynn left the cage door open. She was a vet tech with twenty-five years of experience, and her life was thoroughly wrapped up in her dogs. It was because Lynn cared so much about her dogs, and about Clyde, that Roger had agreed to do this. Lynn said, "Ordinarily, a dog this age with a broken leg would be put to sleep. But Clyde was such a great dog. We decided that if he could get a couple of months pain free, the surgery would be worth it."

Roger looked up from the textbook and glanced at Clyde, who was rousing himself. "Hey, Buddy," Roger said. Clyde had the kind of long, feathered tail that makes Irish setters such handsome beings. His coat had faded from deep copper to a light brown, and he was gray around the muzzle and eyes. On three legs, holding the damaged rear one up, Clyde limped over to Roger and leaned against him. Roger reached down to scratch Clyde on his back above the tail. The expression on Clyde's face seemed to say, You're a good man. Roger turned back to the text, and Clyde hobbled over to where I stood. I also reached down to scratch Clyde, and got the same grateful and friendly response. Clearly, he was a great dog.

Once the sedative had taken effect, Roger and Lynn carried Clyde into the surgery and laid him on the table. Lynn shaved a patch of hair from Clyde's foreleg while Roger put on a smock, cap, and mask and scrubbed his hands and arms. Lynn held the foreleg while Roger gave the anesthetic injection, and down Clyde's head went. Lynn put a breathing tube in Clyde's trachea and connected him to the anesthesia machine, and Roger raised the injured leg and tied it to a hook that hung from the ceiling. The broken leg was shaved, scrubbed, and draped. Not one to omit a detail, Lynn cleaned Clyde's teeth while Roger began the surgery.

He cut through the muscle, now and then referring to the text that he had laid out on the surgery table. When he reached the main femoral artery, Roger paused to look at Clyde's gums. "Still pink," he said. A good sign. Blood was flowing well.

He cut and tied off the femoral artery, the point of no return. Using scissors, he cut away the flesh and bared the bone. It was mottled and discolored, and had obviously been fractured for weeks. The bone was splintered with sharp ends; it must have hurt terribly. When Roger reached in and felt around, a splinter went through his gloves and under a finger-nail. He changed his gloves.

"I don't think I'm going to go fishing for anything else in there," he said to Lynn.

"I don't think you should, Roger," she said.

The severed leg came away easily, with no cutting of the bone needed. Soon Roger was folding skin flaps and laying down a neat ten-inch line of stitches.

"I'm going to make it pretty for the parade," he said. If all went well, the plan was for Clyde to join Bonnie and other Irish setters in a "rescue parade" at a dog show in Connecticut in a few weeks.

All seemed to be going well as Lynn and Roger discon-nected Clyde from the gas, carried him to his cage, and set him on a blanket.

Much of the rest of Roger's day was spent on large-animal calls, mostly equine work. In Alstead, he palpated two mares about to be bred. Roger was developing an insemination busi-ness. He had placed several orders for semen to be shipped from stables in the United States and Canada. Roger used ul-trasound and palpation to do pregnancy checks. Chuck pal-pated manually, but Roger would have none of that. He told Chuck during his job interview that he wouldn't join the prac-tice unless Chuck bought an ultrasound unit, and Chuck had made the $11,000 expense. The machine could do impressive things, such as produce images of follicles and ovaries, and of foals the size of fingerlings.

Roger sedated one of the mares, a fourteen-year-old Egyp-tian horse who had never foaled before and was very nervous. What showed up on the screen was auspicious—an inch-long follicle with an egg. Roger told the owner he would give the horse an injection to make her ovulate just before the semen arrived. The second mare was more compliant and didn't need sedation. Her uterus was looking healthy too. Roger said he would get the mares in a synchronized cycle and inseminate them both in one trip.

On the way to his next farm call, Roger stopped in at the clinic. Clyde had woken up and was whining and moaning in postanesthetic torpor. Lynn said he had already stood up. She had set a blanket on the floor for him, where Clyde now lay, raising his head to speak in protest of how he was feeling.

"Oh, come on, Clyde," Lynn said. "It's not that bad."

Roger left on a call to Marlow to treat a donkey and a Belgian draft horse. The owners, a couple living in a mobile home while they rebuilt an old farmhouse, had gotten the donkey to provide companionship to the draft horse, but it seemed to work both ways. The Belgian needed dentistry. Since this was his first time, Roger sedated him and used a steel speculum to keep his mouth open. While Roger floated the teeth, the owner stood close behind him. This man had abundant affection for his animals. He had rigged a cart up so the donkey and horse could pull together—what a sight that must have been. Now he came around and kissed the horse on the nose while Roger changed files.

The next farm call was in Westminster, Vermont, where Roger examined a mare belonging to Jane Fitzwilliam, another attentive owner. Two winters ago Haddie, her Dutch Warmblood, had slipped on ice while being chased by dogs. The bone above her hoof fractured, and Jane took her to the Tufts Veterinary School hospital to have the bone pinned. After that, Jane could no longer ride Haddie, but she had turned her into a brood mare. Haddie was about to foal. Roger had agreed to come in the night if needed. "I've never wanted kids," Jane said. "But this! I was born for this!"

Jane asked questions about pre-foaling and post-foaling

treatment, and Roger answered all he could until he finally said he had to get back to the clinic. In the truck he said, "She talks a bit sometimes, but she'll spread the word. She's going to be a great client and a good friend. And her horse is going to produce a beautiful baby."

The day had been a rich one, but the excitement cooled when Roger returned to the clinic and saw that Clyde was coming out of surgery, again. Chuck was there, and he explained what had happened. The afternoon receptionist, whose name was Susan Armstrong, had called Chuck at a dairy farm and said, "You better get back here now, there's blood all over the place." Clyde had hemorrhaged. The femoral artery had torn loose. "I had to go back in another two inches and tie the artery off," said Chuck.

"I'm sorry, Chuck," Roger said.

"It's not your fault, Roger."

Perhaps Clyde could have survived the first surgery, but the second proved to be too much for him. A few hours later he hemorrhaged again and died. Because he had taken a chance on this case and left Roger to do the surgery, Chuck did an autopsy. He found lesions on the liver, possibly cancerous, and he found what appeared to be cancer around the broken bones.

The next morning, Chuck said, "It was a pathological fracture, in which a condition weakens a bone and then some event causes the bone to break. This is the kind of situation where the vet gets stuck in the middle because we're going on very little information. It can be a recipe for disaster. I wish Clyde had lived. He was a great dog, and I'm sorry he didn't get another six months. It's the kind of thing you can beat yourself up over, but I'm not going to do that."

Chuck reasoned that he had taken a worthwhile gamble. "First of all, I wasn't going to tell Lynn she couldn't bring the dog up here. This is a passion thing for the rescue people, and once they learned about the dog's history, they got all worked up about it. I knew I was putting Roger on the line, but I also knew it would be a useful experience for him. I would rather have been there, but it's not often you get that kind of opportunity. I wouldn't let him do this with one of my clients' dogs, but this was a last chance for Clyde."

Roger had had a restless night. He kept replaying the day, second-guessing himself, thinking that Clyde's death had been his fault. That he might have tied off the artery incorrectly. That if he had given Clyde a postoperative sedative, Clyde wouldn't have gotten out of the cage so soon.

"I beat myself up pretty bad," he said the next morning. Then the day's cases began—a cat with a blocked bladder to be examined with ultrasound, office appointments, and farm calls in the afternoon. Clyde drifted off into the wake, into the realm of experience and regrets.

As for Bonnie, Clyde's sister, she found a home in Washington, D.C., with another rescue dog named TS, for Truck Stop, after the place where he was found. The word came through the network that Bonnie and TS took nightly walks around Capitol Hill, stopping by outdoor cafés for friendly moments, and that TS had taught her how to approach tables at nose level. Together the two marched in the following year's rescue parade, going around the ring with others, found here and there, great dogs all, under the eyes of their new and admiring owners.

4.

Roger was looking forward to his impending vacation, his first trip back to Alberta since he'd joined the practice. Even after eighteen months he sometimes felt worn down from the stress and demands of the work. As Chuck put it, "The second year is the toughest year of practice. You think you've seen a lot, and you have, but you haven't seen it all. You tend to get over-confident. If you can get through the second year, you'll prob-ably be okay." Roger was more than ready for a visit to the ranch, where, he said, "My mother can feed me, and I can rope some calves."

In the week following Clyde's surgery, Roger had a chance to do a bit of roping when he made a call to castrate a calf. The owners hadn't been able to catch him so Roger rigged up a lasso and roped him. At another farm he caught and re-strained a powerful Limousin bull and put a ring through his nose.

From that farm he went to the clinic to perform a difficult spay on a dog that had had a litter of puppies and grown fat. "Fat is your foe," Roger said. It reminded him of his first spay, when it had taken him almost two hours to work through fat that was like a slab of bacon. "For about three months after that one I wouldn't do another spay without Chuck being in the office."

With the dog anesthetized and restrained on her back, Roger cut through the skin and the subcutaneous layer, along a fibrous medial line in the belly that doesn't bleed—the line of separation, it's called. He reached in with his forefinger and felt around for the uterus, then pulled it up. "You just get to know how they feel," he said. There was a lot of uterus, com-pared with the younger dogs just out of puppyhood that were usually spayed here. Roger said, "These dogs that are older and have had puppies are not a lot of fun. People think dog spays are routine. They don't realize that it's major surgery, a complete ovarian hysterectomy." He ligated and severed the ovarian artery and vein and tied them off twice to make sure they wouldn't bleed.

Laurel Gibbs was assisting Roger with the spay. She had studied wildlife biology at the University of Vermont, and after working at the clinic for four years, she was about to leave to attend a program in veterinary technology in New York. Like the best veterinary technicians, she was adept at making animals feel at home. She also liked to tease Roger.

He removed the uterus. He lifted the abdominal wall and looked into the belly, this way and that, checking the condition of the uterine stumps, the arteries and ligaments. "No blood," he said. "Chuck always tells me that if there's gonna be a problem, there will be blood coming out of your incision by the time you're done." He sewed up the body wall and closed the incision, then began to clean up his scattering of instruments. "Everybody likes it that I'm so clean," he said, smiling.

Laurel looked at the rolling table with the instruments and said, "You threw the uterus crap on there, and there's blood all over, even on the instruments you didn't use."

"Chuck always told me all you need is a live dog and a clean incision."

"Take a look at your truck!" she said. "It's a total mess!"

Roger grinned. He liked this kind of teasing—perhaps it was a sign of his confidence. He liked Laurel too and had introduced her to Jeremy Benoit, the herdsman at Windyhurst Dairy. Recently they had become engaged, and Roger said he was taking the credit for it.

The following day he went on a call to a house in the small town of Westminster West, Vermont. It is a place with an elementary school with two teachers, a place sometimes dubbed "Tofu West" for the New Age and alternative leanings of its population. The client was a woman who lived with her three kids in a lovely log house at the corner of a big mowed field. The house, she said, had been built by her grandfather, her father, and her boyfriend, from trees planted by her grandfather.

Roger walked down a hill behind the house to a paddock, where he looked at an old white horse that had gone lame. Roger examined his hoofs and legs, then recommended a farrier—a good trimming of the hooves would help cure the problem—that and less food to help him lose some weight. Roger gave the horse a round of shots and a dewormer, then did the same for another horse, a miniature less than four feet tall that the woman said she'd rescued from "terrible conditions," living in a garage where tack and saddles were sold. "I bought her right then and there, with a credit card." She smiled. "Spent a lot of money on her."

A very elderly dog, a brown-and-black short-haired mutt with a bit of German shepherd in him, had ambled down to the paddock, trailing behind Roger and the family. The dog was stepping gingerly, but he seemed happy to be out for the walk. He sat down on the grass and watched. When Roger finished with the horses, he walked over, greeted, and examined this dog. His name was Lukas, the woman said, though she called him Buddy.

Buddy was a dog with many maladies. Roger looked at his teeth, brown and ground down. One tooth was infected. He looked at a growth under Buddy's eyelid, a tumor on his chest, and an infection under his tail. Roger examined his hollowed abdomen too, looking for tumors. The abdomen was in reasonably good shape, he said.

They talked about the prospect of surgery for Buddy's problems, but the owner was concerned about how the dog would respond to anesthesia, which Roger said was a valid concern at his age. But he would take some blood for testing, and said he could remove the tumor with a local anesthetic, scrape the teeth, and maybe do something for the infections.

The woman patted Buddy's stomach while Roger took the blood sample. "He was my first puppy," she said. "I've been doing what I can to keep him alive, feeding him liver, giving him lots of attention, and working on his self-esteem."

"How do you help a dog's self-esteem?" Roger asked.

"Tell him he's wonderful. And give him treats."

When Roger was done, he and the woman helped Buddy stand up. "He can walk," she said, "but I usually have to get him up on his feet."

"I'm sure we can do something for him," Roger said.

But first there was the trip to Alberta, for twelve well-earned days.

3

OLD HOME DAYS

1.

I really like this cat," Chuck said. The cat's name was Vinnie, and he was in for a biopsy of a skin problem. While he was sedated, Laurel cleaned his teeth. A gorgeous cat with long, soft white hair, Vinnie was a cat made for petting. "Vinnie is Hobbs's sibling, you know," Chuck said. "He's owned by Hobbs's former owners."

Perched on a shelf nearby, Hobbs seemed to be glowering. But it was hard to tell with Hobbs. He could be winking with affection and rubbing against you one moment or have smoke coming out of his eyes the next. Hobbs was not a cat for petting. He might allow it at times or even seek the stroking hand, but he could just as easily turn and bite a moment later if touched the wrong way. He might roll over and display his white belly, then dig his claws into anyone who touched him there.

He also had a tendency to attack anything that sounded like a howl. This could have been a result of his feral life as a marauding male cat. But even now, after three years of domestic habitation, Hobbs could still revert to his wild ways. Once, when a cat howled while Roger was examining it, Hobbs barreled across the room and climbed up Roger's leg as if it were a tree trunk. Hobbs had attacked nearly everyone at the clinic at least once.

Yet as malignant as he could be, here he remained, with a devoted following. The clinic kept a photo collection just of him—Hobbs inside a grain bag, Hobbs sitting on the seat of the riding lawn mower and ready to mow, Hobbs riding in a little red wagon with a kitten and looking disgusted, Hobbs wearing a Santa hat, Hobbs watching a party from under the Christmas tree, Hobbs rolling on his back in a pile of hair in the surgery. Chuck had said, "That cat has a lot of personality," and this was the trait that saved him.

Hobbs was lucky—he had been in the right place at the right time at least twice in his life. The first was when he wandered into the backyard of the house in Walpole (Vinnie's house) just a few days after that family's cat had died. They saw Hobbs and put out food for him, and a few days later opened their door. Hobbs came in, ate the food, and even got up on a chair, but he wouldn't let anyone touch him. He moved into that house once the weather got cold. One afternoon, when the father of the family was sleeping on the couch, Hobbs jumped on his stomach and then jumped right off to the floor. That was their first physical interaction, but it opened the way for others. The father began to play with Hobbs, and liked to tickle his stomach while Hobbs clawed him. But Hobbs was not a lap cat, and the mother of the family wanted a cat she could stroke. Even after two years, Hobbs still bit and scratched when the mood struck or when anyone touched his stomach.

One day when the mother was washing dishes, she turned the faucet handle, and it made a howling sound. Hobbs came barreling out of another room and climbed right up her back.

Though the father didn't want to do it, he brought Hobbs to the clinic and paid the fee for euthanasia. He was told the clinic policy, that they would accept payment but try to find the cat a home. The man said Hobbs would make a good barn cat, but not a house cat.

That was when Hobbs got lucky again. Just before he arrived, an elderly clinic cat had died. Hobbs came in on a Friday, and over that weekend Roger let him out of the cage and the kennel kids played with him. He was a funny-looking cat, with stiff gray hair, short legs, a pendulous belly, and green, smoldering eyes. He bit when they tried to touch him, but he was a great friend at feeding time. On Monday, when Chuck watched Hobbs, he knew it would be nearly impossible to place a cat with a biting habit. Chuck also enjoyed watching Hobbs and the part of his personality he called the "enforcer element." After a day or two Chuck said, "We're keeping him."

Hobbs couldn't have been in a better place or with people more capable of handling him. He became the clinic cat, the cat who didn't leave. Chuck set some rules, about diet and about being out front. But the rules weren't always followed. Hobbs put away two donuts left on the staff-room table one day, a bologna sandwich another. He often made his way out front and perched under the desk, and was talked to sweetly there or even offered a bite of people food. Hobbsie, he was called out there, sometimes.

2.

During his first weekend on call when Roger was away, Chuck did a DA at Westminster Farms, followed by a house call to put a dog to sleep. A shipment of horse semen arrived from California for the two mares in Alstead, and Chuck inseminated them on Saturday and a second time on Sunday to make sure they were covered. He did the treatments and office appointments and adopted a kitten found in a warehouse. Chuck was certain he could find a home for him. One of the kennel kids put a sign on his cage that read HELP!

Other animals who were not owned by Chuck's clients arrived that weekend, animals whose regular vets were not on call on weekends. A cat who had stopped eating had arrived without records, and Chuck had to work from scratch, as he put it. An ailing dog arrived too, also without records. His vet left a message on weekends telling her clients to take their animals to the emergency clinic in Manchester, more than an hour's drive away.

These were cases that went against Chuck's idea of ethical and responsible practice, but if they were annoying, they were also common and manageable. He was more indignant at the case of Willie Hanna, a cat who had arrived on Saturday after being treated in Rhode Island.

Chuck had gotten a call from Lucy Hanna, Willie's owner, just as office hours were ending on Saturday. Lucy was in Walpole to attend her mother's eightieth birthday party. She told Chuck that Willie had been having abdominal pain and that he was losing weight. She had received several diagnoses and had spent about $2,000 on his treatment. On Friday, Willie had received a punch biopsy in his spleen and an initial round of chemotherapy, yet Lucy still didn't know what was wrong with him.

Lucy's vet in Rhode Island was not available on weekends and didn't board animals. On Saturday the vet had called Lucy in Walpole and said that she had made a mistake, that Willie's problem was not in the spleen, but in the liver, and that she should take him immediately to the emergency clinic at Tufts University. When Lucy said she was about to leave for her mother's birthday party, the vet said she had to decide whether to go to the party or save her cat's life. Lucy called several clinics before she got Chuck, who spent half an hour with her. He told her he wouldn't do any treatment until he had had a chance to observe Willie. As Lucy later said, that was the most sensible thing she had heard yet. She left Willie with Chuck and went to the party.

Now, on Monday morning, Chuck was examining Willie. Tall and orange, with large gold eyes, Willie was the sort of cat who purred when someone made eye contact with him, purred when someone even walked into the room. He had eaten little over the weekend. When Chuck pressed his hand into Willie's abdomen, the cat cried out. "Sorry, Willie," Chuck said. He told Laurel that Willie's temperature had been 104° on Saturday, two and a half degrees above normal, but he'd managed to lower it with intravenous fluids and antibiotics. A blood test indicated that Willie's red blood count was diminishing, indicating blood loss or destruction of red blood cells.

Chuck was in a mood to express his thoughts about Willie's treatment. He thought Willie's vet was practicing in a way that represented a harmful trend.

"A vet I know says, 'Keep it small and keep it all,' " Chuck said. "Meaning, don't hire an associate. Make it a one-man operation. Less overhead that way. No weekends, no overnights. Refer animals to emergency clinics on the weekends.

"A lot of vets coming out of schools these days have an attitude about being on call. They don't want to be. They say, 'I've got a life,' et cetera, et cetera. There are emergency clinics, et cetera. I say to that, find another profession. Twenty years ago we never even questioned it.

"I know what other vets would say about being on call and having a mixed practice. They would say, 'If you want to kill yourself, go right ahead.' Most of them decided it was more lucrative to do small-animal practice and that it was impossible to keep up with mixed practice, that it's too hard to keep up the knowledge base.

"There's no doubt, if I didn't have to work nights or weekends, I might feel better. But it's the attitude about the animals that worries me. What kind of an attitude do you have if the vet wants to get the animals out the door before five every day and won't see them on weekends? I may be oversimplifying, but if the owner is more stressed out about the animal than the vet, what kind of a situation have you got? It may work for the vet, but it's not good for the animal or the owner."

He asked Laurel to take X-rays of Willie. "He looks good," Chuck said, "but with the low blood count, I'm expecting a crash any minute. I think this cat might have liver cancer."

Laurel picked Willie up and looked into his eyes. "Oh, Willie!" she said. "Don't feel so sad!"

Chuck called Lucy Hanna and told her what he thought. He said he'd keep her informed of Willie's progress, and they agreed to meet the next weekend.

The next morning, Chuck examined Willie again. He palpated his abdomen, felt him over, and thought about what was there. He told Laurel he had tried to call Willie's vet but had been told it was her day off.

"I don't know what the hell she was doing on the weekend if Monday is her day off," Chuck said. "They told me she works only three days a week."

"How does she manage that?" Laurel asked.

"Charge the hell out of them. Live in an area where there's an emergency clinic. Don't rely on veterinary income to live."

"I'd like to work three days," Laurel said.

"The owner is willing to keep going. I'm surprised she speaks so highly of the vet. It's not like she doesn't know what's going on. She's a biomedical statistician. She might take him back to Rhode Island for more chemotherapy. My ethics tell me I wouldn't do that to my cat. I'd put mine to sleep. He'd always be sick, in pain. I told her she should find another vet."

They took some blood from Willie and returned him to his cage. Willie leaned against the door and meowed for some attention. Laurel sprayed and wiped the table while Chuck went into the exam room for the first appointment.

"He's direct, isn't he?" she said to me. "With Chuck, you either love him or hate him. He doesn't pull any punches. He tells the clients exactly what he thinks they need to hear. Some can take it; some can't. Some come here because he's that way. Part of it is his age, his sense of authority. People are going to listen to an older man. If I was the vet and people looked at me, they'd say, 'No way.' And even Roger, people listen to him, but he's got that baby face. With horses, they listen to him because they know he knows what he's doing. But he has to be careful, very cautious in what he's saying. Chuck, he's rugged, older, authoritative. He's the owner. He's direct, and some people appreciate it. Some don't."

3.

Dairy work was at the heart of Chuck's practice, and for a twenty-mile stretch of the Connecticut River as well as in the hills nearby he played an important role at most of the dairy farms. By New England standards, some were sizable farms.

Among them was Peter and Mike Barrett's Stoneholm

Farm, milking 240 Holsteins in the Putney Meadows in Vermont. A few miles north, on the New Hampshire side of the Connecticut, Windyhurst Farm, where Roger and Stuart Adams milked their 150 Holsteins. A few miles north, Boggy Meadow Farm, which dated to Jeffersonian times, milking 300 Holsteins in Walpole. On the opposing bank of the Connecticut, Westminster Farms, owned by the brothers Clayton and Robert Goodell, milking 500 Holsteins. Another few miles farther north, across the Connecticut again on another alluvial floodplain, Malnati Farm, milking 80 cows—the maximum number, Vince Malnati said, for one man and his family to handle. And there was Putnam Farm, in Charlestown, milking 400 Holsteins.

Those were the river farms. Among the hill farms, Chuck serviced Great Brook Farm, in Walpole, where Peter Graves milked 80 Holsteins. Crescent Farm, milking 300 Jersey cows, smaller and less costly to feed than Holsteins, but producers of milk with higher protein and fat content—better for cheese and ice cream. Britton Farm, with 100 Holsteins. Dana Merrell's farm, a few miles north in Langdon, on a bluff overlooking flat fields from a glacial lake bed, milking 60 Jerseys. Holmes Farm, run by Steve and Jeff Holmes, the fourth generation of farmers, milking another refined and high-producing herd of Jerseys. In Acworth, Bascom's dairy milked 250 Holsteins and also made 10,000 gallons of maple syrup a year, the greatest production in New Hampshire. Chuck also serviced Echo Moon Farm, milking 60 Holsteins, and Idyll Acres, with 60 Jerseys and Holsteins, and others, tending to about 3,000 dairy cows in all, and nearly as many calves and heifers yet to be milked.

Chuck did several herd checks during the week Roger was away. He preg-checked and palpated eighty cows at Westminster Farms, as he did every Friday. He worked through the Barrett herd as Mike Barrett followed along with a clipboard. He did the Tuesday night check at Boggy Meadow as the manager and herdsman led in five cows at a time. He did the herd check at Malnati Farm, with Vince Malnati bringing in specified cows for palpation and noting the results as Chuck called them out. And he did the regular Thursday morning check at Putnam's as the herdsman brought cows into the milk parlor one by one for Chuck's examination.

The principle of dairy farming is simply to get the cow pregnant, bring her through a successful calving, and collect her milk through the course of a lactation. Get her pregnant again as soon as reasonable after calving, so that she spends the least amount of time at the tail end of a lactation with lower milk productivity. Minimize the time she spends in a state of dryness, where she makes no money.

Great effort is made to get cows pregnant. Traditionally, this was accomplished by keeping a bull with the herd. But with large herds, bulls are problematic. They injure cows and can spread bovine venereal disease. They get aggressive and attack the help—Chuck has been knocked against a fence by a charging bull. Artificial insemination is a more reliable method of breeding, and can be used to improve the genetics in a herd. A major factor leading to today's increased milk production is improved genetics from the frozen semen of the sons of the very best milk-producing cows.

Some dairy farmers watch for signs of heat, such as when one cow mounts another. Then they mark the cow for insemination or put her with a bull. But heat detection is time-consuming work, hard to attend to in the rush of chores. With uterine palpation a farmer can find out exactly what's going on in the uterus. A skilled palpator can say first of all whether the cow is pregnant and, if he really knows what he's doing, how far into the pregnancy. If the cow is not pregnant, the vet feels along the ovaries and attempts to determine whether a follicle is developing—blossoming into a fluid-filled sac with an egg in it. If that is happening, a cow will soon be coming into heat and can be bred.

Uterine palpation is a strange thing to observe. A vet puts on a thin plastic sleeve, reaches into the rectal passage of the cow, pulls out manure, and plunges in again. Once the passage is clean, he feels the cow's uterus through the thin rectal wall. Arming cows, they call it. It's easy prey for humor or, you could say, the butt of many a joke. If you were overly meticulous about palpation, could you say that you were being anal about it?

But palpation is a true art. When Chuck started palpating cows in the 1980s, he scoffed when he was told that it took five years to master the skill. He thought that seemed far too long. He now thinks it takes about seven years.

The palpator, seeking with thin gloves through the rectal wall, must find the small gelatinous body called the corpus luteum, or CL. The CL sits within the ovary but protrudes through the surface. It serves as a timing device, producing progesterone and keeping new follicles and eggs from developing. Within the monthly cycle, as the old CL regresses, another egg and follicle develop, until ovulation occurs and breeding can be achieved. After ovulation, the follicle turns into a corpus luteum, and if fertilization takes place, the uterus sends a signal to maintain the CL and so maintain the pregnancy.

A good palpator can feel the corpus luteum and determine what stage it is in. That palpator can then recommend when to breed. But the corpus luteum can also be manipulated. In the early days of uterine palpation, veterinarians would "set the clocks"—bring a cow into heat manually—by rupturing the CL like a blister to allow another follicle to develop. The cow would come into heat in three days. But the procedure was risky. If the veterinarian didn't do it properly or at the right stage, or if things just went wrong, the ovaries could be damaged or the cow could bleed to death. But when it worked, the veterinarian could seem a lot like God.

Chuck had followed in the footsteps of a legendary palpator by the name of Wilson Haubrich, who began practicing in Claremont, New Hampshire, in the 1930s. He too serviced Putnam's and other dairies that are now Chuck's clients. Haubrich followed circuits of farms in upstate New York, Vermont, New Hampshire, and Maine, traveling in a five-week cycle that corresponded to the time—thirty-five days—between breeding and when a fetus could be detected by a palpator. Because Haubrich worked in a time before the use of plastic sleeves, he was sometimes called Green Arm Haubrich. But because he was so adept at palpation and at setting the clocks, Haubrich was also called God by farmers and other vets.

Following in Haubrich's footsteps, Chuck knew that he had his work cut out for him, but he didn't have to compete with God. During the 1980s the artificial hormone prostaglandin had become available, and prostaglandin could make a corpus luteum regress and set the clocks safely and efficiently.

One former associate said that Chuck Shaw was happiest when he had his arm up a cow's butt. There was some truth to that. Chuck loved the cow work, and he took it very seriously. He enjoyed being on the farms. "I may spend a lot of time with my arm up a cow's butt," he said, "but I'm also looking at the cows' body condition, their eyes, their udders, and the environment they're in. I ask about bedding and about cow comfort. I ask about nutrition and vaccinations and reproductive history. My major effort at the dairies is to get the cows bred and keep them in production. That becomes even more important when the price of milk goes down."

At the Putnam's check, Chuck wore his short-sleeved blue coveralls, clean but permanently spotted from palpations past, and knee-high rubber boots. He carried a stethoscope in his back pocket and a supply kit consisting of a tray with vials and syringes, a squeeze bottle of clear gel called Lubrivet, and a box of the plastic sleeves, made in France. On the box was the slogan GET MORE COWS PREGNANT.

Putnam's was always a busy place. There were usually half a dozen pickup trucks in front of the milking parlor, which was a crossroads for the farm, with various kinds of heavy equipment—dump trucks, tractors, bailers, choppers—coming and going or being repaired. The milking parlor, a double row with twelve units on each side, was attached to big, airy barns that were full of feeding and lounging Holsteins kept cool by large fans in hot weather.

The herdsman at Putnam's, Scott Kemp, had the appointed cows isolated and ready for Chuck. Scott was a quiet man, which worked to his advantage in this business. A mere hand signal from him could move a cow. Scott was also observant—"a good heat detector," as Chuck said—but he couldn't keep up with the heats of the four hundred cows they milked here.

Scott moved the first cow into the milking parlor. Chuck opened a plastic sleeve by sweeping it in the air, and wriggled his arm in. He pumped a gob of Lubrivet onto the fingers of the glove, raised the cow's tail, made a cone shape with his hand, and plunged in. He pulled back manure, which splattered on his boots, and reached in again.

"Pregnant," Chuck said. Scott made his note—a simple "P"—on the clipboard.

The second cow was pregnant too.

The third cow was more complicated. "She's coming into heat," Chuck said. "A regressing CL on the right ovary. There's no heat now, but we should check her in a week."

Scott stepped out of the parlor into the holding pen, made his signals, and a fourth cow came running in. Chuck stood back to let her go by, and then came up behind her when she'd stopped behind the others in line. "She's coming into heat," he said. "She's got heat tone."

You had to wonder what heat tone felt like.

"Turgid," Chuck said. "A cow's uterus, when she's in heat, goes from being doughy to being firm and turgid. When she's not in heat, the uterus is flaccid, the cervix tight."

Another cow rumbled in and stopped behind the others. Chuck put on a new sleeve and lubricated it. "She's got a nice CL on the right ovary," he said to Scott, who made the notation. "I want you to give her Lutalyse on Monday." Lutalyse was the brand of prostaglandin Chuck used. He didn't give her a shot on this day, a Thursday, because that would have brought her into heat on Sunday, and Scott had the weekend off. A shot on Monday would bring her into heat on Thursday, and she could be inseminated then.

Next, a pregnancy. Another pregnancy. Then a CL, with Lutalyse on Monday.

Jessica Putnam was cleaning up the milk parlor, hosing down the floor and pipes. Granddaughter of one of the owners of the farm, she was home for the summer after a semester at UNH, but had no intention of working on the farm when she finished college. There wasn't enough money in it. Still, Jessica had taken a dairy elective that spring, and she peppered Chuck with questions.

"Why do you like cows?" she asked.

"Because they work so hard and because I thought I could

make improvements in the dairies. I get to work outside." He laughed. "I get to work alone."

"Why do you like dogs?"

"Because they're loyal, and you know that when you come home, no matter how bad your day is going, your dog is always happy to see you. No matter what, your dog will love you."

Chuck armed another cow, raked out manure, and armed again. "You haven't asked me why I like cats," he said.

"Why do you like cats?"

"Because they're independent and have no use for people."

Jessica had seen uterine palpation performed in the course at school. She asked, "Should people palpate their own animals?"

This was a more serious question. "If they want to, they can. The animals are their property. I tell them, if you want to palpate the animals, go right ahead. But they shouldn't."

"Because they don't know how," she said. "Right?"

Chuck let her answer stand.

4.

The Walpole Old Home Days parade was coming up that weekend, and Chuck was in the process of creating a float. He had been waking up at 5 a.m., thinking about possibilities. An idea that kept coming to mind was based on a float he'd seen at a parade in Kansas. The float had a little engine at the back, into which someone shoveled manure dropped by the parade animals. Each time manure went into one hopper, candy sprayed out of another. Chuck liked the idea it expressed—of something from nothing.

On Friday he brought in a teddy bear he'd pulled out of

his barn. There was hay in its fur. He left the bear lying on its back on the treatment-room floor.

"What's this, Take Your Pet to Work Day?" Laurel asked.

"That's our patient for surgery on the float," Chuck said. "It's in the right position. We just have to get it cleaned up."

And he wouldn't say any more about it.

Willie Hanna's red-blood-cell count was continuing to drop. Chuck examined the cat that morning, palpating his abdomen and feeling about his body while Laurel held him. Willie's distress was becoming greater, and he complained more often. "Oh, I'm sorry, Buddy," Chuck said. "Your nose is white. You're not feeling good today, are you?"

"I'm going to miss Willie when he goes," Laurel said. "He's such a good cat. He can be pissy, but he doesn't keep a grudge. Some cats keep a grudge."

"He'd make a great clinic cat," Chuck said.

Chuck had talked with Lucy Hanna after she talked with her vet. "I told her that I hoped the vet had apologized for what she put her through. But on the contrary, the vet told her that life is full of difficult decisions." So Lucy had now moved to another practice in Rhode Island, one with seven vets.

A retired veterinarian dropped by the clinic that week. A big bear of a man, his name was Frank Krohn. Krohn was of the generation between Chuck Shaw and Wilson Haubrich, having owned a practice in Springfield, Vermont, from 1958 to 1984. He liked to reminisce and had a bit of the raconteur in him.

Sitting on a stool in the treatment room, Krohn said, "The big thing in this profession was when penicillin came in, around 1942."

"During World War II," Chuck said.

"I decided I wanted to be a vet when I was a kid, milking

twenty-five cows with my mother. I saw a vet come in and prescribe a dose of penicillin. That was the fastest five bucks I ever saw anyone make in my life."

Krohn grinned. "I got eighteen dollars a day right out of vet school. Graduated with a ringed notebook four inches thick, and that was all I had to go on. Look at what the vets coming out of school have today. It's amazing. You can't keep up with it all."

"It's getting harder all the time," Chuck said.

"When I came out of vet school, certain vets were gods. Haubrich, others, one in Kentucky, another in upstate New York. The impression I had out of school was that I would save everything. It's the impression most vets have. But you learn that the worst situation, the one you want to always avoid, is a dead cow and a big vet's bill. The best service you can provide is to be able to accurately tell the dairy farmer, 'You can keep this, or send it to McDonald's.' "

Frank had done a lot of uterine palpation, a lot of arming. "My wife once said to me, 'Don't you ever work on the front end of cows?' " He smiled. An inside joke if there ever was one.

Chuck got called out to Sonny Greene's farm. Sonny's farm was unlike most of the others Chuck serviced. Down a back road, with low buildings, the place seemed almost subterranean. Sonny walked under those rafters easily, but most everyone else had to walk hunched over.

"Let's see how shitty we can get in a half hour," Chuck said as we drove in.

Sonny's eyes were red, his eyelids heavy. His pants hung low on his hips, and his stomach kept heaving, as if it had a mind of its own. In a stream of heavily accented New Hampshire farm country words that were barely intelligible to me, he told Chuck what he wanted done—check a cow for a DA and check three others for pregnancies. Sonny's helper, Jerry, accompanied Chuck into the barn while Sonny milked his cows at a small four-station parlor with a deep well.

Chuck looked at the first cow, which had significantly reduced milk production. He palpated her, flicked and tapped his fingers against her ribs, and listened with a stethoscope. "It's a DA," Chuck said.

Jerry left, talked with Sonny, then returned and said, "Go ahead and do it." They pushed her into a stall, put a halter on, and tied her in. Chuck asked that they shut down a fan. Jerry got an extension cord for the shaving clippers.

Chuck scrubbed and doused, positioned a drape over the cow's side, and began the surgery. He was soon shoulder-deep in a bovine body. It took him twenty minutes from start to finish. "Small animal," Chuck said. Then the dazed cow was let loose to meander off into the subterranean barn.

Two bulls were wandering about the herd. One was a tall, long-legged Holstein that caused Chuck to say to Jerry, "That is one ugly bull." The other was short and stocky and rust-colored, and had a set of horns. Sonny had said one would be put into the field with the heifers soon. They had been competing. "The one with the horns has been winning," Sonny said.

Chuck looked at a Jersey-Holstein that was off in her milk production. He palpated her and then listened to her lungs. She had an infection, he said. "Pneumonia, maybe." He prescribed penicillin.

Sonny's cows were skittish and fearful. While Chuck examined a Jersey along an alleyway, a group of cows streamed by, headed for a more open part of the barn. But just as those cows were going out, around the corner came the tall bull, rid-

ing the back of a cow, mating with her. She was moving while
he hopped along behind her. The second bull was in the
stream of departing cows, and as he passed by the tall bull, he
bumped into him. That was enough to knock the tall bull
over backward, with a clattering of legs. The other cows scattered. The tall bull tried to get up but couldn't.

Everyone had seen it, but Chuck kept on palpating.

"He fell on his ass," Jerry said.

"He's more embarrassed right now than anything," Chuck
replied. "They can break their penis doing that." He wasn't
amused, but he didn't seem concerned either.

Each time the bull tried to get up, he slipped on the
manure-slick floor and fell back. He didn't seem to have the
energy to make it up. When Chuck finished checking the Jersey, he said, "Get some sawdust under him." Chuck got into a
stall and kicked the bedding, wood shavings, into the alley.
When there was a good amount around the embarrassed bull,
Chuck got in front of him and pushed at his shoulders,
yelling, "Come on, get up!" The bull got his front legs under
him and then rose up on his back legs. "There you go. You got
your legs up!" The bull turned, walked off, and then seemed
to become alert, seeking something, but unsure of what it was.

Sonny was just coming from the milking parlor, and the
scene seemed to make no impression on him. "I want you to
do a preg check on that one right there," he said, pointing to
a large Holstein in a stall down the alleyway. "If she isn't pregnant, I'm gonna beef her!"

Chuck put on a sleeve. It didn't take long to get a reading,
but Sonny didn't like what he heard.

"She's pregnant," Chuck said, smiling.

"Ahh! How much?"

"About five months."

"Ahh, now I've gotta decide what to do. Four months more! Do I keep her or do I beef her? You don't know what she's gonna do even then!"

"It won't be that long, Sonny."

"Ah!"

Sonny pointed to another cow, a skinny and sickly-looking Holstein, and told Chuck to palpate her. This finding didn't take long either.

"She's not pregnant," Chuck said flatly. "And she's not go-ing to be."

"Ah, that makes it easy! We know what we're gonna do with her!"

The sickly cow stood waiting to get free, looking fearfully at the farmer and vet.

Chuck walked out through the dark passageways, clearing cobwebs with his head. Outside, Sonny Greene came to a doorway and said a few tangled words to Chuck, then turned to me and said with a charming smile, "They let you go out alone yet? Just give you a thermometer and stethoscope, few shots of penicillin, you'll be all right! Send you out, and he can go fishin'!"

Chuck backed out to the road. "You know, I could walk off Sonny's farm. But what would happen to the cows? At least this way I can do something for them." Most farms like Sonny's had disappeared, Chuck said. "The farmers around here say he's clever and shrewd. He'd have to be to stay in business. They say he knows cows, but not much else."

5.

On Saturday morning before the parade, Chuck met with Lucy Hanna. Willie was happy to see her, but he was not doing well. His weight had dropped to six pounds, from fourteen only a month ago. Chuck told Lucy that Willie wasn't going to make it, that his liver was failing and there was no point in further treatment. He told her he could put Willie down that morning if she wanted, but Lucy decided to take Willie home, spend the rest of the weekend with him, and have him put to sleep on Monday.

She later said, "It was comforting to me to have a diagnosis, even if it wasn't scientifically proven."

Chuck had told her not to prolong Willie's suffering, and on the drive home Lucy remembered his words. "He cried so pitifully," she said, "that I wondered if I had made a terrible mistake." Late that night, however, something happened that made Lucy feel better. "Sometimes he'd come into my room and wake me up. But on this night he came in and slept next to me. I woke up at 3 a.m., and he was right by my head, purring. He did the same thing the next night too. I thought then that I had done the right thing, to say good-bye in that way. I knew it wasn't for Willie, but for me."

Lucy was already taking Henry, her other cat, to the new practice she'd found, but she chose to have Willie put down at the old practice. She went in on Monday, the vet's day off, and had Willie put down by a relief vet who liked him and knew him well. Two weeks later she returned to New Hampshire and buried Willie's ashes where her family had spent summer vacations.

Old Home Days is a tradition in many towns in New Hampshire and Vermont. The celebration began in 1899, created by the governor of New Hampshire to honor agricultural and local traditions. Invitations were sent out to former residents and their descendants, in the hope of encouraging them to return for summer vacations. There was no specific date or for-

mat for the festivities, other than the stipulation that there be
a parade, and towns celebrated in different ways at different
times. Walpole held theirs every few years and made a weekend of it. This year the program included a street dance on
Friday night, and on Saturday a pancake breakfast, the parade,
a strawberry shortcake dinner, a concert on the town green,
and a play in the town hall.

After Chuck met with Lucy Hanna that Saturday morning, he rushed to the elementary school and joined the others
who had entered floats. At the appointed hour the parade line
assembled and headed toward the village, going past the town
common and looping back along Main Street before arriving
at the judging platform. It was a typical small-town parade,
with state reps and selectmen at the head, followed by the
school band and the town fire trucks.

Two farm-equipment companies rolled along next, first a
line of John Deere tractors driving down the street, then a line
of Kubotas. Hubbard Farms, a poultry company that was the
largest employer in town, went by on a modest float—no
chickens to be seen, but a few employees waving to the many
spectators gathered along the way. The Walpole Valley Folks
to Preserve Good Hay, an archaic club, went by on a float
loaded with hay and pulled by a tractor, followed by the
equally archaic Walpole Society for Bringing Horse Thieves to
Justice, on a float pulled by draft horses. The Historical Society was represented by an antique hearse drawn by a black
horse, with a minister and a widow in black walking behind.

The farm floats, central to the purpose and spirit of Old
Home Days, came next. The Fletcher Farm float had an immense globe revolving on an axis, the continents in black and
white—the Holstein pattern—with a sign that read GOT MILK?
Echo Moon Farm and the Beaudry family float followed,
a hay wagon with Holstein calves, waving children, and a

theme—a robot working a butter churn and a bank of computers, signifying farming in the future. Crescent Farm came next, a tractor pulling a float with old farm equipment, followed by a line of other tractors and a procession of Jersey calves, pretty as deer—a presentation that must have been a hundred feet long from end to end.

Caught up in the flow of the parade, anyone could have missed the approach of the entry by the Graves family and Great Brook Farm. But when the float halted before the judging stand, it was a breathtaking sight. At the head was a covered wagon pulled by an enormous pair of jet-black oxen with ivory horns. Bob and Peggy Graves sat on the wagon, with Bob holding the reins to the yoke while their son Peter, who ran the farm, stood beside the oxen holding a short whip. Peter was wearing a felt hat and a white blouse with billowing sleeves. Peggy wore a long dress and bonnet.

Not every town has an ox trainer, someone such as Bob Graves. Bob's father had farmed with oxen, and his grandfather had trained them for other farmers who used them for farming and logging. Bob had been training them for most of his seventy years, beginning with 4-H events like the ones his grandchildren were entering now. In his teens, in front of a big crowd at the fairgrounds in Keene, he had attempted to have his oxen do a maneuver in which one passes behind the other, switching sides, but when one ox got behind his partner, he mounted him and rode him down the length of the ring—to raucous laughter.

Years later, in a glorious time-crossed moment, Bob's truck stalled after a competition at a fair in Massachusetts, so he hitched his oxen to the front of the truck and had them pull until he could jump-start the engine. Many cars pulled to the side of the road to watch. Bob now owned several matched pairs—one so well trained that he could send them down to the brook that ran by the farm so that they could have a drink, then call them back like a pair of hunting dogs.

As the Graves float stopped at the reviewing stand, two riders on horseback came up, and one of them snatched the original deed to the farm—the deed issued on behalf of the governor of the British province of New Hampshire—and raced off with it. The point was that the farm had been around a long time, nine generations in the Graves family. Peter Graves tapped his whip to the nose of the black ox closest to him, and the wagon rumbled down Main Street. Behind followed a line of Graves's grandchildren, each leading a pair of oxen, each pair matched to the size of that youngster—the 4-H contingent.

The crowd hardly had time to recover from the excitement before the next float rolled up—the Walpole Veterinary Hospital entry, pulled by Roger's pickup truck. Chuck had borrowed a hay wagon from Britton Farm, set a row of potted geraniums along the front, and recruited a group of kennel workers to sit along the edge and walk behind, all wearing polo shirts that read wvh. Like the Graveses', here was another drama, but based on the theme of "something from nothing" that Chuck had seen in the Kansas parade. Chuck and Laurel Gibbs, in full surgical dress—blue bonnet, mask, and gown—stood at a table. On the table was the big stuffed bear, and an IV bag hung from a pole. Chuck had an oversized scalpel in his hand. Sitting next to the table in a rocking chair was Tucker Burr, the previous owner of the practice, in his eighties now.

When the float paused at the reviewing stand, Chuck reached into the belly of the bear, pulled out a handful of gummy worms, and threw them into the crowd. Some people laughed; others groaned. One little boy, the son of a dairy worker, jumped back in horror. Laurel reached in and threw some too. While Chuck and Laurel tossed the worms, old Tucker Burr got up from the rocker, picked up the IV unit, which was filled with red-colored water, and squirted it at the judges.

The Graves family got the blue ribbon for best float, but the clinic won an award for the most imaginative entry.

After the parade, Chuck did two DAs at Westminster Farms. At the clinic, he stitched up the lacerations on the chest and legs of a dog that had run into barbed wire. He gave the kitten they had adopted that week to the daughter of a dairyman. Chuck got sick on Saturday night—something he ate, or maybe some kind of bug. On Sunday he made a house call to put down a dog dying of liver failure. He did a third DA at Westminster Farms. After eleven consecutive nights of being on call, he was thoroughly worn out.

Flowers arrived on Monday from the owner of the dog that had run into barbed wire, with a card thanking Chuck for doing the treatment on a weekend. Ellie picked up the ribbon and plaque for the float and hung them on the reception-room wall. Chuck held office hours, tended to the hospitalized patients, performed a few minor surgeries, and did a herd check at Windyhurst.

Roger returned from vacation the next day. For an hour or so on his first morning back, all that could be seen of him was a lone boot outside the X-ray-room door. He had been thrown from a horse while roping calves in Alberta, and he was taking an X-ray of his ankle to see if he'd broken anything.

When Roger heard about Chuck's week and about Willie Hanna, his response was sympathetic, but he also had this to say: "You can totally burn yourself out being on call. I'd like to eventually not be on call. You can't have a life when you're on call all the time. Chuck doesn't have a life a lot of the time."

He had come back resolved to talk with Chuck about adding another vet to the practice, in fact. "That way we could be on a three-week rotation. Then it would seem like nothing. Then I wouldn't be thinking that I wanted to quit."

4

DEATH WEEK AT THE CLINIC

1.

The night after Roger returned, Chuck at last had a night when he wasn't on call, but sleep didn't come easily. He was dreaming of a storm; the window was open, the wind was blowing into the bedroom, and things were blowing in from outside, when Ellie nudged him awake, saying, "The phone is ringing." Joe Joslin, the herdsman at Boggy Meadow, was on the line. One cow had stepped on another cow's udder, tearing a milk vein. There was a trail of blood on the floor, the herdsman said, and rather than calling the clinic and getting the answering service, he had called Chuck at home. Chuck lived about a mile from Boggy Meadow, so he went.

Ellie thought he should have called Roger. "Ellie doesn't complain often," Chuck said, "but she was complaining from the time she woke up until I went out the door. I made the mistake of telling her to deal with it." Ellie was still awake when he returned at two-thirty, and she was awake another hour after that. Chuck teased her about it, trying to make light of it while he mulled over how much to charge Boggy Meadow. He knew the herdsman had called in a panic. He didn't think it would happen again soon, nor was there much need for discussion. "I don't want them to think they own me," Chuck said, "but I do want them to know I care." In the end he settled on a fee that would cover dinner with Ellie at the Walpole Inn, and he let the herdsman know.

Another vet had told Chuck that being on call was like having a bowl with chits in it, and that every time you went out on a call, you took a chit out of the bowl. Then suddenly one day you ran out of chits. Chuck didn't think he was going to run out of chits anytime soon, but he did say the number of chits in his bowl varied according to how much sleep he got. Roger said flatly, "I don't have that many chits in my bowl."

Roger told Chuck that they could certainly afford a third vet with the income that they'd been generating for the practice, about $800,000 a year.

Chuck told Roger that he'd think about it and discuss it with Ellie.

He knew very well the qualifications he would seek in a third vet.

"I would want someone who can do small animals and has an interest in horses but who will also be willing to spend twenty-five percent of the time going out to dairies. I wouldn't want someone who wants to work with small animals but is willing to help out with large animals only on emergencies. That can lead to disaster. That kind of person would be thinking of leaving within a year and be gone in two years. It has to be a person who is comfortable on the farms. You've seen how the farmers look at you when you walk into their place. Roger does so well because he knows about farms, and they know that he knows. It also has to be someone who doesn't mind going home smelling like cow shit. You've got to find someone who doesn't mind that. That's not easy either."

Such a person could be hard to find, I said to him.

"Actually, that person doesn't exist," Chuck said.

He was thinking hard about the financial challenge of taking on another associate. "You pay a salary of forty-five thousand, but it actually costs you sixty with the equipment, insurance, and benefits. How do you find that? We spend twenty thousand a year on relief vets. You can deduct that and bring the cost down to forty thousand. How do you get the rest?" Roger had increased the business by 20 percent in his first year with the practice, but Chuck was well aware that he was one of the rare few.

Roger wanted to hire someone immediately, but he knew the process would take time. They'd have to place an ad and conduct interviews. The interview process itself could take weeks. As Chuck said, they would most likely hire a fourth-year vet student who would begin after graduation, many months away. Roger knew that they might not find anyone interested in joining a mixed practice. "But we won't think about that," he said.

Chuck told Roger to write an ad for the position. He thought it would be a good way to measure Roger's interest in the practice. Chuck said he would write an ad too and they'd place a combined version in the *Journal*.

2.

Despite the demands of being on call, Roger tried to have a normal life on his call weekends. Soon after he returned from

Alberta, he managed to go out to dinner with a woman he was interested in. But it was hard to plan things on those weekends, and Chuck tried to convince him of that.

One Monday morning Chuck said to Laurel, "Roger is defiant about being on call. He thinks he can be on call and still have a life."

Laurel was holding a cat while Chuck took its temperature. She said, "Roger and Jeremy and I had planned to go fishing on the weekend, but then Roger got beeped and couldn't go. So Jeremy and I didn't go either, because I'd have to drive the boat, and I can't drive the boat."

"Ellie and I threw in the towel a long time ago," said Chuck. "We don't make plans when I'm on call. If we invite friends to dinner and I get beeped and have to leave, it changes the dynamics. Ellie has to entertain alone."

"Don't you ever want to just turn the beeper off?"

"No, but I want to throw it against the wall. I couldn't do that, though, because the answering service would get the calls, and that would be a disaster. After ten at night I don't want to get beeped. Roger wants to get beeped, but I want a call. Maybe it's habit from years past, but I'd rather have the phone ring. The phone is next to the bed. Ellie likes that a lot."

"Yeah, I'd like that too," Laurel said. "Roger went five times to one place to look at a horse. And he yanked a dead calf out of a cow."

"As I was saying, maybe I'm a holdover from my generation, but we have different views about being on call."

"How?"

"Roger doesn't want to be on call."

Roger's weekend had gone as follows:

—Saturday morning to the clinic for appointments.

—A call to the Polly DuPont farm to treat a horse with colic.

—Swimming at Colony Mine.

—A calving at Windyhurst.

—A call to Nancy Kenney to treat a horse with colic.

—A fetotomy, extraction of a dead calf in parts by cutting with obstetrical wire.

—A second trip to the DuPont farm to treat for colic again.

—A second trip to the Kenney farm to treat for colic again, 4 to 5 p.m.

—To the clinic, 5 p.m., for treatments.

—Dinner with the woman he hoped to date.

—Back to Kenney's at 10 p.m., recurrence of colic.

—Two and a half hours' sleep

—Back to Kenney's at 2:30 a.m. after horse developed temperature of 105°.

—Home, another two and a half hours' sleep.

—Sunday, 7:30 a.m., a possible prolapsed uterus at Barrett's, false alarm.

—Cow with udder tear after being stepped on, Rushton's Farm, Grafton, Vermont.

—9:30, return to DuPont's, colicky horse eating gravel, a "gravel colic."

—10:30, Kenney horse colicky again.

—Home, mow lawn, clean horse stalls, lunch, five hours of sleep.

—Clinic at 5 p.m. for rounds of treatments.

—6:30 p.m., Kenney's a fifth time, colic, belly tap, and tubed with oil.

"I can do this now," Roger said after that weekend, "but I don't think I can do it forever. I think I will burn out if I try. I may have to choose one or the other later on, large-animal or small. I'd like to be training horses by the time I'm forty-five. Maybe I'll work with small animals three days a week and do that. Maybe I'll just have a horse practice and work out of my truck."

He had just done an ultrasound pregnancy check on a draft horse in Langdon, and the results had come up positive. On the screen it looked like a little cloud-shaped form in a pocket, where the terrain of the uterus rolled by in black and white, all hills and valleys and plains. Congratulations had gone round. Roger then called the clinic and asked Lynn to get a cat ready for surgery. A young Himalayan named Angel, not much more than a kitten, had been hit by a car and suffered a broken femur. Roger was going to insert a pin in the broken bone, with Chuck's supervision.

Along the way, Roger talked about the ad he would write. He had been composing it mentally. "I think I'm going to include something like 'fun place to work, with room to develop interests.' We've got to emphasize the fun part of the job." He smiled at this idea.

Lynn had Angel ready in the surgery by the time Roger arrived. He quickly prepped and then made an initial small incision on the cat's leg. He called Chuck in, and Chuck instructed him in how to lengthen the incision, how to find the line of muscle in the leg, and where to separate it. Chuck told him how to pull the muscle open to find the bone ends, and he described how to clamp the bones.

Roger opened the bone kit—a sterilized set of tools—laid the leg open, and prepared the bone. He then opened his pin kit and selected a pin of the right diameter—a tiny pin for a tiny leg. One end was sharpened and the other threaded. He turned the sharp end through a length of the bone and out through the flesh of the leg. He then turned the threaded end into the other segment of the broken bone and drew the two pieces together, turning the pin like a screw. Next in this rebuilding project, he twisted wire around the rejoined bones. Roger called Chuck back in then, and Chuck told him how to measure the length of the bone, using the X-ray as a guide. Chuck brought in a set of bolt cutters and set them in the sink in a sterile solution.

Roger pulled the muscle over the bone and sutured up the cat's leg. A pin was still sticking out near the joint. Because Lynn was busy, Roger asked Jen Wilson, one of the kennel helpers, to cut it off with the bolt cutters. She did so eagerly. It was an odd sight, the girl holding huge bolt cutters with handles three feet long over a kitten that didn't even measure twelve inches. Roger placed the cutting jaws against the kitten's leg, pushed them down to get as much purchase on the pin as possible, and said, "Okay, right there." Jen closed the handles together with a little snipping sound.

"Oh, shit, you are some tough," Roger said.

Lynn walked in. "Did somebody say 'Oh shit?' You hate to hear your surgeon say 'Oh shit.' "

"I was just teasing Jen here." They moved the cat into the X-ray room. Roger studied the image of the straight pin passing through the jagged bone, with the wire neatly twisted in place. By the next morning, Angel the cat was standing and mewing for attention.

3.

A vet might want outcomes to develop along lines such as this: A golden retriever named Max lives with his family for many years and makes regular visits for examinations and shots. The children go to college, Max ages, and the end begins to approach. The owner understands, but he wants Max to last until Christmas, when his children will be there. All goes well, and Max seems capable of going a bit further. Finally the owner says, "We will wait until Max can no longer enjoy pizza." The key word is *enjoy*. Max likes a slice of pizza now and then. Then the day comes when Max is no longer interested in pizza or any other food, and the call is made. The vet performs euthanasia. Max passes away at home and is buried there, near the garden. Neighbors miss seeing him on the street and call to offer their sympathies.

Or perhaps even like this one, with Roger's house call to put down a horse in a small community east of Walpole. When Roger drives into the yard, he sees the horse grazing on the lawn. He is not much more than a pony, really, with a long forelock and a gray-and-brown coat. Roger notices that the wings of his vertebrae are showing. The horse looks up briefly when Roger gets out of his truck, then resumes eating grass. The owner, a middle-aged woman named Mrs. Digby, is talking with a neighbor when Roger arrives. "The neighbors are all trying to find something to do," Mrs. Digby said. She thanks Roger for coming. "You were very nice about it. Another vet was not nice about it."

Roger walks over to the horse, whose name is Little Dipper, or just Dipper. He is going blind and has lost most of his teeth. "Eating more and more, and losing weight," Roger says when he looks into his mouth. The Digbys are afraid that Dipper will die alone in the barn in the winter. Dipper is thirty-six years old, and Mrs. Digby has owned him for twenty-six of those years.

Roger runs his hand down Dipper's neck and along his knobby spine, and talks softly to him, calling him Buddy. Roger calls most of the animals he treats Buddy, except cows, which he usually calls Babe. Mr. Digby comes out of the house and puts a lead on Dipper. They walk out to the back-yard, behind a barn, where Mr. Digby has dug a hole with his tractor. Next to the hole is a pair of chains laid out in two lines, with a rope beside them, as Roger has asked. They lead Dipper to the chains and stop.

"I'm going to explain how I'll do this," Roger says. "First I'm going to give him a local anesthetic, to numb him for the bigger needle. When I give him the final shot, he'll go down pretty fast. He might take a couple of breaths afterward, but that's normal. Don't worry about it."

Roger pulls a needle from his pocket and pinches a fold of skin on Dipper's neck. Mr. and Mrs. Digby stand on either side of the horse and hold him while Roger gives the first in-jection. Dipper tries to rear when he feels the needle. The Digbys say, "It's okay, it's okay," while they rub him.

The second syringe is much larger and filled with a blue liquid called Fatal Plus. The Digbys hold tightly while Roger gives this injection, and Dipper jumps up again, but not quite so strenuously as before. Roger slips the syringe back into his pocket and then faces the horse, taking his halter in both hands. Standing square, Roger guides Dipper backward onto his rump and then down to his side, onto the chains. The Digbys get on their knees with him, rub and talk to him while Roger listens to his heartbeat, trying to block out the voices.

"We've had him such a long, long time," Mrs. Digby says. "Twenty-six years." She is shaken and sad, of course, but she has no doubts about what they've done. "This is the right way," she says when she stands up, and adds, "I wish we could be this kind to our fellow human beings, to the old people."

"He's gone," Roger says, and stands up. Mrs. Digby hugs him. Mr. Digby gets up, and he and his wife hug each other, both of them crying. She says, "I'm going to leave now."

"We'll help you get him in," Roger says. Mr. Digby leaves to get his tractor.

While Mr. Digby is gone, Roger says to me, "I know this will sound strange, but my worst fear in the world is that they will get up again."

The tractor comes around the corner with the bucket raised. They attach the chains to the bucket. Roger ties a loop around the horse's head. When Mr. Digby raises the bucket, Roger leans back with the rope to keep the horse's head from flopping down. The gesture seems to bring a measure of dignity.

Mr. Digby swings the horse over the hole and lowers him down. Roger jumps in and takes the chains off, then pulls them away. He grabs onto the bucket as Mr. Digby raises it, and he springs out of the hole. Roger picks up a shovel and quickly throws some sand over the horse's head. This seems to change the moment. Mr. Digby gets down, thanks Roger, and shakes his hand. He gets back on the tractor, and Roger walks around to the front yard.

Mrs. Digby is in the driveway, holding flowers a neighbor has brought her. The neighbor is with her young son. Mrs. Digby says to the boy, "Dr. Osinchuk made Dipper feel all better."

"He's much better now that he won't be suffering anymore," Roger says.

"He died?" the boy asks.

"He's in the big pasture in the sky now," his mother says.

"Running with other horses," Mrs. Digby says.

Another neighbor drives in as Roger is leaving. Roger turns the corner and sees Mr. Digby in the backyard, lifting a bucket of dirt over the hole.

"Some vets won't stay," Roger says. "They don't want to see the people cry. I like to stay, hold the head up. They don't want to see the horse have chains on with his head hanging down."

He has learned this from his father. "When I was living at home, my brother's horse died in the barn one night. He had a halter on, jumped up and got caught, and hanged himself. My brother saw him in the stall the next morning, but he didn't have to bury him. My father and I put the chains on, and he had me put a rope on his head and hold it up when we carried him out. It makes it look so much better.

"I want the people feeling good about what they did, feeling that they did the right thing. They had to deal with a lot of moral issues to do it, to get to the point where they could do it. You have to take into consideration how they got to that point.

"Because you can't put people to sleep, some people question if it's morally right to put an animal to sleep. I don't have a problem with that issue at all. When animals start to suffer, it's cruel to make them live until they die. The biggest issue is quality of life and suffering. Those people were sad, but they didn't want the animal to suffer or die in the barn in the winter. You couldn't find a horse that's as close to a family as that one. It's not hard to be nice to people like that. And when they give you a hug like that, it makes you feel good.

"One extra thing. You put a local anesthetic on, it makes it a little easier for the horse. It hurts with that big sixteen-gauge needle going in there."

The cost for the house call is $77.25 for the euthanasia, $30 for the farm call, $107.25 in total.

"I was shaking," Roger says, "worse than when I get tired. I was worried something would go wrong. They can flip over, go crazy, make you look bad. I like to see them in the hole with some dirt on them."

4.

Chuck and Roger were at Murray's Restaurant in Walpole for their weekly breakfast meeting. Chuck wanted a forum where they could talk about work away from the clinic. The discussions were informal, but they often touched on serious subjects. Roger had been off the day before, and Chuck was giving him an update.

"We put half the world to sleep yesterday. Susan's head was down all day," Chuck said, referring to Susan Armstrong, the receptionist. "We put down a kitten with ringworm. The kitten had been given to some kids, and they brought it in a box. Susan kept coming in to look at it and saying, 'Are you gonna put that cat to sleep?' They should never have let a cat leave the Humane Society with skin lesions."

They had performed eight euthanasias so far that week, including a twenty-year-old cat and a German shepherd that had bitten the owner's grandchild. It was not an extraordinary number by some clinics' standards, but it was enough to create stress among the workers, or what is called euthanasia fatigue or euthanasia trauma.

One euthanasia in particular had saddened everyone, that of a year-old Labrador retriever named Jessie Kennealy. Her case was a prime example of the ethical dilemmas that vets routinely face. Jessie had been leaking urine, because of a birth defect, since she was a puppy. Chuck had warned the owners about it in the beginning. At one point they had given Jessie up to a rescue league, which had arranged to have surgery done to correct the problem and then had given her back to the owners. But Jessie still leaked urine, and the owners had decided to put her down, refusing to try further treatment or even to allow the clinic to adopt her out. Roger had done the euthanasia two days ago. Now, at breakfast, he said, "I won't do one like that again, and I don't think the clinic should either."

Chuck had been as disappointed as the others, but he had consented. "I'd rather put her to sleep than have the owner do something foolish," he said. "She'd probably end up taking her out in the woods and tying her to a tree." Chuck said that the owner had taken Jessie to a clinic in Keene, and they had refused to put her down. She had then returned to Walpole, where Jessie had been treated all along and where everyone knew her.

"They should have brought her to Rowley and had her treated," Roger said. Rowley is an advanced-care animal hospital in Springfield, Massachusetts. "They have the money to do it."

"You read the law," Chuck said, "and you'll see that pets are personal property. You may not like it, but it's the law."

"It didn't make me feel good at all," Roger said. "I don't think I'll do it again."

Their meals came, and they moved on to other subjects.

"I wrote my ad," Chuck said.

"Mine's in my head."

Chuck took a piece of paper from his pocket and gave it to Roger. His was a minimal description, with emphasis on location:

Walpole. Mixed Animal Practice expanding to 3 full-time veterinarians. Small animal, dairy, and equine. New facility with great location on the Connecticut River in a town ideally suited for living.

"I'll have mine in by noon," Roger said.

They talked briefly about methods of informing clients

that a pet had died. Roger said he always labored over whether to call them at work. "If it were my dog, I'd want to know," he said. Chuck said he always tried to call them before they called him. "I tell them I've got bad news," he said. "I tell them that I'm very sorry."

They mentioned a couple of disagreeable clients they'd seen recently. Roger said that if they didn't find a third vet, they should think about weeding out one or two of those clients, especially the vociferous complainers. They took too much time. Chuck then moved to a more sensitive subject, one he might have been saving for the end of the breakfast. "The pig died," he said. "Jennifer Tree."

Roger's eyes went wide. "She did?"

Roger had handled the case originally, going well out of his way in the process. A call had come in on Sunday from Jennifer Tree, who lived south of Keene. She had begun raising pigs two years ago, and like many hobbyist pig owners, she had become attached to them and found it hard to sell or slaughter them. As a result, her collection had become sizable in both number and weight. One of her group included a thousand-pound boar named Brutus, and a few months ago he had gotten into a pen with a young female named Abby, who was a favorite of Jennifer's. As a result of Brutus's visit, Abby had gotten pregnant and this past Sunday had gone into a long labor. Jennifer was in the barn from 4 a.m. on, talking to her, stroking her, and reading comic books to her. By midafternoon, when Abby had still not given birth to any piglets, Jennifer called her vet, but that vet wasn't available on weekends and had left a message on her machine directing clients to go to the emergency clinic in Manchester.

Jennifer then started calling other clinics, and she reached Roger at about 3 p.m. He had been training his year-old quarter horse, Spencer, during a break in the flow of calls. Roger said he would come, but he decided to finish his session with Spencer first. He got to Jennifer Tree's place at about five. For the next three hours he wriggled on his stomach and crouched on his knees while he reached inside the pig and pulled out piglets. All were dead, but Abby seemed to be well enough. Jennifer and her boyfriend were so grateful for Roger's effort that they paid him in cash and gave him a $40 tip, which he split with Chuck.

But Abby had died later that night, and Jennifer Tree had called to report it.

Now Chuck said, "We don't know if it would have happened that way if we had gone out there earlier, at three when she called. I've found that it's better to get out there right away. You get it off your mind. Otherwise you keep thinking about it."

Recovering from the shock, Roger said in self-defense, "Well, I'm not going to worry too much about that one. That pig had been going through problems a long time before I got there."

Chuck didn't push it further. This was a delicate issue, another dilemma of the professional life versus the personal one. But he knew how he felt about it. Later, on a house call, he said, "When someone calls, you just have to go out there. You can't wait until later, because there is no later. Something else is coming later. It's hard, when you become a vet, to make the change in your mind to accept that you can't do anything that can't be interrupted when you're on call. It's hard to understand that it can't be a weekend off."

Roger wasn't ready to accept the whole argument. "I'm going to train Spencer. If anyone calls and they're not a regular client, they're going to have to wait."

After breakfast they drove to the clinic, but Roger stayed outside in his truck for a few minutes and wrote a draft of his ad for the third vet. He brought it inside and gave it to Chuck.

Two person mixed practice expanding to three person. Large animal consists primarily of equine and dairy. Room for the right associate to expand on any aspect of their interest while gaining experience in all aspects of mixed practice. Fun and energetic staff with well equipped clinic. (Chuck can put in salary comments.) Call at home or office.

Chuck was pleased, though he didn't say so. The ad showed that Roger cared about the practice, Chuck thought. He put the ad down and said, "I'll read it when you've corrected it, gotten out all the errors. Not when you've written it in ten minutes."

Comparing the two versions, Roger said, "I think mine's better."

Roger composed a sympathy card to Jennifer Tree. "Really sorry about the loss," he wrote. "Wish we could have done more. But I think we did all we could."

Carol Zachary, the morning receptionist, came back into the treatment room with a card from the owner of Jessie Kennealy. Carol gave it to Roger. The note seemed to be saying that, against their better judgment, the two vets had allowed her to struggle. "Not once did you imply, though it may have been on your minds, that it was time to give up. You allowed me to do what I thought was right for Jessie."

"She's trying to justify it," Roger said, and tossed the note aside.

"I lose sleep thinking about these things," he added. "I want to get strong enough, be a strong enough person so I can say, What are you doing? Do you see what you are doing here? I don't have any trouble putting a dog to sleep. A dog that's mean, a dog that's tearing up the house, a dog that's deliberately peeing in the house, I have no problem putting a dog like that to sleep. A dog that bites someone, I'll put him to sleep in a minute. But I won't do that again. Jessie was cute, cute and goofy. Everybody here loved her."

Carol walked in just then with a cardboard box. The flaps were closed on top. "This is Ophelia," she said. "To be euthanized. They've said their good-byes. They don't want to see it done."

Roger opened the box, and a black cat lifted her head out and looked around.

"What's wrong with this cat?"

"They said she has urinary problems, been peeing all over the place."

Roger sighed and carried the box to the exam table, where he readied a syringe and plugged in the clippers. Laurel assisted. When he was done, Roger put the cat in the box, closed the flaps on the top, taped them, and delivered the contents to the reception area, where a man and his teenage son were waiting. Roger shook their hands and spoke to them. Ophelia was fourteen, it turned out, and had been owned by the man's grandmother. The cat had been disoriented lately, waking up at night and howling, and urinating on the rugs.

Enough said. Roger felt he'd done the right thing in this case.

Still, nine euthanasias, and counting.

Laurel came into the treatment room with a full-size Bouvier des Flandres on a leash. He had a pea-sized growth above his eye. Roger put a muzzle on him. "Good boy!" Roger said as he administered a local anesthetic. Then he used a scalpel to cut away the growth. The dog hardly moved the entire time, though his eyes darted about while Roger did his handiwork. Five quick stitches, and it was done.

"Good boy!" Roger said when he took off the muzzle.

"Good boy!" he said again when he took the dog back to his owner. She was happy to see her dog, who was looking happy too.

5.

Chuck went to Putnam Farms that morning, did the herd check, and spent an hour vaccinating calves. He then drove into Charlestown and headed east up the hill toward Acworth. Near the top he turned into a driveway that led to Joan Beaudry's colonial-style house with its long views across the valley to Vermont. Joan came out, tall and slender, in her Postal Service uniform. She was home on her lunch hour. "She's brought me a lot of business over the years," Chuck said, "giving my name to people coming into the post office."

Chuck got out and said, "How are you?" He had a way of saying this with such sincerity that it could bring you to attention. You felt that you should answer well.

"Okay," Joan answered, in a way that meant she wasn't okay.

They went inside to a den, its windows facing west. The rug had a fine covering of dog hair. A fan was blowing. Two elderly dogs had gotten up to greet their visitors. One was a yellow-gold mutt that resembled a golden retriever. The other was brown and red, with a gray face.

"Well, hello," Chuck said to them. "You're keeping cool."

"We really pamper them," Joan said.

"Do you leave the television on for them?"

"No, but we leave the fan on all the time."

Chuck held up his hands as if to show he was unarmed. "All I've got is a stethoscope," he said to the two dogs.

He first examined the dark-haired dog, whose name was

Lady. Lady was thirteen. "No health problems at all with her," Joan said.

Sandy was twelve, and the daughter of Lady. While Chuck ran his hands over her, she remained standing, but when he put the stethoscope to her ribs, she dropped to the floor.

"Her back legs give out on her," Joan said.

Chuck stood up and looked at the dogs for a moment. He seemed to be considering what to say. He turned to Joan and asked, "What did your husband say?"

She looked away. "It's time," she said.

"All systems are going. I don't know how much longer she's going to live, but it's probably not going to be much longer."

Lady walked over to Sandy and stood over her.

"Yes," Joan said. "That's your baby."

She asked if they could go outside, where Sandy had left some feces on the lawn. She thought Chuck might want to examine them. They went out the back door—the vet, the owner, the two dogs. The sunlight was bright on the lawn. Chuck looked at the stools but didn't say anything about them.

"She was my son's dog," Joan said of Sandy. Almost as if to excuse herself, Lady climbed the steps and went back inside.

"What do you want to do?" Chuck asked.

"Is there any reason we have to do this outdoors? Can't we do it inside where she'll be more comfortable?"

"Sure," Chuck said. He helped Sandy up the steps. She went down the hallway a few feet before flopping on the tile floor. Joan knelt next to her. Chuck went to the car and got his clippers, a blanket, and a syringe, and came back into the hallway.

He plugged in the clippers and turned them on.

"Oh, no," Joan said.

"Do you want to leave?" Chuck asked gently.

"I do," she said. "But I would feel so guilty."

"No animal could have a better owner than you. Look what you put yourself through."

After he shaved Sandy's leg, he squeezed and felt for a vein. This might seem like an ordinary thing to do, but finding a vein on an old dog, even when the hair has been shaved off, can be tricky. The dog could object, and the vein could be elusive. Good vets make it look easy.

"I don't see how you can *do* this," Joan said. "I always thought I would volunteer at a clinic, but I could never do this."

"It's been happening all week."

She stroked Sandy and said, "I'm going to miss you."

Sandy's muzzle dropped.

Chuck pressed the stethoscope to her side. "She's gone," he said. "Do you want me to take her and have her buried?"

Joan nodded. Chuck wrapped Sandy in a blanket and carried her to the car. Joan followed and stood watching. Chuck closed the car door, walked back, and put his arms around her.

"Thank you," she said.

"I'm sorry."

He took the long way back to the clinic, driving along some woodland and farmland roads through Charlestown and Langdon. He didn't talk about Sandy. There wasn't much to be said. But he did talk about Jessie Kennealy and the issues her case represented.

"That was a hard one," he said. "Even Ben, the big football player who works for us in the kennels, said, 'Why couldn't that dog be a farm dog?' A death like that can shake the emotions. And when you see one come in on top of another, it can get hard to deal with.

"Roger says he's going to refuse to do something like that again. My last associate would also refuse to do one like that.

But I don't agree. They are refusing for personal reasons, but that's not what their job is about.

"When I was in vet school, this vet came driving up in a pink Cadillac, and he told us, 'I will absolutely refuse to put an animal down until we do every possible workup.' I got the impression that what he was interested in was the money. Some clinics insist on doing two to four hundred dollars in workups before they put a pet down. We've had many people come in after doing several hundred dollars in workups at another clinic and ask us to put the pet down. They can't go back to the other place.

"In a case like Jessie Kennealy, you say you're not going to put this animal to sleep. Now what's going to happen? Will they go to the Humane Society with it? Leave it to be adopted by someone else? Will they take it to obedience classes? How many will do that rather than have their neighbor shoot it, or leave it on the side of the road, or tie it up somewhere? What are the chances of that pet staying in that home or being adopted if you refuse to put it down?

"We have a policy. The customer can pay the euthanasia fee, and we'll keep the animal and tell them we'll try to find it a home. Some people say no to that. I give them the option to say no. Some people are hard-hearted about it. If they say no, then I begin to think, How am I going to deal with this one? We may come to a point where I'll say, Here is my value system. I want people to know where I'm coming from. My thing is, I don't want to feel guilt about it.

"Jessie Kennealy's owner, she's going to have to live with what she did. I don't think I could live with that so easily. When you have a pet, you take responsibility not only for it, but also for its problems. I would have liked to have seen Jessie have a good life. But the vet can't control all the problems.

"Life goes on," Chuck said. "You keep trying to get better."

Back in Walpole, he drove around to the side entrance of the clinic. Susan Armstrong was at the back door having a cigarette. Chuck got out and headed inside for a cadaver bag.

"Death week at the clinic," Susan said as he passed by.

"Nobody wants to talk to me anymore," he answered.

Hobbs sometimes came outdoors with Susan on her smoke breaks, though he wasn't there today. Hobbs spent a lot of time out front with Susan, hiding under the desk or lying on the floor. She liked to talk to him, call him Hobbsie, and feed him. They both liked to eat Doritos. Hobbs would get possessive about the chips, crouching over and guarding them on the floor. He could be possessive about Susan too. A few days ago she had come into the staff room with a cat in her arms, about to put it into boarding. Hobbs had glared at her. Susan noticed and laughed, and she told Hobbs not to worry, but Hobbs chased after her. He caught her halfway across the treatment room and launched himself up on her backside. Susan was wearing a smock, so his claws didn't pierce her skin, and she just kept walking and laughing, with Hobbs swinging from her butt. Riding her ass, they called it. But Susan's feelings for Hobbs didn't change. She was an animal lover, someone who as a teenager had boarded as many as a hundred cats at a time for a humane society. Hobbs was safe with her, jealous or not.

Chuck came out with the bag and carried Sandy inside.

"It's just so hard to see the young ones," Susan said. "On the way home yesterday all I could think of was Jessie as a puppy. She was so happy to be here. And the kitten. I couldn't stop thinking about the kitten."

She blew out a stream of smoke. "It's too bad their lives are so cheap. All you have to do is go get another puppy, start over."

Roger wrote another draft of the ad, Chuck rewrote it, and Ellie edited the final version. It would soon appear in the *AVMA Journal*, and it read:

Walpole, NH: Mixed practice expanding to three veterinarians. Large animal segment primarily dairy and equine with some small ruminant and beef. Room for a new associate to refine areas of interest while gaining experience in a mixed practice. Fun and energetic staff. Large, new, well-equipped facility on the Connecticut River in an area ideally suited for living. Competitive salary. Call Dr. Shaw or Dr. Osinchuk or send resume to Walpole Veterinary Hospital.

Now it was just a matter of waiting for the right person to come along.

5

TEACHING POINTS

1.

Stray animals came, and stray animals went.

Most of the staff had adopted strays. Carol Zachary, the morning receptionist, found her dog, Annie, at the clinic. The woman who brought Annie in said she had adopted her at the Humane Society, but now she was getting married, and her fiancé didn't want the dog. She didn't return Annie to the Humane Society, because she didn't want her to languish for weeks only to be euthanized, so she had decided to take the direct route and bring her to the clinic. Chuck said, as he had to others, that she could pay the fee, and so on. As the days went by and Carol got to know Annie, she decided she needed a dog. Carol said, "If it were me, I would have kept the dog and gotten rid of the guy."

Chuck and Ellie's dog, Heidi, had come in when an elderly owner died. They placed Heidi, but she was a dog who would run off if you let her out the door, and she was returned by her adopters. One day at the clinic Heidi got out the door and ran off, but Ellie drove after her and got Heidi to follow her home. Ellie and Chuck already had a dog and three cats, all adoptees from the clinic, but Heidi got along well with them, so she stayed. "It took two obedience classes from the Humane Society to stop her from running away," Ellie said. "That dog had no sense of how to act."

Roger had Dexter, the blood donor dog. The kennel workers adopted pets too. Susan Armstrong claimed she wasn't a little dog person—they were the ones that usually nipped, she said—but she adopted Saydie, a little fox terrier, after her owner, Clark Prentiss, died. "I loved that dog from the moment I saw her. Always happy." Saydie and Clark had been favorites among the staff. Clark was something of an Eeyore, one of the receptionists said, tending toward the glum, tending to see the negative in things but willing to do anything for his dog. Ellie had noted Clark's birth date in the calendar after he mentioned it was his birthday at one appointment, so after Saydie had a growth removed, Ellie scheduled the follow-up visit on the day of Clark's birthday, his eightieth. Susan made a cherry cake. Clark was twenty minutes early for his appointment, as usual. When he walked into the appointment room, all the staff were there to sing for him. Saydie smiled and trembled while Clark stood trembling too, and blushing. "I was afraid something like this might happen," he said. "How are you doing?" someone asked. "Oh, okay, I guess. I went to a funeral yesterday," he answered. "What are you going to do on your birthday?" "Oh, lay low," Clark answered.

The herdsman at Boggy Meadow brought in a cat that had been hanging around the barn, a little calico, brown and copper and white, and she got the name Stray Cat. She took up residence in the cat hospital. They usually let her out of her cage during the day, and she spent much of the time sitting on a shelf by the window. Occasionally she came into the treatment room, where she was bound to meet up with Hobbs. He was fascinated with her, though she didn't seem to think much of him. When Stray Cat came out, Hobbs would charge across the room, pull up in front of her, sit, and make himself tall. She hissed and batted at him, but Hobbs didn't flinch. If she moved back, Hobbs would get up close again and stand tall again.

"She likes living here," Chuck said. He mentioned a client whose cat had recently been put down. "That cat would be perfect for her," Chuck said. A few days later, Stray Cat was gone, and she had a new name.

Animals would show up in ways that seemed mind-boggling. A young male cat arrived at the clinic one week-end after his owner had been discovered throwing him into oncoming traffic. Someone had stopped and taken the cat away—an intervention, Chuck called it. They named him Wylie. He was buff and white, and he had a way of getting attention because of his cuteness, but also because of a piercing howl. Sometimes when Wylie started howling, they let him out to play. He was playing in the treatment room, batting a toy mouse around, when Roger found a home for him.

Roger was in the exam room with a client who had five cats and had brought one in for an exam. Four of her cats were ten years old or more, while the fifth was a year old and a terror to the older ones. The client said she had been think-ing it might be a good idea to get a younger cat to balance his energies. She lived on property that had been a dairy farm, but when the farm left, the rats stayed. She'd been thinking she needed a cat who could catch rats.

"I've got a rat-catching *machine* for you," Roger said. He went into the treatment room and scooped up Wylie. On the way back, Roger saw Hobbs sitting on a cardboard box, and gathered him up too. Roger went into the exam room with Hobbs in one arm, poor, glaring Hobbs with his white belly

exposed, and Wylie in the other arm, cute and calm and looking about curiously.

"Take your pick," Roger said. Soon Hobbs barreled out of
the exam room and was halfway across the treatment room
before he slowed down.

"If you recommend him," she said of Wylie, who pushed
up against her neck.

"I highly recommend him," Roger said, and offered to castrate him too. And so Wylie had a home—the magic of something from nothing. When he appeared again weeks later with
a new name, Brinkley, the report came that he wasn't much of
a rat-catching machine ("he did catch a chipmunk"), but he
was quite a companion, sleeping on the bed next to his owner.

Hobbs wasn't one to quickly forget indignities. On the day
Wylie was adopted, Darcie Sprague, the new veterinary technician, came out of the treatment room to find Hobbs sitting
on the box again. When she tried to rub Hobbs's back, however, he swiped at her. "Hobbs!" she said. Already Darcie had
taken a liking to Hobbs, and he to her. She tried to stroke him
again, and again he swatted at her. "Hobbs!"

Hobbs had his good days too, and there was a hidden side
to him, as it turned out. A sales rep for a pet food company
visited the clinic and left an entry form for a contest. Darcie
entered Hobbs under the name of Hobbs N. Forcer, position
of security guard. A few weeks later an envelope came addressed to Hobbs Forcer, and inside was a coupon worth $5 at
one of the burger chains.

One day during lunch break, Darcie and Susan put Hobbs
in a cat carrier and drove off to Keene. As soon as the car was
moving, Hobbs began to purr. Darcie opened the lid of the
carrier, and Hobbs poked his head out. He seemed to be looking out the window, and he seemed to be enjoying the ride.

They stopped at a drive-up window and ordered a burger

and fries for Hobbs, setting a portion on the floor of the car. But Hobbs wasn't interested in eating as much as he was in riding. On the way back, he sat on Darcie's lap, leaning his shoulder against the door and looking out. A few days later they took Hobbs out again, to a convenience store in Westminster, and this time he put both paws up on the window ledge and looked out when they drove.

Chuck told Hobbs's former owner about the excursions, and the man told Chuck that he had taken Hobbs for rides many times and that Hobbs used to ride standing up, with his paws on the dashboard.

Stray animals came, and stray animals went.

2.

The ad in the *AVMA Journal* ran in six issues, every other week from mid-October until mid-December. The Walpole Vet Hospital was up against stiff competition in the hunt for an associate. In one issue alone, 553 employment ads appeared, and among them, 507 were for small-animal practices, 43 for mixed, 3 for large-animal exclusive. New Hampshire offered 15 associate positions, 3 in mixed practice.

Two candidates responded to the ad. Both were veterinary students. One took a cursory look and moved on. The other gave the position longer consideration, but he wanted more dairy work than Chuck could offer, and he chose a practice in northern Vermont, deeper into dairy country. Chuck decided to run the ad again in February. He figured he would have better luck then, when vet students were approaching graduation and thinking more seriously about jobs.

Though the two students who responded to the ad were males, chances were that the new associate would be a woman because of ongoing changes in the profession. In 1928 there had been only twenty-two women veterinarians nationwide, and through the 1930s, 99 percent of vet school graduates were male. Even when women were admitted to veterinary schools, they were discouraged from or prevented from taking courses in large-animal medicine. Naturally, there were groundbreaking women who did large-animal medicine anyway. A Cornell graduate of the 1940s, Dr. Jeanne Logue, operated a mixed practice for more than a decade, until she realized that she had eaten only two uninterrupted meals with her family for an entire year. Through the 1950s, men still made up 98 percent of graduating veterinarians, with only 136 women graduating during the entire decade. The proportion of women graduates barely changed during the 1960s, but in the 1970s, with the passage of legislation barring gender discrimination in educational programs receiving federal funding, the number of women graduates increased to 2,726, or 17 percent, during the decade.

The balance shifted markedly in the 1980s, when women graduates increased to 44 percent, with 10,442 of them entering the field. And during the 1990s the number of women graduates surpassed that of men. The class of 2001 that Chuck was targeting would be 70 percent female. At Tufts University, the school nearest the clinic and the only vet school in New England, the class of 2001 would be 80 percent female. The proportions had changed so markedly that by 2004 there would be more women veterinarians than men.

Some said that the radical demographic changes occurred simply because the doors to veterinary schools opened and women walked into a profession they dreamed of practicing and were well suited for. Some said that with changes in commercial agriculture and the decline of the family farm, the typical aspirant, the boy on the farm—the kind of boy Roger

Osinchuk had been—had also declined. More students were drawn from suburban areas, and the number of practices solely treating pets also increased. Moreover, veterinary incomes had not increased at the rate of equivalent professions, and males were more often choosing to enter those higher-paying professions. The average annual income for an experienced veterinarian was about $60,000 in 2001, some $100,000 less than medical doctors earned. Yet the cost of an education at many veterinary schools could be well over $100,000.

Shortly before Chuck's ad was to make its second run, he got a call from a veterinary student at Tufts. Her name was Erika Bruner. She had seen the ad during the fall run and had thought it described exactly the kind of job she wanted. But she had been in the fall semester of her final year and coping with a rigorous schedule that included travel for externships. As the semester came to an end, she'd done some research, asking a drug company sales representative if he knew of any mixed practices in New Hampshire or Vermont with sizable bovine components. She figured that if anyone knew where bovine work was to be found, the rep who sold Lutalyse would. He referred her to Chuck.

During her semester break, Bruner came to Walpole and stayed at Chuck's house for almost a week. She observed treatments, exams, and surgeries at the clinic, and she went on calls with Chuck and Roger. Chuck answered the usual questions about salary and benefits, work schedules and on-call hours, and the support that would be available during those on-call hours. Bruner made it clear that she didn't want to be left at the clinic doing office appointments every day while he and Roger went out on farm calls. She wanted a good share of the mixed practice.

Chuck liked what he saw. Bruner's questions showed that

she was truly interested, which meant that if she took the job, she might stay. Chuck was encouraged by such simple things as the professional manner expressed by Bruner's wearing a white coat when she observed office appointments. And he was impressed by the cheerful way she interacted with his clients. This meant she would possibly build the practice. When Chuck learned that Bruner had grown up in a cooperative household her mother ran near Boston, he thought that she had probably developed good social skills from interacting with several adults from a young age.

Chuck felt some ambivalence about Bruner's academic background. She had been Phi Beta Kappa at Haverford College and was at the top of her class at Tufts. She came from a family of academics—a long line of eggheads, she told Chuck. Her father was a college professor, and both of her mother's parents were physicists. Her grandfather, Milton G. White, had brought the first cyclotron to Princeton University and had worked on the development of radar at MIT during World War II. Chuck wondered if she might be "too academically successful" for the kind of mixed practice he ran—and if she might get bored. He wondered if she would miss the kind of high-level medical technology she would have been exposed to at Tufts, a school that aspired to a level of animal medicine approaching that of human medicine. He also wondered if she might be unrealistic regarding the difficulty of mixed practice, and whether she might become discouraged because of it.

He also saw a lot of himself in Erika Bruner, more than he saw in Roger. Like Chuck, Bruner had decided to become a veterinarian after doing something else—in her case, historical preservation in Cambridge. Like him, Bruner had decided while in vet school that she would like to work with cows. Like him, she had grown up in the suburbs without much exposure to farm animals; it had been difficult in vet school to compete with the students who had grown up on farms. Chuck suspected that Bruner had also felt compelled to excel in school to compensate for that lack of experience.

During the week of her interview, she asked a lot of questions about bovine uterine palpation. She very much wanted to palpate cows, and she made an effort to learn how. During the fall, she had done an externship with a large bovine practice in California, working under the tutelage of bovine vets who palpated full-time in herds of more than a thousand cows. Bruner wanted a promise from Chuck that if she joined the practice, she would be able to palpate. Chuck told her it would be a gradual process, first working with sick cows and then, as her skills developed, possibly doing more advanced palpation work. But yes, he told her, she would palpate cows.

Roger, who had the most at stake, did his best to turn on the charm that week. He took Bruner out on calls and tried to convince her that it would be fun to work at the clinic and fun to work with him. He said he would show her how to examine a horse with ultrasound and how to perform a C-section, his favorite surgery. He told her he would certainly be available to help her if she needed him, especially when she was on call. He assured her, when she asked, that he would not jump ship and leave her as the sole associate.

Roger didn't think Bruner was too academically successful for the practice. There was plenty to keep anyone interested. The unusual thing, he said, was that she was at the top of her class and wanted to work with cows. Roger's impression was that people who wanted to work with cows were usually not at the top of their class.

Chuck offered her the job, with a starting salary of $45,000. It was a good salary in the current market, almost as much as Roger's salary before commissions. Erika told him that she would seriously consider it. She liked the practice, the staff, and the area around Walpole. She moved on to interview at other clinics, and later that winter she traveled to Ireland, where she made a tour of dairy farms. When a card arrived from Ireland with warm greetings, Ellie hung it on the refrigerator in the treatment room.

"She sent us a postcard," Roger said. "That's a good sign."

The second run of the ad had gone unanswered.

3.

Roger's horse practice continued to grow rapidly. He did things within the realm of normal equine care, such as inoculations and exams and suturing cuts. He floated teeth, advised on nutrition and pasturing, and treated for founder, a foot disorder. He checked for pregnancies and inseminated mares. That winter there were quite a number of pregnant mares about to foal, including two of his own. He practiced acupuncture, a skill he'd learned in vet school, on horses with muscular stress and back pain. He delivered foals and nursed them through their first days. He gave advice on training.

One afternoon in Walpole he castrated three yearling draft horses, one right after the other. First he calculated the horse's weight and gave him the appropriate amount of sedative, and then—as with euthanasia—he held the horse frontally by the halter while guiding him to his seat and then to the floor. He covered the horse's eyes with his jacket, even though the animal was unconscious, so as to block any visual images that might startle him awake. Quickly he tied and raised the stallion's leg with a rope thrown over a beam, like a pulley. He was dexterous but not relaxed—he trembled and sweated, especially when he began to cut and crimp with the emasculator. Anyone watching this might be shaking and sweating too. He tossed the extricated organs over his shoulder onto the barn floor. He untied the horse, gave the reversing injection, and soon helped him up and led him wobbling to the stall. There was a minimum of blood loss, a sign of Roger's skill.

It didn't always go as smoothly. In the town of Unity that fall, Roger made a call to castrate two horses. The first, a young and cooperative stallion, was guided to the floor and tied, draped with a jacket, and quickly separated from his testicles. In the adjacent stall, a more spirited horse had watched the procedure through a crack in the wall. What he saw led him to spin around and come to look again. He would have no part of the vet after that, wouldn't even let Roger get close enough to give him a shot. Roger lassoed him with one rope and then another, cross-tying him, but that didn't restrain the horse well enough for Roger to make an injection. As Roger approached, the horse let loose a kick that shot out only a few inches from Roger's head. "I was standing where I knew he couldn't get me," Roger said.

Finally they brought in an old horse, a blocky thirty-two-year-old mare, and put her into the stall with the randy youngster. They pushed her against him and forced him against the wall, and she took a kick, but Roger was able to get the needle in. Down the stallion went, and soon he was tied. Roger trembled from danger and pride this time, from the rush of adrenaline, he said, in addition to the concern of doing the procedure properly.

One thing for sure, he got out and about the countryside. Late that fall, as the leaves were turning, he followed a road to the top of a mountain, to what had been a homestead farm. A descendant of the homesteader lived in a mobile home next to the old house, which was collapsing on its granite foundation. A trail of trash led out of the old empty doorway. The client, an elderly woman, came out of her mobile home smiling. She had a fresh and happy face. She bred horses, and Roger had been hired to take a blood sample from one of her mares. She told Roger the mare didn't like men, and she gave him an apple and a bucket of grain to appease the horse. The woman thought the mare would need sedation, but Roger managed to push her against the stall while she ate the apple, and he pinched a fold of skin and got the blood without resistance. His quick work got him an extra ten dollars. When Roger mentioned his girlfriend, Danelle Philbrook, who lived in Walpole, the client said, "So that means you'll be staying around? She deserves gold stars for keeping you here."

Roger bought a quarter horse stallion that winter, shipped all the way from Calgary, Alberta. His name was Shawne Lake. He was ten years old, seventeen hands tall, and black with a white blaze on his forehead. Shawne Lake had won Canadian championships in several show-horse categories before becoming a studhorse. With his previous owners, Shawne had bred more than ninety mares in the past three years. Roger had brokered a few of those breedings to some of his clients around Walpole. He owned one of Shawne Lake's sons already and had inseminated his mare again by the stallion. Roger bought Shawne from the parents of one of his fellow classmates at vet school, and because they were impressed with Roger's ability with horses and wanted to help him out, they had offered the stallion at a rate below his value of $50,000 and allowed Roger to pay over several years, which he could manage by selling breedings.

Shawne arrived in January. He was accompanied by one of his progeny, a leggy year-old colt named Junior that Roger soon traded for a pregnant Thoroughbred mare owned by a trainer in South Carolina. Roger had built a separate corral for Shawne, and during his first days there, the horse ran from corner to corner, sliding on the snow like a kid on ice, his head high and his long tail and mane tossing and lifting. He was as black as crow feathers. Shawne neighed in a way that made the hair stand up on your neck.

"All my quarter horse future is tied up in that horse right there," Roger said, appraising him.

He planned to spend the spring collecting and shipping semen to his yet-to-be-determined clientele and, when shipping season was done, to take Shawne to horse shows, so as to advertise him. One trainer, watching the stallion run and neigh, and not knowing much about Roger, said, "You'll never be able to ride that horse." To which Roger answered, "I think I can probably handle him."

4.

As the winter passed and news came of a foot-and-mouth epidemic in England, with hundreds of thousands of animals destroyed, fear hit the farms Chuck serviced. Signs appeared on farm buildings forbidding entry of unauthorized visitors, requiring any people entering to wash and disinfect their boots or shoes. The UPS man wouldn't even get out of his truck when he drove onto the dairy farms that spring.

Chuck was skeptical of the panic mentality he saw rising not only among some farmers but also among other vets. On an Internet news group for bovine practitioners, he read of one vet who had bought a bolt-lock rifle in preparation for a domestic epidemic. "They shouldn't be thinking they're going into the business of killing thousands of cows," Chuck said. "They give the wrong impression to farmers."

Foot-and-mouth hadn't been in the States since 1929. Vets were going to England to get a look at it. "If there was an epidemic here, the result would be different for each farmer,"

Chuck said. "Some would say, 'We're going to buy new cows and start over.' Others, like Roger Adams, identify with their cows so much they wouldn't be able to take it."

But the consequences would be serious. The spread of various pathogens from farm to farm was always a concern, but now it was even greater. "If this disease showed up here, I could spread it from farm to farm without knowing," Chuck said. "It has a twelve-day incubation period. By the time it was discovered, it would be too late." A quarantine within, say, a twenty-mile radius would shut down all the dairy farms the practice served. No stock trucks would be allowed down I-91. Chuck would be out of the dairy business—40 percent of the practice's income.

On his way to do a herd check at Westminster Farms, Chuck said he thought the worst was over in England, and he didn't think the disease would spread to the United States. When he got to the farm, Robert Goodell, one of the owners, came striding out of his office with a paper in hand. A stocky man with muttonchop sideburns and a Dale Earnhardt bill cap, Goodell held the paper out to Chuck. Across the top he had scrawled, "SICK BASTARDS."

Looking for information on foot-and-mouth, Goodell had found a news story on the Internet headlined PETA: BRING ON FOOT-AND-MOUTH DISEASE. The article stated, "While U.S. authorities take precautions to prevent foot-and-mouth from entering the country, the president of People for the Ethical Treatment of Animals, possibly the world's most influential animal rights organization, openly hopes the disease crosses the Atlantic. 'If that hideousness came here, it wouldn't be any more hideous for the animals—they are all bound for a ghastly death anyway. But it would wake up consumers,' said PETA co-founder and president Ingrid Newkirk."

"What if some terrorist decides to bring this thing in here?" Goodell said. "What then?"

"It would be hard for anyone to deliberately bring this to a farm," Chuck said. "They would have to know exactly what they were doing." He talked about biosecurity measures the farm could take. At Hubbard Farms, where he inspected chickens periodically, all drivers entering the property had to spray their tires with disinfectant. Maybe Goodell should put up a fence around the farm and have a drop-off point for deliveries in front of the building, not out back on the farm proper. "And get everyone to wash their boots," Chuck said. "Use bleach. Wash them outside the building and then again inside."

But Goodell seemed more concerned about the news release, the mentality of it, the divide it suggested between farmer and public. "I can't believe somebody would say this," he said, and walked back inside.

Chuck practiced what he preached, filling a bucket with water and Betadine before scrubbing his boots with a stiff brush. He had been doing this kind of boot washing for years. He joined the herdsman, Mike Perry, and walked back to the big open barn where the cows were feeding.

Mike Perry was concerned about foot-and-mouth too. "Everyone is terrified," he said. "We'd all be out of business. They'd come in and shoot all the cows. The farmers are talking about it, but discreetly. We've got enough to worry about. If you worried too much, you wouldn't be able to sleep at night." Mike needed his sleep. His workday started at 3 a.m. and lasted until four or five in the afternoon. During the summer he also ran a sideline haying business after work.

He changed the subject to lighter matters. "Charlie," Mike said, "we're building a new manure pit. We'll press out the liquids and spread them on the fields. The solid will become compost. There's money in it! We know a guy in Massachusetts who's getting ten dollars a yard for dry manure compost. He said, 'I'm gonna cut down on the cull rate. I'm getting more for them shitting than I am for them milking!' "

It was a cool spring day, in the first week of April, but earlier in the week a late blizzard had passed through, leaving three feet of snow. Mike got forty inches at his place in Athens, Vermont, and he rushed to the greenhouse where he kept his tractors just as the roof was collapsing. "I drove my best tractor out of there and said, 'You ain't getting this one.' We've had a rough winter. Too long and too cold. The cows need a break from it too."

Chuck was more of a consultant at Westminster Farms than at the other dairies he serviced. They seemed to need his advice. This was the only farm where, when he made suggestions, he tended to use the word *we*. He would say, "We need to get better genetics into the herd," or, "We need to make sure that when cows are calving, they have more space." He regularly met with the owners, Robert Goodell and his brother Clayton, and sat in on their meetings with nutritionists representing feed companies. Westminster had the largest herd among the farms in Chuck's practice. They milked nearly five hundred cows in an open herd, meaning not all the cows had been raised on the farm. Many were purchased at auction, and the turnover tended to be high. This farm also had the lowest average production, though averages had increased in the last year, rising to some sixty-five pounds per day average per cow. That change had occurred largely since Mike Perry was appointed herdsman a year ago.

Mike was about as Yankee as someone could be. He was in his late forties and had worked with cows all his life. He was lean and rangy, and pithy in his speech, someone who would show up at town meeting in the spring with a list of things he wanted to say. Mike would threaten violence to anyone who mistreated his cows—including his boss, when he put a cow with a fever back into the milking herd. He would kiss a cow on the nose before deciding to put it on the "hamburger truck." Mike's father had run a hill farm, milking forty cows, but when they had to start buying equipment to keep up with modern dairy practices, the farm folded, like many others had. Mike had gone out to work at big farms along the Connecticut River. At one, he worked seventeen-hour days six days a week, nine hours on Sunday. At another, he quit when he was told to go out and work on a tractor in sub-zero weather that had already turned his toes black—quitting not because of the task, but because of the disregard in the order.

Mike's job required a tenacious memory in order to keep track not only of five hundred milking cows but also of the dry cows about to calve, the calves themselves, and the heifers yet to produce calves. His attitude stood somewhere between caring and hard-heartedness. Who but a farmer could understand what it took to do this job right? Who but a farmer, or a veterinarian.

Chuck usually palpated about eighty cows during the weekly herd check at Westminster. He and Mike worked together in the enormous open barn, which had headlocks on both sides and an alleyway wide enough for a tractor down the middle. This morning the headlocks were all occupied with feeding cows, three hundred of them, exhaling steamy breaths. Mike stood in the alleyway with his clipboard while Chuck worked inside the pen behind the cows, standing in two inches of manure and urine. He had on coveralls, and wore a turtleneck sweater with one sleeve cut off. The cows kept his arm warm. The ones to be palpated all had red blazes marked with grease pencil on their rumps and foreheads.

"This one," Mike said of the first cow. "I don't care if

she ever gets pregnant, the way she's milking. She's making 134 pounds." That meant fifteen and a half gallons a day. "She's been unbred a long time."

"She has a CL on the right ovary. I'll give her Lutalyse." Chuck made the injection in her rump.

They moved down along the line to the next marked cow. "This little girl, she's stressed out," Mike said of a two-year-old heifer in her first lactation. "She's milking seventy-eight pounds a day. It's eating her up."

"That's almost ten percent of her body weight every day," Chuck said.

"She goes right through her heat, doesn't even show. She just eats and goes back and forth to the parlor."

"Open," Chuck said, meaning not yet pregnant. "Follicle right ovary. She'll probably be in heat next time."

Mike made the notation. "Charlie," he said, "that black one—arm her, would you please? If she's ready, we'll put her in with John Henry." John Henry was the bull, and cows that had been difficult to breed spent quality time with him. Mike had a high opinion of John Henry. "He's a smart bull. He sits down and rests now and then. Doesn't wear his back legs out from standing to breed, which can put a bull on the hamburger truck."

"Follicle right ovary," Chuck said.

"Just what I wanted to hear," said Mike. John Henry had a date.

And on down the line. Of one large and overweight Holstein, Mike expressed disapproval. "She doesn't work. Produces forty pounds when she should be producing eighty. I just have no sympathy with them when they don't want to work. I know that sounds bad, but that's the way I am. They don't work, they're better off taking a trip to Ronald McDonald's."

"No definite structures," Chuck said. "We'll check her next time."

Another cow: "This is one of my old favorites—234 days, 24,000 pounds produced. She's gonna make 30,000 before she's through. Bred with a bull. She's been milking for eight months. Had a 120 average one month, 130 another, 120, 120. I beg you, Charlie, tell me she's pregnant."

"She's pregnant," Chuck said.

"All right, she told me so! Told me she had the morning sickness!"

On they went: "This one's a workhorse. She's at one hundred fourteen pounds."

And: "This one should be headed for the highway, but she's pregnant. Milking only twenty-two pounds."

"She's still pregnant," Chuck said.

Not all the cows were in headlocks. A sizable number were free to roam in this barn, and many were lounging on beds of sawdust in the stalls. There were actually cushioned pads under the sawdust to make their rest more comfortable and so encourage them to produce more milk.

Mike pointed one of them out to Chuck. "See Number 40? She's been through eight lactations and is eleven years old. She's produced 270,000 pounds." If you calculated that out, even at the substandard price of $10 per hundredweight, Number 40 had made the farm $27,000 after delivering those eight calves. One or two of her daughters were most likely in the herd and milking now.

"She's at the point where they want to send her away. She's got foot problems and leg problems and is having trouble walking. But I'm going to hide her out back. The only one that will know she's here is the computer. If she hasn't earned her keep around here, no one has."

Mike had things to say about many of the cows, but he especially liked the kind of an ending that Number 40 was having. He liked to remember an old cow he had known at his first job at the big dairy in Vernon. This venerable cow had produced 360,000 pounds of milk (41,860 gallons) by the age of sixteen, and the owner of the farm kept her around even after she had stopped producing. When she finally died, one of the hands went about dragging her out of the barn with a tractor. Enraged, the farmer saw this, ran up to him, and said, "Leave that cow there. That cow's more important than you are." Mike ended the story by saying, "He got the front-end loader, carried her out himself, and buried her in the family plot."

"Eighty-one days since she calved, no heat yet," Mike called now.

Chuck plunged and pulled, plunged again. "Follicle right ovary," he said. "She's got heat tone."

"We'll breed her tonight," Mike said.

5.

A week before her graduation, Erika Bruner called Chuck and told him she would take the job. She would start in the second week of June. Chuck and Ellie arranged to have flowers sent to Erika on her graduation.

At Murray's that week, Chuck said to Roger, "Erika said she's told her friends she's starting work in three weeks, and they're all saying, 'What? Three weeks! That's too soon!' I say, Let's get going."

To which Roger answered, "But that's the only three weeks she'll ever have off again, the only time she'll have that long of a stretch."

In the coming days, a refrain developed along the line of "When Erika starts . . ."

"When Erika starts, I'll have more time to manage the clinic. Even my accountant told me I should spend more time managing."

"When Erika starts, we'll have a vet at the clinic at all times."

"When Erika gets here, I'll be able to spend more time training Shawne."

"When Erika starts, Roger will get some relief."

"When Erika comes, I'll be able to do some fishing."

"When Erika comes, I'll have more time to use the Internet."

Chuck had no specific plan for her training. "You learn by getting right into it all. But I'll keep her under my wing at first, until she can go out on her own. It's a big step, getting from when she comes in the door until she can walk out on her own."

Yet she would quickly get her feet in the water. "I'll put her on call right off. It's not like we'll say, You don't have to be on call the first two weeks." She would start with every third night and then take the third weekend.

"She will do a lot of normals at first," Chuck said. "Normal exams, heartworm tests, and shots. Normal office visits where she can feel healthy animals all over and look closely at them. She's done a handful of spays. In the beginning you traditionally start someone off doing cat spays, dog spays, and castrations. That way they can build up their confidence."

Chuck had a few teaching points aimed at avoiding simple mistakes and developing habits of observation. The first was, "For every diagnosis you miss for not knowing, you'll miss ten for not looking." He gave the example of how Roger had recently examined a cow for lameness twice without finding the cause, thinking that it might be an internal problem. Roger had asked Chuck to look at her, and Chuck looked inside the hoof, where he found a roofing tack. It was a simple solution. Roger had put the tack on the bulletin board as a reminder. "You have to teach them that they don't have to rely on high-tech equipment," Chuck said. "They have to learn how to look."

His second point was, "No information is better than the wrong information." You could say that this maxim stressed the importance of an open mind, and that it also got back to the first point, that you had to look.

Another point was simply, "Don't send a pet home with a high temperature, because it will always come back." Which also meant that you should continue to observe.

The aspiring vet should cultivate three essential qualities, Chuck said, which were "availability, affability, and ability, in that order." Roger had all three, he said.

Chuck would also have to think about Erika's ambition to do uterine palpation. "I have to protect her. She wants to palpate, but she can't go out there and palpate her own herds right off. Some of these farmers ask one question, then ask another, until they find the area you don't know about. They'll probe for her weakness. I don't want her to come back with her confidence broken. It will be a lot harder than she thinks."

But she would do some palpation right from the beginning. "I basically want to keep her happy," Chuck said.

He wanted to keep Roger happy too. He bought a new full-size Toyota pickup for Roger to use, complete with hot-and-cold running water and a veterinarian's workbox with sliding drawers. The little red Toyota that Roger had been driving for two years would pass to Erika.

Chuck and Ellie went away for the week before Erika arrived, to attend their daughter's college graduation. It was a busy week for Roger, though he'd have a relief vet to help out.

Roger's weekend was as busy as any. More than a dozen calls came in. A horse with colic right after the clinic closed on Friday, a treatment that lasted three hours, and when that was done, off to tend to a sick sheep in Bellows Falls. Out to the distant town of Sullivan on Saturday to examine more sick sheep. At the Graves farm in Walpole, a downed cow and a calcium treatment. At 6 a.m. on Sunday, a difficult calving at Barrett's farm in Putney, which turned into a fetotomy, the extraction of the calf in pieces.

When Chuck returned the following week, he spent a day getting organized and catching up with cases. The next day, Erika arrived. She moved into the guest room at Chuck's house, where she'd stay until she found a rental.

The third vet had finally come.

6

THE THIRD VET

1.

Walking down the street, they were each statements in color. For Chuck it was red, a red T-shirt with a picture of a Holstein on the front. Chuck sometimes wore red when he wanted to express confidence. For Erika the color was purple, the color of her hair that day. During graduation, to make a statement against what she called the soul-deadening repressiveness of vet school (namely the endless memorization), Erika had dyed her hair blond and then fuchsia and blue, like a bouquet. She had a thing for hair, she said—you could do anything with it, and it would just grow back. She wore it in a style called "boy's regular," close cut over the ears, a side part, and a cresting wave above the forehead—a style so dissonant with her feminine good looks that you had to wonder if dissonance was the point. But of course Erika knew that red-and-blue hair wouldn't fly at a practice in rural New Hampshire, so she had given it a unifying black wash, which came out purple.

Down the street they came that morning, an unlikely pair,

the practice owner of twenty-two years breaking in his tenth associate, and the young woman with vet school now behind her, scared and excited about what the day might bring, her hair full of adventure and hope.

Roger was waiting for them at Murray's. He stood up and shook hands and smiled.

"We've got a new vet," Chuck said as he sat down. "With purple hair." His was a wrinkled smile. "She showed up last night with a car full of stuff, lots of plants, even a full bar."

"Well, first-year vets don't make much, with their loans and all," she said. "Don't be worried by all the people coming up the back steps for drinks."

Tammy brought coffee, took the orders.

Chuck reported that Erika had gotten engaged during graduation weekend. She said it was true. Her boyfriend, Gary Rocha, had gotten on his knees in front of her classmates and presented her with a chocolate ring, because Erika didn't like to wear rings—she had bony hands, she said.

"He waited until she had a steady job," Chuck said.

"The whole weekend was a blur," she said. "We all stood up at graduation and took the veterinary oath, but I can hardly remember it."

She had won some awards, Chuck said. One was a live-stock proficiency award, but Erika discounted it. "There were only three of us interested in large-animal work at Tufts," she said with a laugh. "And one of the others also got an award." She had also won an academic achievement award for having a high grade point average and being in the top tenth of her class.

When Erika told of the academic award, Chuck shook his head as if to say, I don't know, she might be too smart for us.

Nevertheless, he was optimistic. He was wearing red. They moved on to talk of the practice and current cases, and Roger told about how he had been training his stallion. After break-fast, just before he left for Putnam's with Erika, Chuck said, "I've got two high-powered associates now. It's going to be a challenge to manage them."

2.

Erika stood in the well in the milking parlor at Putnam's while Chuck and Scott Kemp worked with the cows up above in the runway. The depth of the well was such that the milker stood chest-high with the udders, and so could reach straight ahead to attach the milking machines, which made it easier on the person's leg and back muscles. But the differing perspectives also made someone in the well vulnerable to the splattering that inevitably occurred in the parlor, especially during herd checks when Chuck was performing his bovine ablutions. One inevitably left the well flecked, but Erika didn't seem to mind. She had on a new set of green coveralls, with the vet-erinary insignia—a staff and snake over a V—in yellow over the chest pocket. She wore silver earrings, and a silver chain around her neck with a veterinary medallion. She talked easily while the shit hit the floor.

At times she and Chuck carried on an informal dialogue about palpation and dairy farming. Chuck said, "There are two heat detectors here. Scott does it visually, and I do it by palpation." And, "They give Lutalyse on Monday so they're in heat on Thursday when I do the check." And also, a point he would repeat, "This time of year, the temperature is sky-high. We've got to check them and get them back into the barn where it's cool."

Erika responded with questions about whether there were fans or water misters in the barn, and who gave the Lutalyse shots. Or she talked in a more general way, about palpation or the uterus. It was fun to listen to her, because she had her own take on things, and a way with likenesses. She said that the uterus is like a garden hose, turgid and springy while in heat, flaccid when not. Or better yet, "The uterus is like a waxing and waning moon. It could be on the way in or on the way out. The information you get while you're palpating tells you which way. What you feel in the uterus should corroborate what you are told by the farmer.

"And it's something you can only understand by feel. You can read about it in books, but you'll never get it that way. You get out of practice. Then just finding the cervix is difficult. With practice, the uterus begins to tell you things. Chuck doesn't even have to think about what he's doing. I have to concentrate."

She had green eyes and a heart-shaped face with broad cheekbones and a strong cleft chin. She had a way of smiling when she was talking, a trait so charming it caused Chuck to say that morning, "I think this practice will work for both of us." Tall and broad-shouldered, she had been an athlete, the captain of the track team at Haverford and the school record holder in the 400-meter sprint.

Her parents separated when she was very young, and Ann Bruner had decided to run a cooperative group household rather than bring Erika up alone. The house was in Newton, Massachusetts, near Boston, and Ann still ran it cooperatively, with the idea that people should know their environment and engage responsibly with it. She had decided that Erika should have religious and spiritual experience, so she took her to Quaker meetings, a factor in her decision to attend Haverford, a Quaker school. You could possibly draw a line of influence from the near-silent Quaker meetings to a time during veterinary school when, after one rigorous and, in her opinion, soul-deadening semester, Erika went to a Buddhist monastery for a week and discovered the techniques of Zen meditation. She adapted and continued to use those ways of stilling the mind, and wished she had learned them earlier.

She had studied architecture at Haverford, and after graduation worked at a historical preservation commission in Cambridge. But immediately she thought about doing something else, and almost immediately thought about being a veterinarian. She volunteered at a clinic, worked as a vet tech, and took the science courses she needed to apply to Tufts, getting A's in all of them. For the spot she landed at Tufts, there had been nine other applicants.

If Roger had come to the profession by way of a youth spent with farm animals, you could say that Erika had come by way of a cat, one who had slept curled up by her head all through grade school and high school. She still had his ashes. Of course there were other cats in her life, and her love of their spirit, their calmness and curiosity, is what drew her interest to cows during her second year at Tufts. Cows seemed calm and curious and wise too.

Standing in the well at Putnam's, Erika said, "Tufts had a program called Adopt a Veterinary Student. You spend a few days at a farm with animals you're not used to. I went to a dairy farm with a friend, another woman interested in mixed practice, and we learned how to milk, learned about reproduction and how to worm calves and other things. I liked the cows, and I liked the farmers a lot."

In a bovine elective she spent a series of afternoons listening to talks about milking machines and farm structures. In a clinical program she learned about cows, horses, pigs, and sheep. She learned how to pick up a cow's feet, examine the lungs and udders, and take sterile milk samples.

"Something must have been germinating. After my second

summer of vet school, I wanted to experience more large animals, especially cows. I went to Ohio, where my dad lived, and called his vet. The vet had a mixed practice, but it was mostly small animals, with only a few large animals that he treated after hours. But he referred me to another practice that was truly mixed, with a significant large-animal component. There were five doctors all doing mixed practice full-time."

Those doctors saw to it that Erika got training. They sent her to a slaughterhouse for a bin of reproductive tracts, and they used them to show her how to palpate. It was a superb way to learn. They arranged for her to do a DA surgery for a farmer undergoing bankruptcy proceedings, offering him half the normal fee. They had her do a lot of spays, well beyond the two she had done in the spay lab at vet school. "I did all kinds of stuff there and got the experience of what it's like to be in a mixed practice. Tufts was good for the basic preparation, but to learn mixed practice, you had to go out on your own."

The next year, she did an externship at a large bovine practice in California, where eleven vets worked full-time palpating cows. Some of the farms they serviced milked as many as three thousand cows, and the herd checks took nearly two days. The vets had to be able to palpate with either arm. Shoulder injuries from noncompliant cows were occupational hazards.

Erika had a defining moment in California—a palpation epiphany, she called it. "I was working alongside one of the other vets, a woman I thought of as a mentor. We were always coming up with the same findings. I had been inside a long time and was about to say, I don't know, when I felt something slide through my fingers. It felt like a grape. It was the calf in an embryonic sac."

The epiphany stayed with her, but she continued to consider options. Surgery was certainly one of them. "At Tufts I shadowed a surgeon, a specialist who did the same procedure four times a day. I thought I might like to do something like that. But with this kind of mixed practice, even though there's repetition and you might do four spays in a day, you have the relationship with the people. That's why I want to do mixed practice." It had been the same for Chuck when he made his decision.

She continued to watch him work as the cows were checked, released, and then replaced with another group of Holsteins. During an interval, when Chuck walked to his tray to get more gloves and Lutalyse, he asked Erika, "Have you seen anything yet that you don't know?"

She didn't hesitate. "There's no limit to the possible things I don't know."

Chuck didn't ask her to palpate any of the milking Holsteins at Putnam's that morning, but he did take her out to one of the pens to palpate a year-old heifer. Jessica Putnam accompanied them, carrying the clipboard. Home again from UNH, Jessica was working as a milker, though you wouldn't know it to look at her. Her nails were done, and she was wearing eyeliner and mascara. "Why shouldn't I look good?" she said as she stood atop a concrete barrier while Chuck and Erika worked inside the pen.

There Erika stood, truly a vet now, her expression going from cheerful to dead serious. She held the glove up over her shoulder like a shield. Her expression fixed, she stared at the ground, bent at the waist as she felt about. Chuck had come over to watch Erika when she said, "I think she's not pregnant, but I'm not sure."

He told her to check the heifer he had just palpated, a pregnancy, while he checked hers. "She's open, Jessie," he said. Erika had been right.

That was the extent of her palpating on this day. They returned to the parlor, where Chuck palpated the rest of the designated cows. After that he took her on a tour of the farm before driving her to the clinic for office hours.

3.

In the treatment room, Lynn Hayes was clipping the hair of a cat, giving him a "lion cut," with the tail shaved down to a ball on the end, the belly shaved, and a mane left around the neck and along the spine. This lion, named Baby Boomer, had a flat face and a perpetual pout. Boomer was sedated for his haircut, but he was doing his best to open his mouth and roar.

Erika had been given the job of examining him once Boomer woke from his sleep. He had been having respiratory problems. After listening to him breathe, she said he had "respiratory crackles"—she could hear alveoli popping open in his lungs. He was laboring for breath because of this. "Now what?" Erika said. "That's the difficult part."

"Wait and observe," Lynn answered.

But Erika didn't wait. She took a medical manual into the staff room and began to read about respiratory diseases.

A woman came in with a Samoyed, a big white puffball of a dog, and told Susan she wanted a heartworm test. Chuck had left to do a DA, and Roger was out on call. Susan said, "I'm not sure we have a doctor here." She went into the staff room, file in hand, and said to Erika, "So, are you doing doctor things yet? This woman brought her dog in for a heartworm check, and she says he has a scooting butt."

"Go check butt," Erika said. She left the room and returned in a white coat, with DR. BRUNER embroidered above the pocket. The brightness of her coat made her colorful hair shine. She looked like a tall candle with an ultraviolet flame.

She paused before the door to look at the file, and said, mostly to herself, "Sadie was hit by a truck?"

"Ready?" Lynn asked.

"Yup."

They walked into the examination room, and for the first time in her career Erika said, "Hi, I'm Dr. Bruner." She stuck out her hand and smiled cheerfully. The owner seemed surprised. Then Erika said, "Hi Sadie!" A mass of white hair shook in greeting.

"I'll do a complete physical exam."

She crouched down and patted the dog, then pulled open her mouth. She looked at Sadie's teeth and commented that eventually they could use some dentistry. She looked into Sadie's eyes and said they appeared to be fine.

"It's always a sign of ear infection when the ears smell bad," she said.

Erika felt about Sadie's abdomen and back legs. Lynn worked up front, talking to the owner about the need for grooming and talking to Sadie, calming her. With each phrase ("You're okay honey," Lynn said, and, "You're being *very* good"), Sadie licked her in gratitude and agreement.

While all this was going on, Erika decided to express Sadie's anal glands, and pulled on some latex gloves.

"Yup, that's icky stuff that lives in there," she said. "I noticed she got hit by a truck. Has she been okay since then?"

It was as if Erika had pushed a button. Out came the story, how the guy who hit Sadie had felt terrible about it, how the woman's husband had wanted to put the dog down, and how she had refused to do it—and now look at her.

While Erika listened, she pulled on Sadie's leg and felt around her hips. "How is she on steps?"

"She goes up and down steps every day. We live on a hill-side."

"She definitely has a limited range of motion in the left leg. Could be the anal sac . . ."

Another magic button. Beaming, the owner said, "She has problems, and we usually have to have the anal sac cleaned out."

The exam continued to the drawing of a blood sample for a heartworm test. This took some effort with such a furry and excitable dog. While Erika shaved the foreleg, Lynn kept charming Sadie, and Sadie kept licking at her, doing her best to be as good as Lynn claimed. At first there was no blood, but then with another attempt, a trickle, and then, relief, a sample. Erika finished off with squirts of a kennel cough-vaccine spray in Sadie's nose.

"Yeah!" Erika said while Sadie wriggled.

Lynn went to the cabinet and got a dog biscuit. She gave it to Erika and said, "Here, make friends with your patient." Sadie was waiting expectantly.

Erika said that by the sound of things, Sadie's heart seemed to be okay. She asked Lynn, "What's the procedure here for the heartworm test?" Lynn told the owner that if she heard nothing, it would mean the results were negative.

"Okay, so I just bring this out front?" Erika asked of the file.

"Write whatever you want," Lynn said, and left with Sadie and her owner. Erika recorded the exam, took the file to Susan, and returned to the treatment room flushed.

"Wow!" Erika said. "I'm in shock! My first appointment! It went all right! I should call my mom!"

Then she said, "Tonight I'll probably think of more things I could have asked."

She laughed, raised her fists, and said, "I could spay something!"

"It's the calm before the storm," Lynn answered. "Wait until the weekend, when you're on call and alone."

This sobered Erika slightly. "I think that's going to be the weekend after next."

Susan came to get Erika for her next appointment, and led her out front to where a man was holding a large tabby cat in his arms. "This is Dr. Bruner!" Susan said, and Erika held out her hand again.

The owner wasn't sure what was wrong, but the cat was clearly feeling sick. He might have been hit by a car or kicked by someone.

"Someone may have kicked him?"

"Well, who knows where he goes."

She felt along the cat's back, then asked to take him to the treatment room. There she and Lynn shaved his back, much to his displeasure. They found bite wounds, one of which ruptured at the touch. A fighter with a history on his back. "Everything that's wrong with you is from a bite wound," Erika said. "You, my friend, are getting some antibiotics."

The cat clearly wasn't in favor of any of it. "Don't bite the doctor," Lynn said.

"Antibiotics and hot compresses," Erika said.

By now Chuck had returned and was looking over the case list. He said, "If I were treating him, I'd keep him overnight. He's got a temperature. My policy is, never send an animal home with a temperature, because nine times out of ten, they will come back again. I'd give him an injection of amoxicillin, see if the temperature is down in the morning, and then let him go."

Holding the cat in her arms, Erika returned to announce

her findings and discuss the case with the owner. She came back in with the cat. "I like Chuck's suggestion that we keep him overnight and make sure he's going in the right direction."

It was lunchtime in the staff room. Darcie was eating a slice of pizza from a paper plate. Hobbs was sitting on her lap, his chin on the plate, looking up at her lovingly.

Erika grabbed some pizza and then went back to examine a cat with diabetes. She conferred with Chuck about the case. She realized that she didn't know as much as she needed to know about diabetes. Next came a more complicated case. A client came in with two old cats, a skinny twenty-year-old female named Nigel and a fat white male, not much younger, named Frances. Frances was "a downright mean cat," the owner said. Erika got his exam out of the way fairly quickly and turned to Nigel. The owner said that Nigel had been with her before her nineteen-year-old son was born.

"How's she been doing?" Erika asked.

"Been doing good until lately. I found out she was malnourished. This one was eating her food." Frances, she meant. "He likes to sit at the top of the stairs and swat you when you go by. Mean, downright mean. He swatted Nigel."

Erika looked at Nigel's teeth and listened to her heart. She giggled and said, "I don't know, Nigel. If you purr like that, I can't hear." She felt Nigel's lymph nodes and her legs. "Okay, I'll take your temperature," she said.

"Your favorite thing," the owner said. "Ooh, you don't like that."

Erika looked at Nigel's eyes. One was cloudy from being swatted by Frances. Erika said she wanted to put a stain in the eye and look at it with a light scope. But she was unsure of what she saw. She left to confer, returned and left again, came in and apologized, said she was still conferring with the other vets, and left again.

The owner looked at Nigel and said, "This stopped being fun, didn't it?"

Outside in the driveway, Roger was doing a pregnancy check on an Appaloosa mare. To save money, the owners had brought her to the clinic. When Erika came out to confer, Roger roped her into holding the ultrasound screen. He studied the imagery, probing shoulder-deep, while Erika stood red-faced in the hot sunlight, her arms wrapped around the base of the screen, inwardly fretting about her patient.

Roger was saying that maybe live cover (natural breeding) on this horse wouldn't be such a good idea, since she had only one good eye—he never did live cover anymore, and even though they saved $35 by bringing the horse in, maybe he could come out the next time; where did they live?—when Erika passed the ultrasound machine off to someone else and returned to the exam room, where she waited with Nigel's owner until Chuck came in.

"Oh, Nigel, doggone," Chuck said. To Erika he said, "You stained it, and it didn't take up the stain?"

"Yeah. You want to look at it?"

"That looks nasty," Chuck said. "How old is she?"

"She's ancient," the owner said.

"This sucks," Chuck said. "Pardon my expression."

"It works for me."

"She's got no tears," Erika said. "That's why it probably doesn't show. She's got an ulcer on her eye."

Chuck stained the eye again and looked at it through jeweler's glasses. The owner said she had been putting ointment in, but only once a day, because once was all she could manage. She hadn't put the artificial tears in at all.

Chuck looked at the cat, and the cat looked at him, and he said, "It may be best to leave her with us for a couple of days." He explained the surgery he could do to trim away the ulcer and suture the inner eyelid closed, covering the eye long enough for it to heal. The owner could drop Nigel off on Saturday.

This was fine for her because she would be leaving that day for the Maine coast.

"Sounds like a plan," she said. "Nigel, you're going on vacation. Not as nice as mine."

After they had gone, Erika was unnerved. "My mind is boggled," she said. "Diabetes, I could read tons about that. Respiratory problems, eye ulcers. I'm thinking there's fifty thousand things I don't know."

"And she'll never know them all," Roger said. If Erika was unnerved, he was elated. This was a first day for him too. "I'm feeling quite overwhelmed," he said with a little smile, meaning it in a much different way, the good sort of way.

4.

On her second day, Erika accompanied Chuck to Westminster Farms for the Friday herd check. Chuck wore another red T-shirt. She wore the green coveralls trimmed in yellow, a gray T-shirt, silver earrings and chain, and floppy black buckle boots, all topped off with the violet hair. This time Chuck had her participate fully in the check, though he tried to make it easy by assigning cows well beyond the thirty-five-day minimum when a pregnancy could be detected.

Because of the size of the herd—300 cows packed shoulder to shoulder and another 100 wandering about or lying in beds—Westminster was not an easy place to do palpation.

The vets had to wade through the thick muck and the smell of ammonia, though on this day the big industrial-sized fans were going, a dozen of them at full speed. The only sound that cut through the drone was the clink of headlocks.

The fans lowered the temperature by about 20 degrees, Mike Perry said, which would have dropped it from the 90s into the mid-70s. The hot air still flowed through. Summer was debilitating for milk production, and these cows had been in headlocks since early morning. Mike wanted to set them free. Though Chuck wanted to tutor Erika, he had to keep moving through the check. He would point out a cow for her to arm, and then he'd move down the line. "She's a good palpator," he said to Mike. "Made sure she got trained for this. But I've got to balance her eagerness with her lack of knowledge. I let her do these on her own, we'll be all day."

"She is good," Mike Perry said. "The problem I've got, it's hot."

Erika was concerned with the part of palpation called retraction of the uterus. Strange as it may seem, the veterinarian hauls the uterus up on the pelvic shelf, like a fisherman hauling a net onto a deck. Once the uterus is retracted, it can be more easily examined with the palpating hand. Erika wanted to know how Chuck did retraction. There are various methods, each according to the individual. "Some scoop around and pull, while others grab onto the ligament between the uterine horns," she said.

"A uterus is shaped like a Y. It's horn-shaped, like a ram's horns," she continued. "The body of the uterus bifurcates into two horns that squiggle off at the ends. They can drape down. The ovaries are at four and eight o'clock. There's a ligament between the horns that connects them. It's called the intercornual ligament. You can pull back on that, or you can reach underneath the entire uterus to retract it. If the cow is pregnant and the uterus is heavy, you won't be able to retract it. That's a sign of pregnancy, if it's heavy."

When she asked Chuck how he retracted, he showed her by hand movements that were almost snakelike—turning his wrist in a way that conveyed reaching under from the right, rotating, and pulling up. Erika could see what he was doing, but because of the fans, she could not understand what he was saying. Finally they both shook their heads. "I'll have to think more about how I do it," Chuck said.

On some cows Chuck left the uterus retracted for Erika so that she could study his findings. He said in one case, "There's a CL on the left side. She was bred twenty-one days ago. You won't be able to tell if she's pregnant for two more weeks, but don't damage the CL, because you'll create an abortion and the farmers will be angry. You don't want to stay in there too long."

She reached in and felt around, perhaps for a minute. When she finished and pulled off the plastic sleeve, she said, "Chuck is very subtle with his palpation. He's gentle and doesn't want to hurt the cow. I don't understand these subtleties yet. He hasn't explained them, but I hope he does. I think my technique is okay. I don't think I've ever created an abortion."

She certainly was a study in concentration. Arm-deep in the cow, she bent over and stared at the floor as if the answer were hidden in the muck. She retracted and palpated. It was, she said, like trying to feel something through a shower curtain while wearing rubber gloves. She considered and then considered more. Ten minutes might pass while she armed a cow and assessed a uterus. Chuck's mastery was evident in their differences, in his half minute to her ten, and she was well aware of it. One time, after minutes of feeling and stopping, with pauses to let peristaltic contractions pass, Erika raised her head and tried to catch Chuck's eye. She was about to call him but then said, "Aha! She's pregnant!"

Chuck called her over to check another cow he'd just palpated. "The hard thing is to tell why they're not coming into heat," he said. "Like this cow. She has a CL on the left side, but there's some damage, probably from the last calving." Erika went in and felt about.

On another cow, after long concentration, she looked to Chuck with a beckoning expression. Mike Perry laughed when he saw this. Chuck said, "It's nice to be needed," and walked over. He armed the cow and said to Mike, "She's open. Let's check her in two weeks." The difficulty had been that there was nothing to tell.

He gave Erika other, more practical tips. She was fully engaged in a palpation when the cow next to her let go with a stream of manure at about shoulder height. Erika just squinted and kept on trying. Chuck leaned in and said over the roar of the fans, "One thing you can avoid. The tail can pick that up and then smack you on the side of the head. When one of them does that," he said, "tell Mike to let her go." He showed her the hand signal for this, a half-turn of the wrist. Mike flicked the headlock, and off, enthusiastically, went a free cow.

Erika said, "Stuff they don't teach you in vet school."

There were other dangers. Farther down the line, one of the cows approached and then suddenly charged by, missing Erika by inches.

"Watch out!" Chuck called. Erika hadn't flinched. Chuck walked over and said, "Keep an eye out for cows walking or running by. You could get seriously hurt."

She squinted as urine misted over her, and kept on working. On one cow, after long study, she said she was feeling something like lima beans, but couldn't really tell. "I don't know," she said to Chuck, and walked off, shuffling in her rubber boots. Chuck armed the cow and said, within a minute, "No definite structures! Check in two weeks!"

Erika spent several minutes pondering another cow before waving Chuck over. He waved back limply, teasing her while opening a sleeve in the blast of the fan. After twenty seconds of palpation he said, "She's pregnant."

Erika smiled. "I was right. That's gratifying. She's at an early stage of pregnancy." But she knew it had taken a long time to make this simplest of calls.

She detected another pregnancy, and then another. "I've been right three times in a row now," she said, "but it's been a fight."

As they neared the end, she said, "You have to be patient with palpation. I expect to be good at everything right off because I've been good before. But I have to accept that this is going to take time."

"Sixty days, no heat!" Mike called out.

"She has a follicle coming in on the right ovary," Chuck replied. "She should be coming in."

No water, no rest. Erika said she couldn't wait until she had a drink. Her face was reddened. She had rolled her T-shirt sleeves over her shoulders. On her last cow, she kept at it determinedly. She thought it was a pregnancy, but called Chuck over anyway. She was right.

She then walked over to Chuck and stood next to the cow he was palpating, his last of the check. "I need to be more confident," she said.

"You were at the beginning of this herd check," he replied, with a laugh.

They stopped in the sick bay, a small room with a set of stocks and three languid cows. Chuck examined them and told Erika to listen to the lungs of one cow. "She's got a temperature of 104°, 105°," he said, taking a reading by feel while palpating. "Chronic respiratory disease. They're not gonna get better in the summer. It's a fact of life. You just try to get them through. They get worse, they get better. They get worse, they get better."

Erika listened through her stethoscope with the same determination. She listened to the rumen too, the large first stomach of the cow, and said, "The rumen should sound like waves crashing on a beach. It's a rhythmic sound, the rumen expanding and contracting." This seemed wonderful—the cow as an ocean. It seemed that Erika could animate these animals in the way that Darcie or Laurel could animate Hobbs or Wylie.

When they were done, as she walked to her pickup, Erika's mind was on the herd check again. "I made enough mistakes," she said. "I don't want to pretend I'm confident when I'm not. I don't want to fake it. I want to be right, and I want to know when I'm wrong. I'm definitely not ready to go alone. But when I can go out on my own and do this by myself, that's going to be the rewarding part."

She returned to the clinic to get ready for appointments, changing into white slacks and her white coat. She hoped she didn't smell too bad. "Maybe later on we can set it up so that I spend one day at the farms and another day at the clinic, so I won't smell. Now that we have three vets," she said, and then caught herself. "Actually, we have two and half right now."

Outside, airing out his car, Chuck said of Erika, "She was slow, but new vets are slow. It's all about confidence. In four weeks she'll be twice as fast. She's got the interest. That's all that matters."

5.

After the weekend, Chuck took Erika to another two farms for herd checks. He wanted her to see Mark Rushton's farm in Grafton, Vermont, one of his favorites. Chuck liked the way Rushton treated his cows, which was partly the old way. Rushton had managed a bigger dairy before leasing this smaller place, and had formed his philosophy there.

On his farm, he wanted to "get all the production we can out of them," but he refused to use BST (bovine somatotropin, or growth hormone). He also put the cows out to pasture. "Four hours, and they came back for the fans," he said. "They dropped eight hundred pounds in production for the farm when we put them out, because at first they ran back and forth in the field and used up their energy." But he persisted for the sake of the cows' feet, to get them off concrete for a while. Healthier feet could mean a longer life span. For anyone who had seen some of the other farms, where cows were confined to a barn, walking on concrete all their lives, a cow eating grass in a pasture was a heartening sight.

Erika detected a corpus luteum on the uterus of one cow, and Chuck concurred, though he said, "I'd call that a diminishing CL." When she found a cyst in the uterus of a Holstein that had not been bred for a very long time, Rushton decided that the time had come to turn that cow into beef. Another cow was a windsucker, her vulva torn from calving. Erika found a cyst in her too, but in this case they would treat her with gonadotropin, a hormone that would bring the cow into heat and, they hoped, would dispel the infection. Before they left, Chuck mended the windsucker.

They traveled along back roads to Barrett's Stoneholm Farm so Erika could see the countryside. The Barrett farm was one of the highest producers among Chuck's clients, and Peter and Mike Barrett also declined to use BST, Chuck told Erika. They didn't hit the cows with canes or sticks to herd them either, because that could cause a drop in production. Mike Barrett said that canes made the cows scared, and that made them shit in the milking parlor, which made for more work. A cause-and-effect relationship, or what Mike called the "we'll be nice to you and you'll be nice to us" approach.

Barrett led the herd check and accompanied Chuck through the barn—a big, open Quonset building with three hundred milking cows in five pens. Again, Chuck pointed out cows for Erika to check. Although she still often called Chuck over to double-check her findings, after three days on the job she seemed more at ease, and a little quicker.

A big Holstein walked up and then quickly ran past. This cow knew what the pink sleeves were all about. Erika noticed, and laughed. "I love it when they sneak by," she said. "To see a fourteen-hundred-pound animal sneak is really funny."

She looked about the barn. "My friends in vet school have no idea why I like this. But there's something rugged about it that's appealing. And it's like being a kid, like playing in the mud.

"It seemed funny at first, in palpation labs at vet school, sticking your arm up a cow's butt. At first it was just, 'All I can feel is shit in here.' But now I don't think about that. I'm just feeling the uterus."

A few days later the cat named Nigel was back, and soon was in a cage in the treatment room, one eye closed, placidly watching the goings-on with the other eye.

By then Erika had studied the blood of a dog with a high white cell count, looking for the cause, suspecting it was pancreatic. She had done an autopsy, with Chuck, on a cow that died of unknown causes at Goodell's. She had examined growths on the eyelid of a dog under the watchful eye of the owner, and decided the growths didn't need to be removed. She did a spay on a cat, though she remembered partway through that she should have checked the cat's temperature before beginning. She did a dog spay, but got delayed after the anesthesia tube went into the esophagus rather than the trachea, only to have the animal wake as she was about to cut, and so had to begin again, only to have Chuck walk in and say, "Who's doing appointments?" Chuck finished the spay in his coveralls while Erika, in her white coat, waited in the reception room for the clients who didn't arrive on time. To Chuck's reminder that she had to keep track of the appointment book, she said, "It was a typical graduating vet mistake and won't happen again." And when he reminded her again, she gave the same answer again.

She was right. They both were.

"It's overwhelming," she said one afternoon, her violet hair tousled, eyes dazed. "So many details to think about, so much happening. In between remembering to keep good records, I have to remember how to fix pets. But my head's not blowing off. I'm okay."

Important successes occurred. One morning Darcie said to Erika, "What did you do to Baby Boomer? He was up and calling to me this morning when I came in!" Erika had given Boomer an injection of dexamethasone, the synthetic steroid, and a long-acting bronchial dilator.

"I made a cat better!" Erika said, with that irresistible laugh.

She talked about doing her first DA soon, though it wouldn't actually be her first, she said. She had done two during her externship in Ohio two summers ago.

"First one you'll get paid for," Roger said.

"When do we get paid here?"

"Today."

"It will feel so good to get that check!"

During that first week, Erika also performed her first euthanasia. She was alone, since Roger and Chuck were out on calls. After administering the injection, Erika spent long minutes with her stethoscope pressed to the dog, trying to decide if he was dead, thinking, What if he wakes up later? She kept thinking about it through the night. She kept seeing the bag move.

The great, pressing, omnipresent responsibility had hit her now.

"I never knew it would be this intense," she said. "They tell you in vet school, your first year is going to be difficult, but I never knew it was going to be like this."

7

WHAT YOU DO WELL

1.

If Roger had stayed in Alberta and not become a veterinarian, he likely would have become a professional horse trainer. The best job he'd ever had before becoming a veterinarian was when he was in college and spent a summer working at a cattle ranch of eighteen hundred head, where he trained three-year-old colts for ranch work and calf roping. He moved cattle to pasture and trucked horses, vaccinated calves and kept records. He worked sixteen-hour days, but enjoyed them because in that northern part of Alberta the sun didn't set until after ten. "The workdays were like now," Roger said, "except a little less stressful."

He said, "A lot of those cattle were rank, and they'd charge you. One time a bull got in with the heifers. He wasn't supposed to be there. I knew that the bull charged horses, so I didn't take my own horse in with him. I took one of theirs. We rode in, and the bull came straight at us, knocked both of us onto a pile of brush. I rolled off on the other side. That horse was really fast and athletic, and just took off. He was kind of ruined after that for ranch work. Whenever any cattle looked at him funny, he got spooky."

Roger worked with horses at home on the ranch too. His father kept about 200 cattle on 800 acres. They released the cattle on the range in the summer and rounded them up with horses in the fall. Roger thought those cattle had a pretty good life compared to dairy cows. "I don't have any trouble eating beef," he said. The horses were often crosses of quarter horses and draft horses, big, strong, fast, and tough.

If you got one going full speed, Roger said, "you were lucky if you could bring it to a stop by the time you got to the end of the ranch." The approach was utilitarian and practical. When horses ceased to be of use, went lame, or were uncooperative, they were auctioned off for the European meat market—put on the plane to Belgium, as they said.

A boy growing up in such a life would get an early start with horses. Roger's first came as a Christmas present when he was six. His father bought a pony, put her in a box in the back of a truck, and told Roger to go out and open the box up. He named the pony Bingo.

"Bingo set me for life, as far as working with horses," Roger said. "She had a lot of heart. In a race, she would run past horses, run just as fast as she could. She would run against my dad's big stock horses, and she'd always almost win." They trained Bingo to jump into the back of a pickup truck. They'd back up to a pile or a hump on the ground to give her a little help. Bingo would run up the pile and leap on. Then they headed into the range, looking for cattle. Once they found some, Bingo and Roger rode after them, herded them to the road, and sent them off toward home. After that, Bingo would jump back onto the truck and they'd go looking for another bunch.

Roger and his brother and sister weren't allowed to ride

with saddles when they were young because of the chance they'd get a foot caught in a stirrup while taking a fall and get dragged. Bareback riding gave Roger a greater feel for the horse under him. When Roger was nine, he spent some of the money he'd earned on the ranch to have an Appaloosa mare bred. He halter trained the filly right from the beginning, and on her second birthday he put a saddle on her. A friend of the family helped him with the initial training. "I rode her on the third day. For the next year, there wasn't a day I didn't ride. I learned that the way to get a horse broke was to ride her every day, so she got rode every day. She was my main horse until I was seventeen or eighteen, and she had a few babies."

To further his son's skills and provide him with a way to earn money, Roger's dad took him to auctions and helped him choose horses that he could train and sell at a profit. Most of them were animals someone else had given up on.

"A lot of those horses we got, they'd try to kill you because they were afraid. One was a mean albino mare. She'd buck every time you got on her, but she was a pretty good horse once you got her going. I got kicked by her once, when I was just walking by. When she kicked one of the men who worked on the farm, Dad made me sell her. I put her in the auction to sell her for meat because I didn't want her going to anyone she could hurt. But I was pretty sure someone would want such a good-looking horse. She was bought by a stock contractor, a guy who leased animals to rodeos, for his string of bucking horses."

Roger has one characteristic that might seem peculiar for a veterinarian. He faints at the sight of his own blood. He was sixteen when he was hired for the first time to train a horse with a bucking habit. The horse was a Thoroughbred, and the owner wanted to ride him in shows. Roger brought the horse home for training. During one session, the horse bucked

using Haddie as a tease mare to get Shawne primed for the phantom.

"Can you believe this? Listen to this!" Jane said of the commotion between Shawne and the paint. But Haddie didn't seem to mind at all, and stayed calm as Jane led her from the barn. She'd heard it all before.

Roger had called Jane a few days ago and said, "Jane, get on your dancing shoes. You've got a baby coming in May," and when they next met, she had thrown her arms around him. She was unquestionably pleased with Roger. "He takes getting his horses bred personally," she said.

Now she stood watching as Shawne trotted from corner to corner, stopping and turning, his mane flying. There seemed to be a kind of agreement in place, an understanding of boundaries. Shawne could have kicked the boards off the paddock and gotten out if he wanted. He had kicked boards off before. Probably he knew his time was coming soon. Roger had his part in this agreement too. Last week, when Shawne had gotten out of hand and reared, Roger had smacked him, but a bit harder than he'd meant to. He knew that a previous handler had been afraid of Shawne and beat him too much. Roger knew that when Shawne was beaten, he lost his libido. The next day, Shawne stood with his head in the corner and ignored Roger when he tried to collect him. The understanding was that they were working together, and that trust had to be established.

Now Roger arrived as Jane was closing the trailer. They talked only briefly, because Roger had to palpate the mare. When he heard what the owner had said about the paint and the breeding chute, he said, "I'll get her in there."

First he had to get Shawne into the barn and out of sight, where he was less likely to rile the mare. Shawne, who knew all the steps in the process, started screaming even more when Roger led him into his stall. He screamed and curled back his upper lip—flehmen, it is called, the flehmen lip curl. He tried to reach his nose over the top of the stall.

In the next stall, the paint was doing her part in this dance, wheeling about with her ears back. She didn't want to come out, but Roger went in, talked gently to her, and managed to get a halter on and lead her out. He walked her around to relax her, and then led her up to the opening of the breeding chute. She stopped short there, planting her hooves, flicking back her ears, raising her head. She had light and ghostly eyes. Roger led her around and up to the entrance again. It was as the owner had said—she was not going into that chute.

Roger put a chain on the lead and ran it over her nose, then tightened the chain and led her around again. This time she reared and flicked out her legs. Roger held on, and when she came down, he gave her a whack in the ribs. He didn't hit her hard enough to hurt her, only enough to let her know he was there and that his will was stronger than hers. "She's trying to intimidate me," he said. "I'm not going to let her."

Again he led her up to the chute, and this time he had me hold a pan of grain at the other end. This offering of food interested her, but not enough to entice her through the chute. He led her around to the opposite end and tried to coax her through, but she dug in her hooves again. Calm but determined, Roger went into the barn and returned with a rope fashioned into a lasso. Again he led the mare around in a circle and up to the breeding chute. When she pulled up at the entrance, Roger twirled his rope and cast it over her rump. He tightened the loop and pulled. Now he was pulling her front end with the lead rope and her back end with the lasso. Roger cinched the lasso rope around a rail on the chute and took up every inch she gave. Although her hooves were still planted and her rump high, Roger had her, and she was becoming convinced. Suddenly she gave in and bolted through. Roger stepped back, caught the lead, and went with her.

Roger's expression had hardly changed all this time, except for the hint of amusement he now betrayed. He was outwaiting the mare, he would say.

Now he brought the mare around again, lassoed her, and cinched her up. She resisted again, digging in her hooves, but was not quite so stubborn as before, and when she finally gave in and bolted through, it was not quite so fast and furious as the first time. Roger brought her around, repeated the maneuver, peeled away when she ran through, then did it all over again, twirling his rope once more. And again, ten times altogether, until she was going through easily. Then he reversed direction and took her through the opposite way. He did this four times and then reversed direction again and brought her through the original way. The route and the release were firmly in her mind now. The next time, when the paint entered the chute, Roger stopped her at the end and offered her a pan of grain. She was interested, definitely interested. On went the back gate behind her, and on went the front gate fastening at her chest, while she ate. She couldn't move ahead or back now. Roger tied a rope across the rails and over her back so she couldn't jump up either.

He brought out fresh hay, which she was also interested in, and ate while he examined her uterus with ultrasound. As Roger pushed the probe into her, the paint's head shot up and her ears flicked back, but she didn't resist, and turned her attention to the hay again.

"She's going to ovulate," Roger said. He led her back into the barn and went to get his collection equipment from the house.

The foremost piece of equipment was the AV, or artificial

vagina. This consisted of a rubber cylinder, double jacketed and about the length of a forearm. Roger filled the jacket with warm water at the bathtub and lubricated the inside with a non-spermicidal gel. On the tip of the AV he fastened a cylinder and sock that looked like a condom. He set the artificial vagina inside a leather carrying case that looked like a rifle holster and headed back to the barn.

You could hear Shawne from the house, but when Roger walked into the barn, the horse blew a powerful string of notes. When Roger pulled a blue hard hat off the wall and put it on, Shawne neighed mightily again. And when Roger picked the breeding halter, a leather halter covered in lamb's wool, off the wall, Shawne let out a screech. Roger got into the stall and put the halter on. He leaned back and looked down, then decided he didn't need to use the tease mare. "I've got to get going before he cools off," Roger said.

Roger had a rule with horses that he always led the way. But as soon as Shawne rounded the corner, he bounded for the phantom, and Roger had all he could do to keep up. Shawne hit the phantom on the fly and clutched the barrel with his front legs. This was a dangerous moment for Roger because now he had to let go of the lead and trust that Shawne would keep his balance while he connected with the AV.

In the literature of horse breeding, there is a juncture called the searching phase. Shawne thrust his way into this phase, and it was very much a hit-or-miss affair. You could also see why live breeding could be so perilous for the stallion. An excitable mare like the paint could kick during this phase, causing significant damage to the important organ. The searching phase was a vulnerable moment for Roger too, who had given up control of Shawne and was now crouched below him. The blue hard hat was only a token gesture of protection against what could happen if the stallion flipped or kicked out. Roger's attention had diverted downward and was focused on the AV, which he held under his left arm while he grabbed Shawne's phallus with his right and directed his searching. He then held the AV like a cannoneer while Shawne heaved against him. This part left bruises on Roger's forearm. There was an emotional quotient too—the process was so dangerous and exciting, and so close to the center of who Roger was, that he was left trembling afterward. Even more so than when he put down a horse or castrated one, he said.

About thirty seconds passed before Shawne produced another thousand dollars worth of seed, thirty seconds before that universal moment when Shawne's head cocked slightly, his mouth pressed toward his chest, and his facial muscles slackened. This too was a vulnerable moment for both of them as Shawne backed off the phantom, almost into a crouch, and Roger took the lead rope again, saying, "Easy, easy," and, "Good boy, good boy." Shawne twisted away and righted himself. Tall again on his tulip-stem legs, he walked to the barn with Roger at his side. The yard was suddenly quiet, except for the sound of his hooves.

With the AV under his arm, Roger headed up to the house again to sort and measure the collection. As he walked up the driveway, he said, "Did you see him give the phantom a little nibble at the end? He gives it a little kiss."

A spare bedroom had been turned into a lab, with a small incubator, a microscope, beakers and flasks, and Styrofoam mailing boxes. Crouching on his knees, Roger unfastened the collection sock from the AV and poured the contents into a beaker for measurement. Shawne had produced 110 cc, a kingly amount. Roger would be able to get three parcels out of it. He took a third for the insemination of the paint and placed the rest in the refrigerator for slow cooling. One degree every five minutes was optimal.

With an eyedropper he placed a drop on a slide and examined it under the microscope. "They're boiling," he said. It was true—billions of spermatozoa, in their own searching phase, flip-flopping in search of the equine egg.

Shawne hadn't been collected for more than a week. Hence the volume, well above the usual 40 cc. The long interval had also resulted in lower spermatic motility. "It's usually about one hundred percent," Roger said, "but this one's about eighty-five." In the breeding trade, such an output is called a rusty load.

It was the paint's turn again. Roger prepared for the insemination by mixing the semen with a liquid extender and pouring that into a syringe. He put the syringe in his pocket to keep it from the light, even though the sun had set by then.

When Roger walked into the barn, Shawne announced that he was ready for another round. Roger looked into the stall and said, "Oh, no, Buddy. Put that thing away."

With the excitement and unfamiliar surroundings, the paint had regressed in her training and didn't want to go into the box again. Roger anticipated this, and had the lasso ready, and a pan of grain. After he pulled her through once forcefully with the ropes, on the next round she was ready to stop at the end for a bite of grain. We fastened the gates, but Roger didn't need to put a rope over her back this time.

He attached a long pipette to the syringe and inserted it well into the mare. She only raised her head momentarily, though quizzically, while a billion little Shawnes shot into her and began the race for her egg.

Roger left the mare outside in Shawne's paddock for the night, where she nickered and snorted and pranced from end to end, raising her tail and running. Shawne screamed at her from the barn.

"I could do that all day long," Roger said over a beer back at his house. And he actually hoped to someday, with a viable stallion station in combination with some level of veterinary work. If he could make fifty shipments a year with just Shawne, many things were possible, starting with the payment of the loan for Shawne's purchase. Then a ranch maybe, a base of his own. And there would be training—of Shawne's progeny, he hoped. The stallion's foals would carry the good news.

Leaning back in a kitchen chair, Roger said, "You know that trick of tightening the rope over her butt? That's something I learned from those old-time trainers back in Alberta. They sure helped me out a lot."

He talked about Erika, the struggles she was having in her first days and would certainly continue to have. He said it was so hard in the beginning, when you want to be good but can't help feeling that you're not very good yet.

"You try to be really good at one thing, and try to do all the other stuff well," he said. "Erika wants to palpate cows. I have no interest in palpating cows at all. But I can do the horses really well, and that makes me feel I'm really good at something."

3.

Erika's first call weekend wasn't as busy as it could have been, but it was challenging nevertheless. On Friday night she got two calls. The first was to tend to a whippet that had run into the woods and, after the owner heard a crack, had come out again howling. She had run into a tree branch, and a sharpened twig had shoved into her side under the skin. Erika went to the clinic at 7 p.m. to meet the owners, but she had to call Roger down to show her how to operate the X-ray machine and how to put a drain in the wound. She did the procedure and kept the whippet overnight. The second call was about a cat with a wound under his collar. The owner had used release collars previously, which the cat could get out of, but this time had put on a collar without a release, and the cat had struggled until he tore open his neck. Erika kept this cat overnight, and on Saturday would scrape down and sew up the partially healed wound.

She returned to Chuck's house at eleven and tried to sleep, but couldn't. She was "buzzing," too excited about having been on call and alone at the clinic. She tried some deep-breathing exercises, and they helped to relax her, but she kept thinking that she needed to sleep, and that thought kept her awake.

On Saturday she did the clinic treatments, which included checking the sutures in Nigel's eye following his corneal surgery, cleaning the ears of a boarding dog, giving an enema to a constipated cat, checking another cat for ear mites and fleas, removing the bandages from a cat who had been declawed, examining the postoperative incisions on two dogs, examining the whippet and giving her antibiotics, and treating the cat with the infected collar wound. She got a call about a cat with respiratory difficulties and treated him with steroids. She got another call about a dog with shut and puffy eyes and treated her with antibiotics. A call came in about a horse with green stuff coming out of its nose, which Erika referred to Roger. Another call came about a horse with pus coming out of its eye and was also referred to Roger. She got a call about a lamb with an injury, and made a farm call to treat the cut on its leg.

One call came from a client who said her cocker spaniel was screaming and losing her balance. Chuck had seen this twelve-year-old dog two months ago, in April, performing surgery and removing a cancerous mammary mass. The owners had opted not to have chemotherapy, deciding that it would only postpone the inevitable, and now the inevitable had come.

Erika recorded the visit:

> Quiet, seems a little disoriented. Owner describes yelping, trouble standing, difficulty breathing over the past few days. Has lost a lot of weight. Heart murmur loudest on left side. Very large mass occupying most of abdomen—in abdominal wall on left caudal side, extending from left hind leg to caudalmost rib. Extremely thin. Advanced cancer has progressed to point of affecting lungs, brain, and other body systems. Could do more diagnostics, but would probably not affect outcome. Owner elects euthanasia, will take body home. Euthanized with 9 ml Beauthansia IV.

Chuck was at the clinic to be on hand if Erika needed him, and was reading a medical manual in the staff room. She didn't ask him to help with the euthanasia. She asked one of the kennel workers, Nicole Guerriere, a high school girl who was herself considering becoming a veterinarian. "Have you assisted before?" Erika asked. The girl said she hadn't but was ready to try. Erika told her what to expect. "The dog may struggle, so you have to hold on. I'll be shaving the leg, and you'll help hold off the vein." They went into the exam room, where the owner was sitting on the floor with the cocker. He had wrapped her up in a wool comforter. His wife had left a few minutes earlier.

When Erika reemerged, she said to me, "It's done." There had been the same uncertainty as before, during her first euthanasia, "of knowing when the animal is dead. You listen and listen, but you can't keep the owner waiting forever. And he took the dog home. You wonder if she will wake up.

"It's such a fine line between life and death. What is it? If you see a cow that's been dead for two days, that's one thing. But an animal that has just been put to sleep? When is it no longer alive, when is it dead, and how do you know? You listen, you don't hear anything, and you just hope you're right. It's a matter of experience, of confidence again."

Aside from the technique, there was the emotional part to contend with. "You try to feel what the people feel, but not fall into it, so that you can do this. I don't mind doing it, because I feel like I'm doing a service. When an animal is suffering, I don't mind putting it to sleep.

"But you have to learn how to talk about it. When I was in vet school, I was the director of the pet support hotline, and I learned how to talk about it. I noticed when I was in school that some people couldn't talk about it. And if they couldn't talk about it then, they probably won't be able to talk about it later. They'll carry all this stuff inside, build up this big, expanding thing they're carrying around."

At the front desk Erika finished her record keeping and wrote out the charges. She decided not to charge an emergency fee. "I think that we shouldn't charge for euthanasias at all," she said. "It feels terrible to take money from people when you put their pet to sleep. Especially if you've been treating the pet for years. If people come in only once in a while, you should charge them, but if they've been regular customers and spent a certain amount over the years, then I think you should do the euthanasias without charge. That's the way I'll do it if I ever have my own clinic."

She said, last of all, "This was the first time I've actually told the people that their animal was ready to be put to sleep. I think it went well."

After her call weekend Erika drove to Concord for her licensing exam. On Tuesday she worked at the clinic but also spent time outfitting her truck with supplies. She bought tackle boxes for a foot box and a vaccine box and a syringe box. She bought a cooler for the equipment she'd need for doing DAs—the cooler could also serve as a table, Roger told her. She conferred with Roger about the drugs she'd need, and he filled her in on "the little cocktails" he used to sedate horses. She loaded her truck with a supply of bottles taken from the storeroom, filling trays with dextrose, calcium, electrolytic powder, and other medications. She said, "I'm so jealous of Roger's new truck, with all his neat compartments." Someday she wanted to have a truck with flames painted on the side. She had begun giving her red Toyota a personal touch, however, clipping a leopard-skin organizer to the visor and hanging a Rosie the Riveter air freshener from the mirror.

She was on call Tuesday night, and answered the phone when it rang at Chuck's house at six in the morning. At Boggy Meadow, a cow had milk fever, a depletion of calcium in the blood experienced early in lactation, when so much calcium is going to make milk. Chuck heard Erika talking in the hallway and called to her through the closed bedroom door. Did she want him to come? She said no, she'd go alone. He told her the remedies he used for milk fever, the injection of calcium foremost. The herdsman was still on the line. At the end of the call Erika said, "I'll be there, maybe with Dr. Shaw," and immediately thought, Why did I say that? She left for the farm alone, and the drive, she remembered, was much scarier than the confrontation that awaited her. Actually there was no confrontation at all. When she arrived at Boggy Meadow, the cow was up and walking, "which was a pretty good sign that the milk fever had abated."

4.

Break time in the staff room, and four hot coffees from Dunkin' Donuts. Hobbs was on the table, resting his chin on the lids of the coffee cups, for the heat apparently. Carol came in and sat down, and Hobbs jumped on her lap. Roger came in and opened a sandwich, and Hobbs jumped up on the table. Roger said, "I don't allow cats on the table, especially gross ones," and dropped him to the floor. Hobbs jumped up on the seat next to Roger, and Lynn sat down on that chair with Hobbs. She began to eat a bagel, which Hobbs wanted a share of. When he bit her, Lynn cried, "Hobbs!" and he jumped down. The conversation continued, and Hobbs jumped up on Carol's lap again. When she didn't give him anything, Hobbs bit her. "It's not really a bite," Carol said. "He just sort of grabs on." Hobbs jumped down, went underneath the table, jumped up on Lynn's seat, and sat next to her, his head between her elbow and side. His eyes followed the bagel.

He was looking cute, which inspired Darcie to get the new photos out. Hobbs on a stool with a full-size surgery cap on his head. Hobbs being pushed in a cart, his ears back as if he were going fast. Hobbs rolling on the floor in hair from a golden retriever. Hobbs with a mouse. Hobbs in the microwave. Hobbs smelling flowers at the front desk. "He doesn't just smell them," Roger said. "He pushes his whole face into them."

"Oh, what would we do without Hobbs?" Darcie asked. "He's above us all."

Earlier, Hobbs had tried to attack a cat that was dead. The owner had brought her in with her toys and asked that they bury her. When Nicole Reinhart brought the box to the treatment room, Hobbs trailed behind her, and when she set the box down, Hobbs tried to jump in after the cat. Nicole took the cat out of the box and put the box over Hobbs. He moved around the treatment-room floor, the box rising up and down, with everyone watching.

Erika did the few appointments of the morning while Chuck worked in the surgery. One of his procedures was the spaying of a Saint Bernard. Chuck and Darcie put a muzzle on her for the first injection of sedative. In the surgery Darcie asked to put the muzzle on again before lifting her onto the table. "She's too goofy to bite," Chuck said, but they put a muzzle on anyway. "You never know," he said. "For all the size they have, Saint Bernards can be pretty shaky creatures when it comes to self-confidence." They lifted her together, holding the dog from opposing sides. They went around a couple of times like square dancers, laughing.

A young woman studying to be a veterinary technician was working at the clinic for the summer. Her name was Kat McClenning. Chuck gave her a lesson on the shaving of a dog's belly. It is important to get above the belly button, he said, and down to the lowest part of the belly. "If you don't get below, and we need to make a larger incision, then we're screwed. The only thing the owners have to judge us by is the shaving and the incision. That's all they can see. And you don't want any blood on there. That's not cool."

Kat clipped while Chuck watched. He said to clean the stubble by going against the grain and by shaving away from where the incision would be. "And then use the vacuum to clean up all the hair," he said. "I don't like to open the kit until you've got it all cleaned up."

When Kat was done, Darcie scrubbed the exposed belly with disinfectant. Chuck used a tape roller to remove the hair from his smock, then put on a cap and gloves. He had just begun cutting when Erika walked in, finished with appointments. She said, "Darcie, do you want to go kill a horse too?"

"Sure," Darcie said. She wanted very much to be outdoors on this beautiful summer day, and Chuck had already given his permission for Darcie to accompany Erika on a house call.

"We're going to call you the grim girls," Chuck said.

"Doctor Death," Erika said. "That's me."

They left the clinic, and Erika drove toward Charlestown. "We'll kill the horse first," she said.

"I've never killed a horse before."

"Neither have I," Erika said, and laughed at the weirdness of it.

She said that the owner had not been listening to them. "The horse has impacted bowels and was dehydrated so bad that Roger couldn't get blood yesterday. She's been keeping it in a greenhouse with a tub of dirty water. Roger tubed the horse yesterday and gave it fluids. He told her that we couldn't save the horse by doing surgery, but she could send it to a referral hospital in Rochester or at Tufts, and they might be able to save it. But she didn't listen. She has a good heart, but something is not connecting."

As soon as they drove into the yard and parked by a barn, a little girl came running up. "The horse died," she said.

They walked around to the back of the barn. Inside a pen with a tarp roof was a woman sitting on the ground with her legs straight out. The horse lay in front of her, and another girl, of about twelve, was stretched on the ground, her head on the horse's neck and her arm over its head. She was rocking back and forth and moaning. The woman was staring at her, speechless.

Behind her were Holsteins in the barn, and some were reaching their noses through a break in the wall. In a pen nearby, other ponies and horses grazed. This was a leased farm, owned by one of the big dairies. The girls were foster children, and the ponies were theirs. There was another girl, who was handicapped and in a wheelchair. One of the ponies had been trained to pull a cart for her.

Erika crouched down and got into the pen beside the woman. She put her arm across the woman's back and held her. Darcie got in the pen on the other side and put her arm on the woman too and rubbed her back. They didn't say much, just held her and massaged her while the girl turned on her stomach and moaned.

The woman looked back and forth at Darcie and Erika, but she didn't move much at all. Cows, horses, the vets, the mother, all watching the girl writhe on the ground. After a good five minutes of uninterrupted wailing and thrashing, Erika said, "You did all you could," and she and Darcie crawled out of the pen.

"I don't know if I could put my hand on a Bible about saying that," Erika said when she got back into the truck. "We thought she had been told. We thought we had been pretty clear. She didn't seem to grasp how bad the horse was. When Roger visited her yesterday, he told her it was really, really bad."

Roger was off today, or he would have made this call. Luckily, Erika had been spared the task of killing the horse.

"But she owes us money. Maybe she thought she couldn't afford us. She called last night but then waited until the last minute to put it down, when the animal was really in bad shape. Maybe money was a factor."

"She really tries," said Darcie, who knew the woman from her many visits to the clinic. "I think she gets up every morning and how the day ends is how it ends."

They drove south through Walpole for the next call. A cat

had to be euthanized. A man who had recently moved to Spofford from New York City had heard that the Walpole Vet Hospital made house calls. Chuck was about to begin surgery when the call came in, and he had said that Erika could go and take Darcie with her.

It was a newly painted house with a freshly cut lawn. A man came out—in his fifties, with long gray hair and a pony-tail. He had a German shepherd with him, and the dog had a muzzle on, which seemed thoughtful of the owner. He led Erika and Darcie through a garage to a deck at the rear of the house, overlooking a steep drop-off into the woods. A crew was working down there, clearing brush.

On a lawn chair, stretched out on a towel, was a very old and emaciated cat. He was blind but could hear. He lifted his head and tried to look about when Darcie talked to him, and he looked for Erika too. He turned to find one and then the other.

"We adopted him a long time ago in New York," the man said. "He's a crossbreed, Abyssinian and Maine coon cat." He had a coat like a red fox, but silver too. "A vet I knew told me that cats rarely turn silver with age, but this one has."

One of the cat's eyes was swollen. The man said it had happened yesterday and that he might have had a stroke. He had been diagnosed with a liver condition in October. Erika thought the swollen eye was the result of a tumor, but didn't say so.

She went to the truck for a syringe and fluid, but when she returned and looked at the cat's paw, she said it would be hard to find a vein. "Do you have a disposable razor?" she asked. "I don't have any clippers." One item that hadn't gotten into her truck yet.

The man said he did, and he went to get one. But when Erika tried to use the razor, it didn't remove the hair.

"These work on cows," she said.

"And people," he answered.

She pulled out a pocketknife with scissors and clipped away the hair. Even then it was proving difficult.

"Good luck finding a vein," the man said, and walked off into the garage. However he soon returned and sat down and leaned in close when Erika inserted the syringe. When a little trail of blood came out, he sighed and leaned back in his chair.

Erika had difficulty pushing fluid into the vein, and she pulled out the needle. "Now that I've tried that, I'm going to inject into the chest," she said. The man got up and walked away, into the house. Quickly Erika felt for the heart and fired. The cat's eyes fixed, and it was gone.

Darcie and Erika folded the white towel over the animal, and the man returned.

"This cat had a wonderful owner," Erika said, putting a hand on his shoulder.

"He had a good life," he said. He tried to pay with cash—$79—but couldn't come up with the exact change, so he went to get a check. Erika and Darcie looked down from the deck to where the men were dragging away loose brush.

"We're getting married this weekend," the man said when he returned. "This property goes all the way back to Chesterfield Gorge. We fell in love with the place. We feel really lucky to be here."

He said they had been hoping the cat would last through the weekend, but that's how it goes.

"What do you want to do?" Erika asked. "We have a burial service."

"We're going to bury him right here. We have a place."

Erika put a hand on his shoulder again and did what at this stage she was really good at, it seemed. The kindly rapport, the doctorly way.

"Do you have someone to talk to?" she asked.

He seemed touched and even surprised. "Yeah, yeah, I do."

"Have a nice wedding."

The man thanked her, and she and Darcie left for a lunch stop and then back to the clinic for the afternoon's appointments. Another house call under her belt, another matter of experience achieved.

8

A HORSE RESCUE

1.

Erika beat herself up over her first DA, at Westminster Farms. It had gone about as well as could be expected for a first-time vet, slowly and haltingly. Roger had done one before her, taking about twenty minutes to do the procedure. Erika had taken about an hour and a half. She had made typical first-time mistakes—in her nervousness forgetting to put a sleeve on and reaching into the cow with a bare, scrubbed arm; reaching again and again for the abomasum but not finding it, finding the rumen instead, until Roger went in and found it for her; struggling over the suturing, forgetting what she had learned in school while she trembled, leaving deep creases in her fingers from the strain of pulling on the twine. She kept saying to herself, Breathe and sew, breathe and sew, hoping the mantra would see her through.

She had thought it wouldn't be a tough one, but it was, and she wished it could have gone better. Outside the barn in the heat, her face reddened, she said, "One thing this teaches you is not to be a perfectionist. This is a Zen thing, being a vet. It teaches you not to be attached to a specific thing. To let go."

Roger agreed. He told Erika that his first DA took a long time, and in the following days he had gone back and checked on it five times, but the cow had recovered well and produced again. Roger said of Erika's struggle, "She has to learn to accept that everything can't go perfectly. That's one of the things I learned on a farm, that it's different all the time and things don't always go the way you want."

"I had to think about everything, every step," she said. "I even had to think about the sutures, because it was just not flowing. I was trying not to think about stressing and just sew. Problem is, when you get stressed out, you don't pay attention. I'm not happy about the way it went. I have to struggle not to beat myself up over it."

By the next day Erika was feeling better, even a bit elated after vaccinating some calves and treating two sick cows at Barrett's on her own. To help her in her trials, her stepmother had sent her two homeopathic remedies, one for self-confidence, another to eliminate dread. "Not that I believe in that stuff, but I took it. It felt like what I really was taking was my stepmom's concern. Took four doses, four little drops, and the dread seemed to fall away.

"I don't talk about my feelings all that well," Erika said, "but if you read between the lines, dread is there. Sometimes things seem too easy, and sometimes things seem unbearably difficult. The DA was unbearably difficult. The vaccinations were about as difficult as I thought they should be. The sick cows were relatively easy.

"Sometimes it's so difficult that I wonder if I'm doing the right thing. And then that is passed by the feeling of, Hooray, this is great! Deep down I know I want to do this. I just don't like not being as good as I want to be. I know that eventually

I'll feel accomplished. I just wish I could drink something to make me feel that way."

2.

A few days later Roger left for his summer vacation in Alberta, taking Danelle along to meet his family. With Erika on board, the departure was much easier. He didn't have to feel that he was leaving Chuck alone.

Erika had moved from Chuck's house into a small and lovely house in Westmoreland that sat in a maple sugar bush on the grounds of an old farm. Gary had joined her and was working in Walpole with a group of carpenters. A former elementary school teacher, he loved the satisfaction that building brought him. Gary was Erika's strong source of support; he had been with her all through vet school, living with her at her mother's house. When she stayed up late at night, her head inside veterinary textbooks, she had asked Gary not to say good night, but rather, "I hope you'll be joining me soon," to make the deprivation feel less sharp. Now they were living together, engaged, thinking they'd get married in Walpole eventually, and Erika had her buddy, as she said, to talk to about her trials on the job.

While Roger was away, her week began with a normal mixed-practice day on call. After appointments, she delivered a calf at Westminster Farms and returned with her shoes soaked with amniotic fluid—getting her feet wet, you might say. After the clinic closed that evening, she went on a call to treat a llama. She stayed until eight o'clock. "The llama had a cut on its throat, cellulitis maybe. The owners wanted to yack. It was anytime of day for them. But I wanted to go home."

She was still charged up when she got into bed, and though Gary was asleep, she couldn't stop thinking. To calm herself, she recited in her mind the Buddhist chants she had learned at the Zen monastery.

The first was "Sentient beings are numberless; I vow to save them."

No, Erika thought, I don't want to think about that. That's what I do all day long. But, she thought, by sitting and meditating, you do save them. You create the proper mindfulness, and the saving has begun.

The second chant was "Desires are inexhaustible; I vow to put an end to them." This is good, she thought. I can put an end to the desire to go back and check on that calf I pulled today and see if it's all right—see if those were twins, if there was another calf in there. If I put an end to the desire to go back, I put an end to worry. There's calmness in that idea.

The third was "The dharmas are boundless; I vow to master them." This is good too, this paradox. There's calmness here too, in the acceptance of the impossibility and the truth of it. You always vow to achieve mastery. You would make continuous effort despite the unknowns.

The fourth chant was "The Buddha is unattainable; I vow to attain it." The best one of all, she thought. Even the masters never attain it. Enlightenment is always a struggle, always. It's in the doing that you achieve, in the attempt to attain. You never move beyond the attempt.

Breathe, she thought.

The next morning, after office hours, Erika was on her way to work on some sheep and goats. The windows of the truck were open. Erika had placed a feather from a red-tailed hawk in the sun visor. Just below was the air freshener with Rosie the Riveter and the slogan WE CAN DO IT. She had just pointed out the hawk feather to me when the wind caught it, and it sailed out the window. She watched it fly, laughed, and said, "Oh well, it's important to let go."

While driving along the back roads, she talked a bit about the variations in approaches to vet practices. "There was a professor at Tufts who wasn't my mentor, and couldn't be, because she was against the commercial use of animals. And I had a friend at school who believed that people shouldn't own pets unless they have the money to treat them. She believed that unless you are willing to do all the treatments that a dog or cat needs later in life, you are not a responsible pet owner. The question she asked, the code phrase was, 'Do you want *this* dog, or *a* dog?' I think she got the wind knocked out of her a bit when she did her rotations at vet school. But she'll be working at a small-animal practice in New York City, where clients can afford to take it to the limit."

This was an interesting ethical consideration. If you're not willing to spend, say, $250 on a medical procedure for your pet, should you own a pet? What about $2,500 for a hip replacement? If the pet is part of the family, how far do you go? If you aren't interested in spending $2,500 for a hip replacement or $10,000 for some other procedure to save your family member, then just what kind of person are you? How far to take a pet into the people realm?

Or, to use a philosophy that was in the air that day, if your cat or dog needed a big-ticket procedure, and you said, I'll stop here—couldn't you take on another animal, save another sentient being? Wasn't that a proper ethical approach, in the attempt to save another being? Wasn't there enlightenment in that, of a kind? Could not *a* sentient being be as important and worthy as *the* sentient being?

It would never be an easy or a simple decision. But with the proper approach it could be rewarding.

Erika stopped at an old Colonial-era house, a small farm run by, as Chuck put it, "a city girl who married a country boy."

The client was raising goats and sheep, and there were some cattle up on the hill behind the house, though they belonged to a neighbor. Erika had come to give shots to the younger sheep and to castrate and dehorn a two-week-old goat. This is something Roger might have done had he not been in Alberta—Roger could castrate a goat in about two minutes—but Erika knew how to castrate and was game to make the call.

The woman came out—healthy, sun-browned, in bib overalls, about Erika's age—and led Erika to the animals. Erika went about getting some vials and a dehorner and scalpels out of her truck, and she told the client she wouldn't sedate the goat, because it might upset his rumen. But when she got a look at the goat, all twenty pounds of him, a big, strong guy for his age, she said, "I'm going to sedate him."

Erika measured out a shot, a tiny amount, a hundredth of a cc diluted down, and gave it to him. She laid the goat on some hay in the barn while the sedative took effect. The woman then gathered the sheep in the paddock and held them while Erika gave vaccinations.

Then the woman brought the goat from the barn. He was as limp as a towel. She laid him on the lawn, and they crouched down beside him.

"This is terrible," the woman said of what was about to happen.

"Welcome to the world of large animals," Erika said.

The woman looked at the goat and said, "You're gonna hate me for this."

Just then a call came in on Erika's cell phone, and she got up to take it. What she heard unnerved her. Two horses were stuck in the mud in Swanzey. When Erika returned, she said, "I don't know how I can help those horses. They need to be sedated. How do you sedate horses that are stuck in the mud?"

But she put that thought off until later, and went about dehorning the goat with the bud-ex, a tool that looked a bit like a branding iron with an O on the end. Erika turned it on and pressed it over the goat's little horns, and smoke rose up with the smell of burning flesh. Concerned about frying his brains, she went lightly, hoping the horns wouldn't grow back in a stunted form—another concern. She cut out the goat's testicles, pulling the cords until they snapped, and the goat cried out from his deep sleep while his owner stroked him and apologized. Erika stretched him on the slope of the lawn, put a rock under his head to keep it elevated, and watched him.

In five minutes the little goat got up on his feet, but then he slumped to the ground and fell asleep again.

"Standing is always a good thing, even if you can't keep it up," Erika said.

"I see a tail wag," the owner said. She sighed. "A neighbor who's an old-time farmer told me I'm a terrible farmer because I care about the animals too much. They have Scottish High-landers that they sell for meat. I have to stay away from them so I don't get to know them."

"I don't want to leave him," Erika said. She listened to his heart and pulled on his tongue and examined his mouth. She lifted his head and stroked his side, called him "little guy," "popcorn," "sugar," and kept talking to him while he snored. She said she wanted him to wake before she left, but eventu-ally she had to go.

The muddy horses were about half an hour away. Anxiety set in as she approached. She felt confident around cows, she said, but she was suspicious of horses. They spoke a language she didn't hear.

"I don't know what they want me to do. Sedate, I guess. I certainly don't feel very useful."

On she drove. "This is the kind of thing where I'd like to ride along, where someone else is doing it and I could learn so much from them. But to be on my own, I just don't want to do something wrong. Like how much do you sedate a horse in the mud? I wish I could call Roger, but he's in Alberta.

"When I rode with mixed-practice guys on the ambulatory rotation at school, they were always saying, 'Wing it,' and I was saying, 'Wing what?'

"I feel stressed. In vet school I read book after book, studied and studied, but the learning doesn't seem to be of any help now."

She got lost, retraced her route, and found Old Swanzey Road. Along this unpaved road an emergency vehicle approached. She reached out and waved.

"Did they get the horses out?" she asked.

"They're out," the driver said.

"Thank you!"

Farther down the road, Erika saw a group of people walking. She stopped and asked, "The horses are out?"

"Yes," a man said, "and they're coming down the road. Best to stay out of the way so they can come through."

Then along came a kind of procession. First a group of girls leading a wet and muddy horse. The horse was draped with several blankets, and at his neck was an IV unit with a bag of fluids. One of the girls walked beside the horse and carried the IV bag. Behind the horse were other people, adults and children. Then a line of pickup trucks.

Erika pulled over and got out to walk up the road. One of the trucks stopped, and a window went down.

"Are you Erika?" a woman asked.

"Yes."

"I'm Dr. Jerilyn Jacobs." She smiled. "I've been working with this horse for two hours."

"Do you need any help?" Erika asked. Jacobs said to follow them.

They went into a yard up the road and took the horse into a barn that had been offered by one of the rescue crew.

Two teenage girls had been riding horses in a state park and wandered off the trail. When they reached this neighborhood, they came to a small snowmobile bridge built over the inlet to a pond. When one of the girls tried to walk her horse across, the bridge collapsed, and they went into the water. Neither was hurt, but the horse was soon deep in the mud. When the other girl went in to help her friend, her horse jumped into the water too and also got stuck. The girls ran to get help, and help began arriving. One of the horses was younger and stronger, and they soon pulled him out. The older horse was in the water much longer. Someone brought in a backhoe and dug a trench. They covered the horse's eyes and began to pull. Jacobs got into the water with him, and at one point the horse rolled over on her, but she managed to push herself away. By the time they dragged him out, the horse was severely dehydrated. Jacobs attached the IV line, and a group of neighborhood girls led him away.

The girls who'd been riding had left to get treated for cuts and bruises.

Jacobs was about forty, slender, with long hair. She wore full-length coveralls with an elastic waistband. She was a partner in a five-vet practice in Vermont. At the barn, she asked someone to bring more fluids from her truck. She had one of the girls feed the horse some hay and try to give him some water, but he wouldn't drink. Jacobs tried to wipe mud off the cuts on his legs, but that irritated him too much. She said they would take him outside and hose him off.

Jacobs smiled at Erika and said, "So, you've been at Walpole for a year now?"

"I just graduated, from Tufts."

"Oh, so you're brand-new!"

"Yeah."

"I went to Tufts too."

"When did you graduate?"

"Seven years ago."

"Do you know anything about llamas?"

"No, nothing. We refer all our llamas to"—and she mentioned a clinic. "I stay away from llamas. Can you keep an eye on the fluids?"

"Sure." They led the horse outside, with Erika carrying the bag of fluids and the IV line.

Jacobs took the hose and washed the mud off his legs. "Erika, how's his nose?" she asked.

Erika leaned and looked and touched the horse's nose. "It seems to be okay."

One of the girls said, "Oh, it's good to know there's another horse vet around here." Erika didn't say anything in response. She didn't want to pretend, but she didn't want to sell herself short either. She thought that in two years she might get called again, and by that time, she might be a horse vet.

Jacobs went to her truck for another bag of fluids. "Erika, do you have any penicillin?"

"Just the long-acting kind."

Jacobs sprayed a topical anesthetic on the cuts and bruises. Her treatment was straightforward—Banamine and dexamethasone, a pain reliever and a synthetic steroid, the basics that Erika would probably have prescribed too.

They took the horse back into the barn, where Jacobs gave him some hay and got another bag of fluids connected. Just then the owner of the horse, the father of one of the girls, came to the door and looked in. He seemed uncertain about his role. Jacobs said to him, "You're going to trailer him home?"

"They said something about maybe leaving him here overnight?"

"He needs to go home. Do you have a trailer?"

"No," the man said. "But I have resources." He said he thought maybe he could get him home.

Jacobs said with a laugh, but forthrightly, "We got him out of the swamp. You can get him on a trailer and get him home! He's going to be very sore tomorrow. You need to get him into a stall."

"Will he be able to go out in the pasture tomorrow?"

"He'll tell you that. He's going to be sore. You'll have to talk to him."

"He doesn't answer me."

"He'll answer you."

With that, the man left to find a trailer. Erika was about to leave too. In parting, Jacobs told her that she could call if she had any questions.

So she had someone after all, someone to learn from. The sort of vet she might be in seven years.

"I hope so," Erika said to me. "She's competent."

On the way back, Erika remarked, "They said in vet school, 'Unless you're lost, you won't be able to find yourself.' And that's kind of how it is."

The next morning at breakfast at Murray's, Chuck said, "It's always horses that are getting into that kind of trouble. It's never cows."

"No one's trying to ride a cow over a tiny little bridge."

Erika had a question about the goat she had worked on yesterday. She wanted to know about a growth under his neck. Was it part of his anatomy, a characteristic of the breed, of Nubians? Chuck said that it might be, but that it could be a cyst, that they get things like hay or sticks caught in their throats at times and the pieces work into the flesh.

She also talked about the dehorning and said she was worried that she didn't dehorn him enough—worried also that she had fried his brains.

"Erika will worry for fourteen hours about a goat she worked on for fourteen minutes," Chuck said.

He told her, "It's the ones with the crooked horns that live forever, you know. And the customers will say, 'Dr. Bruner fixed that one!' You kind of wish they'd fall over, but they just keep going on and on."

An e-mail arrived from Alberta:

> I hope that Erika is doing OK and relaxing. We are having a great time. Physically tired though. We moved over 500 pairs of cattle on Tuesday and today my friend and mentor here castrated 14 horses. I knocked them all out and he castrated them and we did them all in just over an hour. All the cowboys were amazed and I think it will be the talk of the town for a while. This guy has 80 Brood mares and a whole shithouse load of babies, yearlings and 2 year olds. Say hi to everyone but to be honest with you I am not really ready to come back yet.

3.

That summer when Erika was breaking in as a vet, the American Veterinary Medical Association held its annual convention in Boston. Among the many talks and presentations was one given by Dr. Carin Smith, a veterinarian and writer, on the effects of the increasing number of women in the profession.

Smith made the point that this trend could be catastrophic because of how women are viewed in the workplace and how women sometimes view themselves. Jobs filled by women have less prestige, Smith stated. People predict a higher value for work done by men.

"Discrimination takes the form of stereotypes about women's personalities and inherent abilities. Assumptions are made about what's important to women," she said. "True or false? Entry of women into the profession is a good thing, because their nurturing and empathetic nature enhances their work with clients and pets."

No one denied that it was true, that feminine empathetic nature was in fact a good thing. It seemed to be the strong point for women vets.

"Such assumptions can backfire," she said. "They lead to other assumptions, such as that men are not good at such things as nurturing and empathy. Women could be held to a higher standard. And veterinary medicine could become a woman's job. Ultimately it leads to the assumption that it's okay that we make less money. A trade-off, of empathy for income.

"Men don't say it's okay to be empathetic and earn less. They shouldn't earn less. But today the stereotypical male who wants a high income doesn't go into veterinary medicine.

"Women charge less," Smith said. "Why do women accept less? Because they have always accepted less.

"When a man and a woman are doing the same work and women are paid less, we assume the performance isn't as good. When women and men are doing the same work, women tend to judge themselves more harshly. Women will rate themselves lower and admit mistakes more easily than men. When men are asked to value themselves, they usually set their value at higher rates, and they don't easily admit mistakes." Nevertheless, Smith said, what women want in the profession most of all, more than money, is respect.

After the lecture, standing in the hallway, Smith, who did not seem one to pull punches, said, "There's an economic crisis in the profession. That's the dirty little secret no one wants to talk about. Students are coming out of vet schools with $100,000 in loans and making $45,000 a year if they're lucky."

Erika's loans amounted to $104,000 when she graduated. She had worked out a ten-year payment plan of $1,100 a month. "I knew I could have bought a house with that money, but I went to vet school. I call it a mental mortgage." For now, Gary would carry the major household expenses while Erika worked down her debt.

Smith had made some interesting points, well worth thinking about, but you had to wonder about the strict division of her definitions along gender lines. Erika was quick to admit mistakes, no doubt about it, and even more ready to admit her shortcomings. And without a doubt, what she was seeking was respect.

But so was Roger, the farm boy who saw a C-section and decided he wanted to be the special person who did that procedure. And Chuck, he wanted respect too, when he drew up a list of career components and decided that being a veterinarian was a good way to play an important role on farms and in the community.

And Chuck certainly seemed to have that feminine nature when it came to charging, or charging less. He was always discounting according to the circumstances, and he had not even collected on many accounts. He sometimes worked for free.

Admitting mistakes? Hard to tell. Perhaps that fell into the realm of confidence building. Could you say that a male felt it was counterproductive to talk about mistakes, while a female felt it was healthy and productive to admit hers? Weren't those assumptions gender stereotypes too?

But Smith drew that line. Males overvalued themselves and charged more, and females undervalued themselves and charged less, she claimed. True or not, it was a provocative idea, and made you think about your assumptions, about approaches to this profession, and about work in general. And that was partly her aim—that and the point that vets should charge more.

4.

Erika came in one morning after Roger had returned and said, "I'm happy."

This feeling was contrary to others she'd been having. Erika was scheduled to go to Westminster Farms to check on some sick cows and possibly do a DA. She was pleased to be sent on a farm call by Chuck, but she still felt that she was going unprepared. She had been feeling anxious most mornings. "I'm sitting and doing meditation, but it isn't helping," she said.

So she had worked out an agreement with Chuck and Roger. She would go to the farm alone, check the cows, and cut the cow open if she had to, but Roger would arrive when she was about to deflate the abomasum. What she felt happy about was that she had negotiated this supervision and mentoring.

"I have to take care of myself," she said that morning. "I told myself that by the time I was thirty, I would know what I want and I would get it. I decided to become a vet, that was one thing. Now I have to do what's necessary to eliminate stress. I have to be able to say, I'm not ready for this! I want to plunge in. I want to do it, but I want some help, some support.

"Here in the clinic doing appointments, I feel okay. I can handle anything, and if I have questions, I can ask someone. But out there, I'm alone, and I'm thinking, What if this goes wrong? What if this happens, and I go—ahh! Things would probably be okay if I did the DA by myself, but I just need to feel there's someone there for support. Roger was willing to just plunge into things, but I'm not that way. We're different. And I'm psyched that I was able to state it, to work it out. I feel like I just had two espressos!"

Erika went off to Westminster, and as promised, Roger followed half an hour later, but he said, "Erika needs to realize that everything is going to be all right. She's stressed more than she's letting on, but everything is going to be all right. Chuck has been worrying too, about money, and he should probably slow down too."

Erika was shaving the side of the cow when Roger walked into the sick bay. She had diagnosed a DA, but she asked Roger to examine the cow too.

"It's a DA," he said.

Erika asked him to hold the rolls of sutures while she made the initial incision. She smiled and said, "It's good you're here."

He smiled back. "I'll just hold up the wall." He wanted to help, but he felt that this doubling up of duty was slowing the practice down.

There was some discussion of DA technique, with the conclusion that you had to do what works best for you.

"Whatever yanks your crank," Mike Perry said.

"Whatever floats your boat," Roger said.

"Whatever blows your hair back," Erika said, and laughed. "I like that one."

Erika prepped and prepped. She scrubbed and scrubbed. She moved back and forth to her kit. She cut the cow open and trembled. She tried to tear the fascia, like Chuck and Roger did, but she didn't stand in the right position for the right leverage to use her body weight. Roger helped her with this. "It bleeds less if you tear it," he said.

Mike left to tend to some cows. Erika wondered if he left because he couldn't bear watching her.

She put on a sleeve, went in with the needle, and began to deflate the abomasum. In mid-process she asked Roger to check her progress.

"You got it," Roger said.

She began to tie the omentum, the layer of fat, to the body wall to anchor the abomasum. She said she wanted to tie it in a way different from Roger's.

"Whatever floats your— Whatever blows your hair back," he said.

She began to sew. The sweat was running down her face.

Roger said, "I'll go talk to Mike," and he left.

In a moment Erika said, "Roger knows the value of confidence. He's leaving me alone knowing I'll learn from it."

Roger told Mike about Erika's stress. He came back with Mike and watched a few minutes longer before saying, "I'm going to go work on some horses."

"Thanks for coming," Erika said.

She continued to sew, with difficulty—it was a hard thing to push a needle through a cow's hide. She said she didn't like the needle very much.

"Charlie probably sends them out to be sharpened," Mike said. "I'll try to sharpen it for you if you want. I'll take a stone to it. I've got one in the barn."

"No, that's okay."

Mike leaned on the cow's tail while she sewed. To lift her

spirits, he said he had called the clinic that morning and was told that Dr. Bruner would be coming. " 'Dr. Who?' I said. 'What's that last name?' I said, 'Oh, Erika! I'm just a farm boy. Let's keep it simple.' "

When she had closed the incision, Mike helped her with the infusion of dextrose, holding the bottle as the contents drained in, and when Erika apologized that it was not going quickly, he said, "You can only get it to go so fast through that needle."

When it came time to tube the cow and fill her stomach with liquid, Erika wanted to put the tube through the cow's nostril, as she had learned on an externship. But it didn't go well.

"How do you know you got it in the right place?" Mike asked, meaning in the stomach rather than the lungs, and when Erika finally pulled the tube out, Mike said, "Here, let's try it this way. I do this about fifteen times a week." He pushed the tube down the cow's throat and held up the five-gallon bucket. "This is my job," he said.

Mike said to the cow, "Okay, darling, you're done now." About two hours had passed.

"Okay, Mike," Erika said.

"Done already? Damn, you're good. Can you ding that one over there for me?"

"You mean, you want me to check for a DA?"

"Yeah, she's right over there. Ten fourteen." Mike showed her the stall.

Erika pushed herself in and said to the cow, "Okay, I'm getting in here." With the stethoscope—her badge of honor—she listened and pinged and listened some more.

Mike told a story about a cow he had once known and worked with. "You remember the cow I told about that was buried in the farmer's plot?" The cow had produced phenomenal numbers for many years. A working Holstein's life span is about three to four years, but this one had lived into her teens.

"This cow, her lowest year was 25,000 pounds. Her *lowest* year. She was twelve years old, and they did a DA on her. She didn't care if she moved after that. I got into the pen with the shocker, and shocked her till she moved. I shocked her again. I got her so mad she started coming after me, ran me around the stall half a dozen times until I jumped out of there. But she started milking again. She was okay with everyone else, but if I got in there, she came at me. That was okay," Mike said. "Kept her alive."

"She's got a DA," Erika said.

"What do you want to do? How do you want to do it?"

Erika said she didn't know right now, that she would have to talk to Chuck. "And we'll get back to you."

"Whatever blows your hair back," Mike said. He led Erika to the hose for the boot washing.

Erika really washed hers. "They're clean now, but they won't be clean long."

"It's a never-ending battle."

Outside at the truck, she said, "I feel it went better. But only a little better."

Looking back at this day and others with Mike, including calvings, Erika would eventually say, "He was teaching me things, and it was so gentle, so subtle, his coaching, that I didn't even know he had done it until much later."

Some of the best learning came that way.

9

FEELING BOVINE

1.

Chuck had his hard days and rough nights too. He came in one morning and told Erika that he had been awake since three, thinking about clients and animals. There were other things weighing on his mind, the many problems of being a clinic owner. Equipment problems, income problems, personnel problems. He had said to Ellie that sleepless night, "Do you think it's time to sell?" But Ellie knew it wasn't a serious question, that it was the kind of thing said under stress.

One of the cases troubling Chuck was that of Burt Davies, a Scottish terrier owned by Dottie and Donald Davies. The trouble began when Chuck picked up the work list one morning, read through it, and said, "What! Burt Davies! We're gonna kill him?"

"The owner brought him in," Erika said. "He bit her when she was trying to catch him. As he was running away. Required three stitches. I'm turning him over to you, Dr. Shaw."

"That's okay, I'll take him. He's one of my babies."

"He's a CPS client," Roger said, meaning Chuck's and not his.

"He needs to be placed in a new home," Chuck said.

Out back in the dog kennel in a cage was Burt, about a year old, handsome and energetic, black curly hair and glittering black eyes, panting and licking at the outstretched hand. And barking, really making some noise—12 beats per five seconds, 24 per ten seconds, his ears cocking back each time his jaw opened. On his cage was a card that read "E and B." Euthanize and bury.

Erika was packing a toolbox with supplies for calf vaccinations. "I'm not saying I'm for dogs biting their owners," she said, "but something could be done with him. Three stitches is not that much. Sometimes it just happens with dogs."

Chuck said he would call the owner. With a red marker he scrawled across the card on Burt Davies's cage, "DO NOT EUTH."

In the fall, Chuck had put down the Davies's previous dog, another Scottish terrier, after he developed a malignant tumor under the shoulder. Chuck had gone to the Davies's house early in the morning before the clinic opened. When he was stopped by a friend in the center of Walpole, with the dog's body on the seat next to him, wrapped in a sheet, Chuck had explained and said, "And that's how I started my day."

The Davieses had found the Scottie after Donald had a stroke, and Donald fell in love with him. "It broke his heart when we had to put him down." Mrs. Davies soon replaced him with Burt, but Burt turned out to be a management problem. Just recently on a visit to a neighbor's house he had jumped on a coffee table and knocked a vase over. Now he had bitten Dottie Davies—again, as it turned out.

"She does everything for Donald," Chuck said. "And she's probably worried that Burt will bite him." Of Burt he said, "Scotties are an independent breed. They have a lot on their mind, and it's usually not people. He was probably thinking he was going somewhere, and she grabbed him. What we will do is go through the client base, look up the people who have had Scotties, and contact them. One possibility is a couple in Alstead. They waited to get one. I bet they wouldn't mind having another."

Mrs. Davies had called the clinic early that morning before the vets arrived. Darcie was opening up and feeding the animals. Mrs. Davies told her she had a dog she wanted to put down. Five minutes later she came in crying. She quickly gave the necessary information to Darcie, said to Burt, "This is for the best, I love you," and rushed out.

When Chuck phoned her, he said, "So you're not having a very nice day?" Mrs. Davies said, "We put Burt down." Chuck thought, No you didn't, and we're not putting him down, but he said, "Maybe it's time for him to be with some younger owners." He became chatty and friendly and told her about the obedience classes at the Humane Society in Keene that a new owner might take him to. He mentioned a behavioral therapist to whom he sometimes referred clients.

Then Chuck said, "Epileptic?" and went quiet. When he hung up, he shook his head and wrinkled his nose. He said to Darcie, "You know that Scottie out there? He's a fly biter."

"Fly biter?"

"It's a petit mal kind of thing. The animal bites at the air, at things it can't see." Another vet made the diagnosis, Chuck said. "He prescribed phenobarbital. Her husband is on phenobarbital. The idea of giving it to both of them terrified her." Chuck thought it was a false diagnosis.

Roger said, "Have you ever seen him fly snap? I never have, not once."

Erika said that at Tufts she had seen dogs come in with fly-biting diagnoses, but none had ever shown fly-biting behavior.

Chuck decided to call for more information. This was a shorter conversation. "I know, I know, I know," he said. "You don't have to worry about a thing. You thought about this all night, didn't you?"

He told the rest of the story to Roger and Erika. A friend of Dottie Davies's had taken her dog to this other vet and gotten a fly-biting diagnosis, so Dottie had gone there too, with the same result.

Chuck became very quiet. At the lab table he set up a slide on the microscope, a sample that needed to be checked for a pathogen.

Perhaps he was doing diagnostic thinking. Maybe he didn't want to criticize the other vet any more than he just had. As with M.D.s, it was an unspoken rule of the profession not to publicly criticize another veterinarian. Maybe he was silent out of his feelings for the Davieses. Maybe it was a combination of those reasons.

He stared into the microscope, scanning the slide, as five, ten, twenty minutes went by, until he was late for a herd check.

The following Monday, Darcie said, "The little mouth is still here."

"I almost euthanized him yesterday," Roger said.

Chuck said, "She called me yesterday. She's got the neighborhood involved. A woman named Alice Ross might take him."

Alice Ross was in her fifties, charming and energetic, a bit of a powerhouse, and an animal lover who already owned quite a few animals. She and her husband, Vince, had been engineers before moving to Walpole and starting a business. When Alice arrived for her appointment with Chuck, a few minutes ahead of Vince, she said she had known Dottie was having problems with Burt and had told her she'd help if she could.

"I just don't want the dog to die," she said.

"I won't kill him."

"And I don't want my husband to leave me." Alice smiled in a way that seemed to mean that leaving was unlikely, but she loved him enough to care about it anyway. "We have eight cats and a dog. My husband said that if we get one more animal, he's going down the road. I would prefer that wouldn't happen."

Chuck told her about the communications he'd had so far with Dottie Davies. Alice knew about most of them already. "She was in my kitchen when she called you on Sunday. I'm sorry about that."

"Oh, that's all right. She can call me anytime. She does anyway."

When Vince Ross poked his head into the door, he said, "Are we done here? I got a message to come by at four-thirty. Are we done here?"

"No," Alice said. "I just explained to him that I don't want you to leave me."

Vince was bearded and heavyset, and had a dry sense of humor. You had to think, watching him interact with Alice, that he would no more leave than he would spread his arms and fly. "So are we finished here?" he repeated.

"Let's just see the dog. Just meet him. Can we meet him?"

"We can meet him. But we're done here, right?"

Chuck sent Darcie out back to get Burt. While they

waited, Alice told Chuck that both of their mothers had died that year. "We don't have any kids," she said. "I'm an only child. The animals are all we've got."

"We're parentless," Vince said. "It's weird."

Alice said that Burt got along well with their dog, which was a mutt, "a beagle something. We're not purebred people."

"Yeah," Vince said.

But she seemed willing to make an exception.

Darcie opened the door, and Burt sprang in. He ran to Alice and jumped on her legs, then on Vince's, went to Chuck and jumped on him, barking and springing, barking and springing. He seemed to be saying something along the lines of Hey! I'm here! I love you! Let's go somewhere! Right now! Hey! Hey-hey! At about 120 beats per minute, with ears flicking simultaneously. While this was going on, Chuck talked about the biting incident, the neighbor's table, and the flowers getting knocked over, the boot he would have put to Burt's rear end if it were his table, and the behavior training he would need if they adopted him. Last of all, he said a few words about the fly-biting diagnosis, and then left the room.

"So we can ruminate," Alice said, smiling.

Chuck gave them sufficient time, then opened the door to check on them.

Vince asked right off, "What's fly biting?"

Chuck explained the petit mal thing. There was an expulsive laugh. "Did I say the wrong thing, Vince?" Chuck asked, and closed the door again.

When Chuck returned to the meeting, Burt started springing again and barking out his refrain. "I don't think you could get a better example of the breed," Chuck said. "When I heard you were going to take him, I thought, Good, this will work."

"You heard we were going to take him?" Vince said. Alice gave him a guilty smile.

They discussed the fly-biting condition. Chuck talked of the probability of a misdiagnosis, and of the benign nature of the condition should it exist.

"It's probably nothing to worry about," Chuck said.

"It's probably not even there," Alice said.

Vince said, "So if Alice starts doing this, should I be worried?"

"I'm persuaded," Alice said, "but he's not. Let's go home and massage it a little, and we'll call in the morning." She turned to Vince. "We can think about it, can't we?"

"We can think about anything."

Whatever they decided to do, Chuck said, he would keep Burt for at least ten days, for what technically could be called a quarantine period, since he had bitten someone.

2.

On Friday night a dog that had been hit by a car came in. He was a stray with a broken leg and cuts to be sutured. Chuck stabilized him that night but postponed the leg surgery. He worked all day Saturday at the clinic, until 7 p.m., when he was called out to euthanize an old dog. When he arrived, the dog had already died. There were phone calls all day Sunday. On Sunday night Chuck put an old golden retriever to sleep after she had spent two days in distress at the clinic. He took a walk outside with the dog and her owners before putting her down.

By Monday morning the HBC was no longer a stray. His owner had made calls to various clinics and had come in on that Saturday. "Stray!" she said when she saw the card on his cage. "You're not a stray! You have a name! Hunter!" She crawled into the cage and threw her arms around him. Now, on Monday morning, Hunter was about to have surgery. He sat in his cage, a forepaw held up limply.

Lynn sedated him and led him into the surgery. He was a large dog, and Lynn's face turned purple when she and Darcie lifted him onto the table. "He's part Lab and part something big," she said. Chuck told her to shave him over most of the right shoulder and down below the elbow joint. He was studying Hunter's X-rays, which he had hung on the window. It would be a tricky procedure, since a dog's humerus is a curved bone and this was a long humerus. He'd have to hit the bend just right with the pin, like a long shot on a curved fairway.

Chuck pressed deeply into the broken leg. "We'll open it up here," he said to Lynn. "We'll get the bone stabilized, but everything is going to look like mush in there." He said they would have to identify the large cephalic vein and the radial nerve, and avoid damaging them. "The good news is that when he came in, he had feeling in his toes. So we hope we won't cut that nerve, of course." He put on the surgical cap, scrubbed, put on the gown and the latex gloves, and began.

From a back room came the familiar though muffled sound of "I love you . . . love me too . . . let's go somewhere, hey!"

"She called me Sunday night at seven," Chuck said of Dottie Davies. "She said to me, 'Did you have your dinner yet?' I said, 'No, but let's talk now.' She told me that she and Donald have been coming down here, sitting in the parking lot, and watching him in the runs. But she still thinks she's doing the right thing in giving him up.

"She talked to Alice Ross. She realized that Alice is trying to do a good thing, be a good Samaritan. Alice has to realize that it's okay not to take him. Her husband doesn't want the dog. I can understand why they wouldn't want a little Scottie running around the house with eight cats.

"Now Dottie and Donald have to think about it. I told her there's a client in Alstead who has a Scottie, saved up four hundred dollars to get one. I said he would probably love to have another one."

While he was talking, Chuck opened up Hunter's leg. He soon found the big vein and nerve. "Damn," he said. "Everything is awfully close together. We've got a little window here to work in." A window between the nerve and vein, with the broken bone sitting below. "Okay," he said, "now we know where everything bad is."

"Now let's find something good," Lynn said.

"And here it is." He lifted out a flake of bone, a loose piece that had seemed to be floating in the X-ray image.

Whenever Chuck was in surgery, he rarely did only that one task. He was always managing too. Carol came in and asked, "Did you euthanize Misty?"

"Yes."

"Her owner was just in to pay his bill. He wanted to say thank you to whoever did it, and say that the staff were all kind and made things easier."

"Good."

Erika came in. She had been to Boston over the weekend and gotten a fresh haircut, boy's regular, though the color had now faded to a rosy rust. She had a question about Jane Fitzwilliam's colt, whose cut she had sutured after he jumped into a fence. Jane had nearly fainted when Erika sedated him. "I told her to look away," Erika said. Jane had sent a fax stating that Erika had done a fine job, but now she had called because there seemed to be a touch of infection, which had improved slightly overnight.

"If he's improving, I wouldn't worry too much about it,"

Chuck said. They worked out a treatment—hot compresses alternating with cold water from a hose, three times a day.

Chuck fastened a clamp on the lower section of Hunter's broken humerus. "The body is an amazing thing," he said. "Already the end of the bone is forming a callus and beginning to repair. It would have healed on its own, though he would have been gimpy."

Now that Chuck had opened the leg, identified what needed to be identified, and stabilized the bones, his next step was to thread an eighteen-inch pin through the two sections. First he drilled a pilot hole through the upper end of the humerus, at the shoulder. Then he turned the pin into the hole with an electric drill set at low speed. He told Lynn to take over at the drill while he guided the pin.

"How do we know how to point it?" Lynn asked.

"That's a good question. You're gonna follow me."

Chuck looked at the X-ray again and at an anatomical drawing of an intact humerus. He told Lynn to turn the pin in further. Then he stopped to examine the X-ray again, had Lynn back the pin off a little bit, and moved forward again.

"Whew, that's not a straight bone," Chuck said. "Hopefully I wasn't too ambitious with my diameter of pin. All right, go ahead." Lynn started the drill and sunk the pin deeper while Chuck grasped a section of bone in each hand.

Darcie came in and said that Hunter's owner had called. She wanted to know if she could visit later that afternoon. "We'll wait to see how he wakes up," Chuck said.

Ellie came to the surgery door. She said that Sonny Greene had called about a milk fever cow. "Right," Chuck said. "I'll go later, at about noon, after we finish up here. We won't subject Erika to Sonny Greene just yet."

A high school boy shadowing Chuck for the summer came in and wanted to know what to do. He was Bob Graves's grandson, Tyler Westover. "We're not going anywhere for a while, Tyler," Chuck said. "You can come back at noon or you can weed the garden. Do you know how to weed?" Tyler said he did. Chuck was pleased at that. He told Tyler to weed the garden by the big sign out front.

"Okay," he said to Lynn. "We're just getting into crunch time here."

"You don't mean crunch literally, right?"

"I hope not. We're close, damn close." He got another pin and held it next to the leg for a length comparison, then measured the pin against the X-ray image. He put his gloved fingers inside the leg and muscled the lower piece of bone toward the upper. Both were now skewered on the pin.

"Just have to do some worrying of these pieces here," he said. "At the old clinic when we fixed these things, it was all brute strength." Once again he turned to look at the X-ray, holding his bloody hands upright to avoid touching anything nonsterile.

"Now you have to start drilling," he told Lynn. "No time for weenies."

Lynn turned on the drill and pushed, her face reddening.

"That's better," Chuck said. "Two more turns. It's a little rotationally unstable because of the fragment we removed, but you know what? He's gonna heal just fine."

"He might be a good candidate for a cast or crate confinement," Lynn said.

"Time is what he needs. Call the owner and ask if she wants to have him neutered while we've got him on the table."

Chuck inserted a pair of retractors to spread open the muscle. He pulled a strand of wire around the joined bone, wrapped it again, and twisted the ends to tighten the coil.

Lynn got on the phone. "We're close to finishing. He's not neutered. Would you like to castrate him? Okay, we'll take care of that. He's gonna be okay. You need to keep him quiet. Do you have a crate? Well, keep him off steps then, and give him lots of bed rest. Don't let him jump off the couch."

Chuck coiled a second wire around the joined bone, but became concerned about an exposed nerve. "Got to keep that nerve from rubbing against that fracture," he said. "I'll sew something between them as a cushion."

Darcie came into the surgery again. She had just taken a call from a woman who owned a pig. The pig had stepped on something, and she wanted to know the price of a farm call to Westminster.

"How big is the pig?"

"I didn't ask."

"I'll call her in a few minutes, when I finish here."

Lynn brought over bolt cutters. Four inches of pin remained protruding from Hunter's shoulder. Chuck pressed the cutting head down on the muscle to get a good purchase. Lynn's eyes went wide as she squeezed the jaws. Snap went the pin.

Chuck turned to suturing, sewing the cushion between bone and nerve, and closing the incision. Tyler Westover came in, wanting to know where the weeds went— Over the bank, Chuck said. Carol came in with a client's question about antibiotics—Chuck said she would have to bring the animal in, that he wouldn't prescribe antibiotics without seeing her. Erika came in with a cat she thought had ringworm, according to the tests, but she wasn't sure. Chuck said the cat had ringworm, and he told Erika to treat for it. "Am I missing something?" she asked. "Is it obvious?" "It's hard to diagnose," Chuck said.

They turned Hunter over, and Chuck quickly neutered him. They carried him to the X-ray room for a picture of the leg. Ten minutes later Chuck assessed his work. "There's about a fifteen-degree rotational error," he said, "because of the missing piece." The photo showed the pin entering at the top of the humerus, barely touching against the inside curve, and then exiting at the center of the bone again. Pretty much a perfect shot, right down the fairway.

Hunter's owner was told an hour later that he had already wagged his tail when they called his name. She visited that afternoon and again crawled into the cage. The next day, Hunter limped on three legs to the dog runs, where Darcie and Nicole ran cold water on the swollen leg. A day later he went home.

3.

Mrs. Davies was calling Chuck every day, he said. "Donald misses the dog. He feels terrible about losing him. She took him away for the weekend, thinking it would help him forget, but when they came back, they drove into the parking lot and sat there waiting for him to go out into the runs. But it was the wrong time, not nine or five, when the dogs are out.

"Donald says he wants the dog back. I said to Dottie, 'It's really up to you. You have to learn how to handle him.' She may take him to a trainer. But I don't know, he's such a brat. Right now he just thinks he's at camp."

Another couple had volunteered to take Burt, but Chuck had fended them off. "If I give him away, I'm going to give him to a client," he said. "I'm responsible for him right now."

Susan Armstrong had decided to leave, and Chuck now had to find another afternoon receptionist. He didn't have to look far. He had hired a woman named Jennifer Schreiter during the winter to work as a kennel helper, but Jennifer's skills were beyond that job. She was the daughter of a veterinarian and had worked for her dad through her school years. Jennifer had first won Chuck's admiration when she shoveled stools off the dog runs on a cold January day without having been asked. Jen wanted to work in the back with the animals, not out front with the customers. She said she had enough of that when she worked at her father's place. She had a bit of a cynical streak about animal owners. Of the relationship between owners and animals, she liked to say, "It goes right down the leash." In another reference to human and animal relationships she had said, "Don't tell me about human nature. Getting a divorce, kill the dog. Moving, kill the dog. Had a baby, kill the dog. I've seen it all."

But Chuck convinced Jen to move out front. The salary would be more, he told her, and that's where she was needed.

Did Hobbs know that Susan was leaving? He did seem to turn quite affectionate, walking about brushing into people's legs as if he were dispossessed already.

At her good-bye party Susan got a cake and a bottle of bourbon, and said, "I was hoping to get away without this." She said she had told Hobbs that she was leaving, and would say good-bye privately.

Hobbs joined the party and sat on one of the chairs, looking for cake—even a bit of frosting would do. When Erika noticed this, she said, "No way, Mister. I'm not going to be part of your problem." Hobbs looked about charmingly, squinting at whoever noticed him, and eventually got some frosting from one of the high school kids, Nicole, fed by fingertip. "I can't believe you're giving him that," Erika said. She had just come off an appointment with an overweight dog who was regularly fed mashed potatoes, and she was in no mood for nutritional malfeasance.

Hobbs was losing Susan but gaining Erika, which could

have been to his greater good. No Doritos! No donuts! No sandwiches!

After the ten days, Burt Davies was gone. The Davieses had met with Chuck and decided to take him back. They agreed to take him to a behavioral specialist, and Chuck set up the appointment. "They're really happy I didn't put him to sleep," Chuck said.

Dottie Davies said, "Donald and I went away for the weekend last week, and we talked about it all weekend. We decided that we are going to take that dog back, and we're going to do it right. Burt is not bad. He's good. He's the way he is because of me. He's always had his way. When I go to the appointment, I'm going to write down the most important things I want him to do. It's my problem. I have to do it the right way."

Chuck said, "I think he's too much dog for them."

Later, Dr. Myrna Milani, veterinarian and animal behavior therapist, concluded that the root of the problem was in the owners' faulty relationship with the dog. From a dog's point of view, the Davieses were a pack, and he, Burt, was the dominant member. Dottie and Donald had reinforced Burt's assumption by acting like subordinate pack members and, when Burt had become aggressive, by doing what he wanted and ignoring his bad behavior. Milani believed that domestication suspended an animal in an immature state, and she recommended that the Davieses become the adults within their pack, that they become adult dogs relating to a pup.

"It's hard for a four-legged nonverbal creature to lead bipeds around in their daily lives," Dr. Milani said. "In that household, in any household, a Scottie is a powerful dog with powerful jaws, comparable to a Doberman's. And this dog is a butt biter. He lacks confidence, and so he waits and bites on the rear end. Dottie told me she was black-and-blue on her rear end for the first month she had him. And she was blaming herself for it. That's subordinate behavior."

At their meeting at Milani's office, she asked the Davieses to sit quietly and ignore Burt. At first he tried to leap on the counters, and he dug at the doors. He even defecated by the door, but without response. Eventually he settled down, but Milani noted that he sat next to her, not his owners. She concluded that he recognized that it was her place and she was in charge. With any movement from his owners, Burt got up on his hind legs—a dominant act.

"I associate this behavior with an intelligent dog that has been put in charge," Milani said. Milani also learned that when he was at home, Burt expected to be let out on demand whenever he sat by the door. If he wasn't obeyed, he would urinate. She learned that he had nipped the sleeve off a child's sweater, and he had often tugged on Mr. Davies's arm. Burt's behavior had been dismissed as playful, but Milani was concerned that the small dog might "grow into his mouth." She could see that he didn't hesitate to use it.

"With this dog it's going to take more than love," she said. "This is something I see all the time, the idea that the human-animal bond is about unconditional love. It's not. It's conditional on both sides."

Milani thought the dog and his owners were a poor match, but she concluded that there were few options left for Mrs. Davies, who felt obliged to keep the dog her husband loved. Because of the biting, she felt she couldn't morally place him with another owner. And she couldn't put him down—Chuck had taken away that option, Milani said.

Milani added, "I see that my job now is to support her in whatever she decides to do, and not to put obstacles in her way."

Dottie Davies said, "It sounds crazy to me, but we're try-ing. The dog thought he was the one to be in control, and that was a lot to put on him. I'm being a little stronger. I'm making him sit. He's been good since he came home, or bet-ter. The idea is that we're in control, and he knows it."

Mrs. Davies began using a "gentle leader" head collar, a kind of halter and muzzle, when she took Burt for walks or when visitors came.

4.

Weeks later, Chuck was doing the herd check at Putnam's. In the milking parlor—a floor grate, a line of sunlight along it, a brown boot, and manure falling.

"I was at the Cheshire Fair last night," Chuck said to Scott Kemp, "sitting in the stands watching the ox-pulling event. This guy sitting next to me is a dairy farmer from up north, in Orford. He told me he's doing his own DAs. I said to him, 'If you want to do your own DAs, go ahead. They're your cows.'"

But Chuck had mulled it over and done the math. "They have to have a hundred percent success rate to make it work. I know I can get ninety percent. If they lose one cow, they're losing money at it. His cows are worth two thousand dollars. Some cows at other farms are worth three thousand. Some are even worth four thousand. One DA costs two hundred dol-lars. Ten DAs are two thousand dollars. If they lose one cow, they haven't gained anything.

"Give this one Lutalyse," he said.

"If they want to do it, let them. I'm beyond the point now of telling the producers what to do with their animals."

Erika had asked for a two-month review, an assessment of her work. Chuck had met with her and told her she was doing well, and offered examples in the reports he'd gotten from clients. But Erika had pointed out that all the examples he'd given were from office appointments and that she hadn't done any palpation since her third day on the job. She asked to get out more.

"It's the old tug-of-war," Chuck said at Putnam's. "Erika wants to work on cows. And one way to keep her happy is to keep her arm in the cow business."

To use an apt phrase.

"I think this one's gotten through a heat. Ovulated left ovary," he said to Scott, who made the notation.

"Erika knows a lot. She just hasn't seen a lot. One way for her to gain experience is the way we're doing it now. Roger on horses, me on cows, and Erika at the clinic and going out on calls. But when you've got an associate who's burning to do production medicine, you've got to give her what she wants."

Chuck said he had told Erika to be patient. "I hope to have her up to speed by March first or April first, so that she can do eighty percent in a very timely manner. That's when we get busy, April, May, and June. By May, I've got to—"

"Go fly-fishing," Scott said.

"That's right."

After the herd check, Chuck drove to the Graves Farm to take blood samples for a neosporosis testing program that Peter Graves was participating in. Neosporosis is a pathogen that can cause abortions in cows, among other things. Chuck worked with Peter for about two hours, taking blood samples. Chuck seemed happy to be on a farm, less tense there.

On the return drive to the clinic, he talked about various financial concerns. The gross income of the practice was roughly the same as a year ago. When the economy goes into a downturn, Chuck said, as it had done sharply that year, some people stopped taking their animals to the vet.

There was also Erika's salary to factor into the overall economic equation. "It's hard to have the expense of a new vet when the income is the same as the year before. We have to make a thousand dollars a week more to pay for that salary."

There were expenses for equipment. Erika's truck had broken down—Chuck had an appointment later that day at the Toyota dealership to look at a newer one. A major component of the X-ray machine had also broken down and would have to be replaced.

And other economic challenges. "At the end of the year, I pay eighteen thousand dollars on the drug bill, a prepurchase with a discount, which gives tax benefits. But if I don't have that money, I have to borrow on the credit line, and that means interest.

"I pay my taxes quarterly, and that's always a bite. Last year I didn't pay my taxes in January, because the money wasn't there, so I had a bigger payment in April. That on top of the health insurance premiums for my employees.

"It's crucial that the farmers pay their bills. They pay the vet with the second milk check. They get paid on the fifth and twentieth of the month, and the vet bill comes out of the payment on the twentieth. Some of those payments are the profit for the month. We have some farmers who owe anywhere from two thousand to five thousand dollars for the month. If that doesn't come in, we're in trouble. It can make the difference between the clinic running in the black or in the red.

"We run out of money in the winter and make up for it in the busy season."

Chuck said that a new vet starting in June after graduation did not get a fair impression of the job. "The busy time is from March to June. That's when it gets frantic. Next year by spring, Erika will be eighty percent with it, ready to do DAs and rectals.

"If she goes out now and palpates five cows and comes back three hours later, we haven't made any money."

Add it all up, the uncertainties, the expenses, the demands, and throw in difficult cases like Burt Davies—such were the makings of a sleepless night.

"I'm a worrier anyway," Chuck said.

5.

Chuck soon arranged for Erika to do some palpation. He asked Mike Perry to pick out twenty easy cows to give her for a light herd check, and on that Friday he left with Ellie for a long weekend in Maine. He also arranged for her to do another check the following week, at Ken Young's heifer farm in Springfield, Vermont. He told her it would be relatively easy, that she just had to determine if the heifers were pregnant and approximately how far along.

Erika was coming off an encouraging stretch. She was a worrier too—"Worry, worry, about this, about that, but everything that has come recently, I've been able to handle. Nothing's been so terrible that I haven't been able to do it." She had done a DA at Barrett's, and though she called Roger in, she had done the procedure on her own. On call over the weekend she had done another DA at Westminster Farms. She had gone to the Graves Farm to treat a milk-fever cow. When she drove in, Bob Graves had gotten off his tractor, walked up to her, and said, "You're a pretty good-lookin' woman."

"Smart too," Erika said.

"I suppose that's useful."

"Better to have a vet that's smart than one who's good-looking."

"You've got a point there," he said, and led her into the barn.

After the DA at Barrett's, she had walked into the Westminster General Store with a bloodstained shoulder and ordered lunch. The owners of the store wanted to know what she had been doing, so Erika explained the DA, and they were amazed. She had begun to feel like she owned some of the jobs, "rather than them owning me."

The Young Farm was an idyllic place, with solid old buildings, some red, some white, and fields along the west bank of the Connecticut. Ken Young's father and grandfather had owned it before him. Ken had stopped milking, but his teenage son thought he might want to get back into it. Dairying had become a little more appealing with the price of milk approaching $18 a hundredweight. The foot-and-mouth epidemic had stopped imports of dairy products from Britain, so beef prices were up too.

The Youngs were about to ship thirty-eight Jersey heifers to California. That had been a good business for farmers in this region too, selling Jerseys to the big farms out west at a premium because of the high fat and protein content of their milk.

Young and his wife and son worked with Erika, isolating a cow, driving her to the end of the barn and into a chute, closing a gate behind, and pushing her into a headlock. There Erika palpated, listened to the lungs, gave shots, and put on ear tags, as each cow demanded.

Erika was happy. Like Chuck, she seemed more at ease on a dairy farm, especially a gorgeous farm like this one on an 80° day. It was perfect haying weather, and the Youngs planned to be doing that in the afternoon.

Erika looked almost ethereal, an oracle of the uterus.

"Four months pregnant," she said. "Two months." "Six months." All based on the uterine feel, the buzz of the uterine artery. With one cow she said, "She's swimming away from me," and then, catching up, she happily pronounced, "Six months." Another time, after putting in an ear tag and trying to press a stethoscope to a reluctant cow's ribs, it was, "So you don't like my tender ministrations?"

Yet this was time-consuming work, and Erika was looking pale before she finished. They examined a last cow and gathered up all the spent sleeves, and Erika scrubbed her boots and said her good-byes.

Driving down the road, she said, "I feel really good about that. I'm feeling bovine. I've wanted that."

This could be an elusive thing, this feeling bovine.

"To me it feels like work. Sweaty, honest, gross achievement. I don't like to get sweaty at the clinic. I'm not normally a sweaty person, but I don't mind getting all bloody and sweaty at the farms.

"I like the cows. To me they're calm, calm and quiet. They're like cats in what they give off. I like their fuzzy ears. And their eyes. And their necks, the way they reach out to you, so curious.

"I think now if I had to pick between large and small, I'd pick large, if I had to pick one or the other. I did a whole herd check. I've done two herd checks. I've been feeling much better these last few days. I don't feel like a big faker anymore. I don't have that feeling of dread I was getting in the morning, especially when I'd had a day off. This morning I was thinking I would be doing a herd check, it was on my mind, but I didn't have the dread."

Over the months, in the village of Walpole, most anyone could see a gray-haired, fit woman walking a Scottish terrier, the two of them quickly walking along, she holding the leash, he with the complicated collar, she sometimes talking to him as they walked. If she was walking down the sidewalk and someone else was coming, she'd move to the road, avoid the passerby, and talk to the dog.

"She still has him," Chuck said months later. "He's the same."

He thought for a moment and said, "She loves him."

10

THE LINE OF SEPARATION

1.

Chuck and Erika were at Murray's for the weekly breakfast when Tammy brought over a pot of coffee and a phone. She handed the phone to Chuck. He listened, then straightened and said, "Okay."

"Holly is dying," Chuck said. "I'll go down there and take care of her." He got up and walked out. Erika wondered briefly what to do, then said, "I want to be there to see it."

This was a difficult case, Erika's most difficult yet. Holly Butler was a miniature dachshund, the adored pet of a family from Westmoreland. Erika had spayed Holly two weeks ago. In the interval she had gnawed off her stitches, developed chronic nausea and depression, and now had returned with a blood disease.

On the way to the clinic Erika said, "I don't know if it's the spay, or the reaction to the spay, or a reaction to the drugs we gave her. Or none of that. But there's clotting in the blood." The dog had developed something called disseminated intravascular coagulation, or DIC. "In vet school we called it Death Is

Coming," Erika said. She had been intensely worried not only about the dachshund's outcome but also about her relationship with the owners, who had made a direct correlation between the spay and their dog's illness. As Erika put it, "I feel we're not working as a team. They're making me feel guilty, and I'm already feeling guilty on my own, even though it's unjustified."

Darcie had been the first one in that morning, and she had discovered Holly lying on her side, with her mouth and eyes open. She thought Holly was dead. She checked for a heartbeat, found she was alive, called Erika, then paged her, waited five minutes, and called Murray's. "I need your help!" she said to Chuck.

Chuck had told Darcie to move Holly into the surgery and give her oxygen. Amy, a new kennel worker, stood next to the surgery table, rubbing the dog.

Chuck also asked Darcie to bring her Rottweiller, Lita, out of the kennel and into the treatment room to serve as a blood donor. Darcie had been bringing Lita to the clinic since she had gotten her as a wedding present, when Lita was a puppy. Now Lita was well beyond the puppy stage, a full-grown Rottie who could get exuberant at times and by Chuck's orders was kept caged in the kennels during the day.

They lifted Lita to the exam table. Darcie hugged her from behind, pointing her nose toward the ceiling while Chuck shaved a patch and quickly pulled 60 cc of blood out of her.

"Payback time," Chuck said. "You hang around here long enough, somebody's going to take blood from you."

Back in the surgery, however, Chuck had a difficult time finding a vein in Holly's leg. There wasn't much blood pressure. "These dachshunds," he said. Darcie tried to get a temperature, but it wasn't registering. Chuck said, "Go into exam room number one and get me the eye loupe"—the jeweler's magnifying glasses.

With the loupe on, he turned Holly over and tried the other leg. He searched about, squeezed and pressed, and did find a vein. Erika watched, and when Chuck placed the catheter and started to feed in the blood, he said to her, "How much, how fast, can you put it in?" It had been a while since he'd done a transfusion, he said. He was seeing Erika as a resource then, a bright student fresh out of school. Maybe even testing her too.

"A drop per ten seconds," she said.

Chuck was going faster than that, putting the blood in as quickly as it would go. "Seems to me whole blood is just the thing she needs in this sort of crisis," he said. Then to Erika, "Figure out and prepare the right amount of vitamin K for this dog, in case we're totally off on this." He meant in case the dog had eaten rat poison. It wouldn't harm her to give the K, he said.

The transfusion took perhaps five minutes. Chuck asked Darcie to bring Lita out again for another donation. "You are the best girl," Chuck said as he turned on the clippers and shaved a patch on her other leg.

"Sit," Darcie said. Again she pressed her chin to the back of Lita's neck and raised her nose while Chuck took 60 cc more. "She behaves when it counts," Darcie said. Lita seemed more proud than before, as Darcie stroked and petted her.

Chuck returned to the surgery with the blood and said to Erika, "When this is done, get her into the cage and on a heating pad, give her fluids, and watch her temperature."

In surgery they always watched the color of an animal's gums, an indicator of blood pressure and other conditions. Holly's gums had been yellow, a sign of jaundice, but now they were looking a healthier pale pink. The whites of her eyes were becoming less yellow too.

Quietly Chuck said to Darcie, "You did a good job."

Lita was standing at the surgery door just then. Chuck looked at her and said, "And you did the best job of all. You've got roaming privileges."

"For today," Darcie said.

Erika took over and supervised the rest of the transfusion. When most of the second 60 cc were in, Holly began to whimper and struggled to move. She was coming to life again—she had Rottweiler in her veins.

With a stethoscope and timer Darcie checked the heart rate. "Eighty," she said.

"Don't stop giving her antibiotics," Chuck said, "and keep her on steroids."

The mood had relaxed. "At least we had time," Chuck said. "It wasn't like she was hit by a car, when you could lose her at any moment."

Chuck left for Murray's to resume the breakfast. Those Thursday mornings were a tradition not lightly broken.

Of Holly he said, "Her red-blood-cell count was at 40 when she came in, and yesterday it dropped to 26. It dropped through the night, must have been 10 by this morning. When Darcie found her, she was suffering from hemolytic jaundice. That's why her gums and eyes were yellow, from the decomposition of blood parts. Below 10 on the blood count, that's time for a blood transfusion.

"It's hard to say how this came about. Twenty-five percent of these cases that go into teaching hospitals don't make it. We just try to give an animal with that condition a blanket treatment. It's not like we have the backup of a hospital or an emergency clinic, where she could be watched overnight. We have to do everything we can, cover the bases."

Holly's case brought up other issues, such as Chuck's concerns about employees and their feelings. Specifically he was thinking about what Darcie encountered that morning when she found Holly.

"You know, one thing you don't want to happen when you have a clinic, you don't want your help coming in and finding an animal dead. It's hard for them. It upsets them. Most of your employees are women, and they tend to feel more.

"In the old days, some vets would attach an apartment to the clinic and make a deal with a tenant to watch the animals at night and check in on them. When I first started, I used to take the animals home with me, put them in a box, and bring them into the bedroom. But eventually you have to decide that if you're gonna have a life in this profession, you have to set some boundaries."

Off Chuck went to Putnam's for a herd check.

2.

Holly's owners were called, and Erika met with them that morning. The entire family came, a mother and father, a teenage son and daughter. They huddled around the cage, and Holly seemed to respond to their visit. The father then talked to Erika off to the side. His eyes filled when he told her that the dog was very close to his wife. She had had surgery for ovarian cancer recently, and Holly had been her companion. "She's been with her all through it," he said. "I don't think I can take any more of this."

His name was Tom Butler. He was about fifty, and worked as an EMT. Butler was intent on providing for his family, and an important part of that provision was in the animal realm— two horses, a goat, a full-grown pig that was a pet and would not be slaughtered. The pig had been a house pet and used a litter box.

Now he said of Holly, "Whatever it takes. It doesn't matter how much money." Erika stood beside him and rubbed his arm.

Butler watched his wife and kids huddled at the cage. He said that at horse shows the dachshund had been the center of attention—though he wasn't sure she was a miniature, as he'd been told; those legs were getting quite long. He talked about his kids. His daughter wanted to be a vet, his son a doctor, he said. He gave a little laugh and said he'd heard there were educational grants out there. And his wife—they didn't know if it would recur, the cancer. And his job—some of the things he saw as an EMT, he said. And the cause of Holly's problem—could it have been the spay? He had studied the sutures.

With these many complications, issues, and feelings, Erika was herself at a high pitch. After the Butlers left that morning, she said she felt better about their interaction, that they seemed to be on the same team now. "I thought that they thought it was my fault. They wanted to know why. I asked why they waited two weeks to bring her in if they were seeing problems. Now that I've talked with them again, I think I know where they're coming from. They know we're doing all we can and that her problem is not"—she tried to laugh when she said this—"because I'm some kind of sucky vet. At least we're treating now for that specific thing. That's covered."

She said, "I'm seeing now that I have to learn that you have to wait, that outcomes don't happen immediately and you don't always know why."

Erika put on her white coat and began appointments. A stray cat named Dropper was in for a first exam. "She adopted us a week ago," her new mom said. "Just showed up and stayed. We drove around the neighborhood, and no one knows her."

"Why do you call her Dropper?"

"She likes to hang upside down from the porch and drop to the ground."

Erika ran her hands over the cat's body. "Her teeth are good. A little tartar, but they're healthy."

"That's because she eats so many chipmunks."

"We all know the health benefits of eating chipmunks."

Stomach good, hips and joints okay, eyes good. The question was, had she been spayed? "There seem to be bumps on her stomach that could have been from sutures. If she goes into heat, bring her in."

"How will we know?"

"She'll put her butt in the air every time you touch her. She'll roll over and make a lot of noise."

"Oh, don't do that," the owner said, and stroked her.

Erika took Dropper out to the treatment room to take blood and give shots, the standard round of rabies, distemper, feline leukemia virus. She met the owners in the reception room. "I'd keep her inside awhile until you find out if she's going to go into heat or not," she said.

Darcie had been training Amy, the new kennel worker. Amy was about twenty years old, and she was deaf. Nevertheless, she had taken up talking to Hobbs. Amy was seeing new things here. She had left the surgery in tears that morning when Chuck was determinedly searching for a vein to start Holly's transfusion. To make communication easier, Darcie had learned some basic sign language. Now, in a more routine moment, Amy signed the name of a pet, spelling out J-E-S-S. She put her fingers to her mouth, the sign for feeding, and threw her hands up in question. Darcie signed back, yes, a little dry food—"little" as in two fingers pinched nearly together, "dry" as in D-R-Y written in the air, and food as the fingers bunched to the mouth.

Amy didn't hesitate to get a pad and write notes if necessary. Darcie had also put up a list of signs to help others communicate. Some were:

VETERINARIAN—a V sign over the wrist at the pulse point.

CAT—whiskers with fingers, brushing out.

DOG—a circling arm brushing the leg, and snapping the fingers for "come."

BITE—close the teeth.

NEEDLE—point at inner elbow.

WATER—W on mouth.

SHIT—the finger drawn out from a ring of thumb and forefinger.

PEE—the finger going in that ring.

STUPID—smack the forehead.

When Roger read the list of signs, he quickly put the signs for stupid and shit together, grinned, and pointed to himself. Amy enjoyed that one.

Cars outside the clinic that evening—not a good sign. Holly had begun vomiting again. They put fluids into her and gave her another transfusion, and she seemed to be improving, but during the night she died.

The situation that Chuck had warned about, and hoped to avoid, had also happened. Amy found Holly and came running to Darcie with a handwritten note.

She handled it okay, Darcie said. Amy was busy feeding the animals that morning when Chuck was in the surgery and the call came in from Tom Butler.

"I hate to be the bearer of bad news," Chuck said. He told Butler that 25 percent of dogs with this condition didn't make it. He listened, then said, "That must have been her purpose in your life. Sometimes an animal is here for a purpose, and then they're gone." He got off the phone, let out a breath, and went back to the surgery.

Carol came in and said that someone had called and wanted to know if the dog died. Mrs. Butler had just run out of her workplace. "I didn't think I would be breaking confidentiality, since you already told them the dog had died."

"It's all right," Chuck said.

3.

For Erika, the worrying didn't stop there. It took another five days for Holly's death to fully manifest itself.

Chuck was on call that weekend—all day Saturday at the clinic, a DA both days. Roger was on call Monday night, Erika on Tuesday. That day, as afternoon appointments were ending, a woman came in and said she had a "ram problem." Erika asked if she wanted to wait until morning, to avoid the emergency fee, but she wanted Erika to look at him right away. Just as Erika was about to leave, she got a call from a couple who needed to have their Newfoundland put to sleep right away. They had intended to have him euthanized several days ago, but hadn't been able to bring themselves to do it. Now the dog was in distress. Erika went there first. The couple apologized to her for bringing her out at such a late hour, and said they were sorry to meet her in that way. She told them it was all right, no problem.

The woman with the ram had thirty other sheep and was living in a tent behind a cornfield. She had just separated from her husband and moved from Maine. "No electricity, and using a kerosene lamp," Erika said. She looked at the ram and thought it might have pneumonia, but she wasn't sure. "Wouldn't it have a temperature?" the woman said. "That's why I said maybe," Erika answered. She wanted to prescribe antibiotics, but the woman was using homeopathic treatments and didn't want to compromise them. The ram hadn't been eating, so Erika decided to force-feed him with intubation as she did with cows after a DA. She didn't have a tube in the truck, so she substituted a syringe case, which eventually worked, but it was a struggle. The sheep owner added to the frustration by talking to the ram and explaining the proce-dure, which made them all seem ridiculous.

"I basically did nothing, but had to charge her all this money," Erika said. "I was charging a hundred dollars with the emergency fee. Working in the dark. She had no money. And I was charging her for basically nothing."

Another late and fretful night, an anxious morning.

Now Erika was in the surgery, about to spay a cat. The minister of the Congregational church had several cats living in his barn, and he had been trapping them and bringing them in for neutering. This young cat had been a reluctant pa-tient that morning, clutching at the cage door when Darcie tried to take her out, swinging on it until Darcie pulled her off.

Erika had scrubbed up, put her gown and gloves on, and was about to begin. Her hands were poised over the animal's abdomen. But there they stayed. The thought had come upon her that she had no idea where to make the incision. Her hands began to shake. Holly's illness had come after a spay. Here she was again, doing a spay, and paralyzed with doubt.

Darcie came out to Chuck and said, "You better get in there with Erika."

He walked into the surgery. "Do you want me to do that?" he asked.

"I don't know," she said. "I want to be good at this. I feel like a flag flapping in the wind."

"You have to ask yourself, What can I do next time that will be better? I'm sorry we had to lose her. I wish she could have made it."

"I don't know what to do with this feeling that I'm faking it."

Chuck said, "I wish you could have been a fly on the wall three months ago, when I told Ellie that you would be hitting a slump after three months. All associates go through the three-month slump. They just have to suck it up and get through it. It will get worse before it gets better. It will be November or even March or April before it's over."

The talk went on a few minutes longer, just the two of them in the surgery, Erika in full dress and Chuck in coveralls, the unconscious cat between them on the table, Chuck talking and Erika nodding. Finally he said, "This is why mixed practice is so hard," and he left to get ready for a farm call.

Outside at his car, Chuck said, "This is when associates decide it's not for them. You look at the number of people who go back into internships after their first year. Those positions start in May or June. They had to apply in November. They had to have come to the decision before then.

"She just hit the three-month slump. I made that term up in there, but that's what it is. She's discovered that she went through vet school, thought she knew it all, and has now realized that she knows practically nothing."

Inside, after her pep talk, Erika relaxed and found her way. She remembered where the "line of separation" was, where an abdominal incision can be made with minimal bleeding. At first her hands shook, but the task drew her in. She excised, clipped, tied off, and sutured. Lastly she put a line of sterile glue on the incision.

The storm had passed—for now, if Chuck was right. Erika held up the little limp cat and said, "Ta-da! A shpayed kitty!"

At a cookout at Roger's house a few days later, she was smiling when she said, "And then I suddenly didn't know where to cut. I had done who knows how many spays, and then I didn't know what to do."

Roger had told her not to beat herself up too badly over it, just as he had told himself before. "She's doing okay," he said. "She's got to take it easy on herself, though. She's a lot better than she thinks she is."

Chuck had given Erika another pep talk on the day that she broke down. To make things more difficult, a DA Erika had done at Barrett's had displaced again and needed to be re-done. Chuck did these secondary DAs by "turning the cow over," putting her on her back, and going in through the abdomen.

Erika had called him and said she felt terrible about the DA coming up again. Chuck said not to worry, he'd take care of it. He told her to go to the Sawyers' Crescent Farm, examine two sick cows, and do a DA. Erika did one successfully.

Later at the clinic, Chuck told her she was doing fine, that everything would be all right. He gave her a hug.

"That's what I needed," Erika said at the cookout. "It was the second time he'd hugged me. The first was when he hired me."

"I hope she makes it," Chuck said a few days later. "She feels she isn't real, that she doesn't get it, that she isn't doing us any good, all those things first-year vets go through."

By way of illustration he told a story about a dog named Sophie Beauregard. She had come in for a routine exam a few weeks before, and Chuck had found a large growth, a tumor spread out along her side. The owner hadn't noticed it. The surgery was a difficult procedure, and it left a big divot in Sophie's side. She had spent a few days out in the kennel with a wide bandage strapped around her ribs.

When Sophie returned for her follow-up exam, Chuck was at the end of a hard day that included a difficult euthanasia of a dog. But when Sophie walked in, happy and smiling, glad to see the vet, Chuck had said, "Thank God for dogs like Sophie Beauregard."

There were so many times when you couldn't figure things out or make them better. You had to deliberately appreciate those cases like Sophie Beauregard's, the ones that made you feel good about what you were doing, and about the profession.

"The same will happen for Erika if she hangs in there," Chuck said.

4.

A few weeks later, Erika felt she was in need of another pep talk. She'd had another difficult night. She cried in the shower that morning, as she had been doing every day lately before going in. She wrote in her journal and meditated, but meditation wasn't helping. At the clinic she was still feeling emotional, and she went to talk to Chuck.

"Maybe he didn't hear the part about needing another pep talk," Erika said later.

And maybe her timing was off. The attacks on the World Trade Center happened that week. Chuck had a fishing trip scheduled up north, but he was feeling more like heading south, feeling that he wanted to reenlist. In Erika's mind, Chuck had blasted her, saying, "You think you're the only one having a hard time? You've got to buck up." Erika thought, Maybe this is what I need, and she also thought, I just want a hug. When she told Roger about it later, he gave her a hug.

She found herself wishing she had a more normal job. "That it wasn't life and death every day, that I wasn't so worried that I'm going to make a mistake." She had been talking with her friends from vet school and learned that they had been feeling the same way. "That they don't know anything, that they feel like they are asking questions all the time, that they feel like when they're giving a diagnosis, it's, Could be this, might be that, might be this too, but it's probably that."

Of those fellow graduates she said, "They are not easygoing, most of them. We all got to vet school by being smart and pushing ourselves. We weren't motivated by money. We just want to do a good job. But you get out there in practice, and you think, This is like being in school, so stressful, so filled with unknowing."

Erika knew she had been luckier than some of them. "My friend Michelle looked all over New England for a mixed-practice job like I have, and she couldn't find one. Either it wasn't a true mixed practice, or the place was crazy. She's working at a small-animal clinic now." She also knew that some of her stress was self-induced. "There's no salary problem, because I asked for what I wanted and got it. I asked for a truck and got that. I'm not in a place with a staff problem or high turnover. All things that can be controlled are good. I have a good, moral boss, and I like working with Roger."

Following the "bad interaction" after September 11, Chuck told Erika that if she "needed to go out and whack trees, go ahead." If she needed to take a day off, go ahead—the work would get done. Soon after that, one afternoon, Erika did take some time for herself.

During the morning's appointments, she and Darcie euthanized four dogs. One had needed it, Erika said, but three were old dogs taken over by family members who just didn't want them anymore. Two were littermates, beagles, eager and energetic. They had to be sedated first, and before it was over, both Erika and Darcie were crying. When Erika was out having lunch, she began thinking she should get right back to the clinic and take care of a list of things. Then she remembered what Chuck said, and she thought, Schedule some farm calls, get out of the office, a day and a half of appointments is enough. "So I just scheduled them. I didn't check with Chuck and Roger. I just looked at the schedule, saw that Roger was on but didn't have any calls, and scheduled one for myself."

She went to the farm of an elderly woman, Alice Hadley, who lived in Bellows Falls. "Alice has sheep and a dog, Watson. I vaccinated some of the sheep and worked on Watson, putting flea treatment on him. Alice wanted me to teach her how to do it. She's old, and was shaking and having trouble. But I told her how to do it. It just felt nice to be there. She asked me at the end if I wanted some brandy and water, and even though I didn't want one then, I took it, so I could spend more time with Alice."

Erika had been calling her mother all along to tell of her successes and express her doubts. Like Erika, Ann Bruner often thought in metaphorical ways, and while Erika was passing through her three-month slump, Ann told her about learning to walk. Could there be a more basic metaphor, or someone more able to convey it? Ann reminded Erika that though she was verbal at nine months and fluent at a year, she didn't walk until she was eighteen months old. She had crawled about until the knees were worn off her pants and the toes were worn off her shoes. Erika's mother had finally taken her to a shoe store, where the salesman fitted her with a pair of boxy shoes with platform soles. He plunked her down right there, and she stood waving about. A day later she was walking barefoot.

Ann Bruner thought that Erika had lingered in some preliminary phase that most children pass through quickly. Ann found the quick transition remarkable, and she had seen evidence of that kind of learning since. She told Erika she had often seen her in a kind of slow climb with a long self-doubt phase. Then something suddenly clicked, and she took off. Running had been like that for her. Ann told her that it would probably happen again, that she had been preparing for it and acquired lots of information for it, that the persona would fall into place. She thought Erika needed to grasp it intuitively, grasp a feeling, just as going from the knees to the feet had been a feeling thing and not a verbal thing.

In December, Erika went to Chuck's house one night after work to again discuss her progress, a sixth-month review. Chuck told her that she was doing well and again gave her examples of feedback he'd gotten from clients. He told her she had to reduce stress and develop the ability to put things in proportion, to decide how much time should be spent on something relative to other things that had to get done. He told her she should think about coming in on her day off once in a while when something interesting was happening, as a way to learn more.

The next morning in the surgery, spaying a cat, Erika said, "I was hoping he would say, You're wonderful, and everything you're doing is absolutely perfect! He didn't say that, but he did say some good things. And I said to him that it's time for me to grow up a bit. I've never been in a position where I've had this much responsibility before."

Chuck thought that was a significant thing to say. Most people couldn't admit they had to grow, he said. "It usually involves pain, and people retreat from pain. So many times I've had people come in here, even in their seventies, who say they didn't make the right choices in life, or make the decisions they needed to make."

5.

One morning in January, Roger and Erika were doing the treatments and talking about calls in the night—venting, actually. The previous night, Roger had gotten a call at 2 a.m. from someone who had been bitten by a cat. "They wanted to know my opinion on that. I had come to the opinion that they were idiots and told them to call a doctor. I'm thinking that when my foal is born, I'll call up people early in the morning just to let them know."

Erika said she'd gotten a call a couple of days ago at two or three in the morning about a sick cat. She had called the owner back at 7 a.m. to give him a bit more diagnosis. "He'd said, 'It's early,' and I said, 'Yes, but that's the way it goes, isn't it?' " Then she asked Roger, "Do you have any tips on how to trim llamas' feet?" She had an appointment to work on some llamas that afternoon.

"The trick is to get them to hold still," Roger said.

The week before, Erika had worked on some alpacas in Vermont. "The owners were a dream. They had the meds out and the animals restrained when I got there. On the drive there, I was so worried that I talked out loud to myself about what I was going to do. The whole year has been like that, not knowing what you're going to do, not having anyone with you, and getting used to the idea."

"You'll be all right," Roger said.

Things did seem to be looking better, Erika said that afternoon when she drove to Stoddard to treat the llamas.

"I think I've gotten over the hump," she said. "Except for that truck accident." She had recently slid backward down a hill and into a ditch, she said.

When Erika first got the newer Toyota truck, she had read through the manual and thought she understood the four-wheel-drive system. She didn't understand, however, that she had manually locking hubs, that she had to get out of the truck and turn them into position. So when she thought she was in four-wheel drive, she actually wasn't. Coming down one of the big hills into the center of Walpole during an ice storm, she had hit the brakes, spun around, and slid into the ditch. A tow truck had to come to pull the truck out, and the tires had to be reinflated. At the service station, Erika said, "They had a good time telling me what was wrong." Chuck hadn't been very pleased either.

The ground was covered with snow on this day in Stoddard. Lessons learned—before turning onto an unpaved road, Erika got out and locked the hubs and shifted into four-wheel drive. She drove through the woods to a large colonial-style post-and-beam house set on a small hill. Next to the house was a fenced pen with two llamas inside. They were watching their visitors with rapt curiosity, their camelid heads posed high.

Josh and Verna, the young couple who lived in the house, had recently gotten the llamas from a friend who told them that llamas were nothing but big lawn ornaments. Josh and Verna were learning how to train them. They had plans to use them for trail excursions as part of a bed-and-breakfast business. The llamas would carry provisions and equipment for day hikes, maybe even for an overnight. But they were far from ready to be pack animals. Josh said that one of them, named Frosty, shaggy and mahogany-colored, was especially attracted to people. He seemed to think he was a person.

While Josh was building a shed for them, Frosty had spent much of the time at Josh's side with his nose under Josh's armpit. The second llama, named Zanzibar, or Zanzi, was more aloof and kept his distance. Josh hadn't even been able to put his hand on Zanzi's head without him recoiling.

Other animals had been dropping by to view these lawn ornaments. A moose had broken through a fence in an adjacent pasture and spent a few hours in the company of Frosty and Zanzi. Josh had moved the fence next to the house then. A deer jumped into that pen, stayed awhile, then ran and leaped out. The llamas bounced along with the deer, right up to the fence.

Erika explained thoroughly what she intended to do that day. She talked about the rabies vaccine and its purpose, and the tetanus shot, and she said that the leptospirosis vaccine was especially important with deer in the area. She explained how she would give the shots (while everyone held the llamas) and where (in the armpit, less hair). She described the features of the sedatives she'd use, what the mixture consisted of, how the two components worked together and how they would have worked separately, how the animals would react, and how long the effect would last. She talked about the composition of llamas' hoofs, and how she would trim them.

Josh and Verna listened patiently, adding an occasional comment based on their own observations. When she was done explaining, Erika returned to her truck and prepared her kit. In a tray she placed three syringes of vaccines for each creature, and she carried a pair of clipping shears and set of cutting tongs. Josh went ahead to make an offering of food.

Now Erika and Verna walked to the gate, where the llamas came up to greet them, bending their long necks down to their faces, getting nose to nose with each of them.

The greatest challenge was as Roger had said, getting the

llamas—350 pounds and capable of pogo-ing like an ante-
lope—to stand still. For all her doubt, Erika went at it like a
paratrooper. Her strategy was to sedate Zanzi first, since he
would be aloof and probably resistant. Erika thought that they
might not even need sedation for Frosty, since he was so com-
panionable.

Erika, Josh, and Verna got into the pen, and with arms
outstretched they made whispery sounds and walked toward
the llamas. Both animals immediately became suspicious, raising their heads high and looking askance at the foolish creatures approaching them. But Zanzi was wearing a halter, and
Josh grabbed onto it.

Maybe Frosty was trying to show his worth as a human being. Maybe he wanted to be on the right side of things, on the
winning side. Whatever the reason, Frosty turned on Zanzi
when Josh took hold of him, leaping at his pen mate, spitting
at him, and biting his ear. Erika tried to move in close with syringes while Josh was holding on and Frosty was striking out,
but it couldn't last. Josh let go, and both llamas, reunited in
purpose if not identity, bounded away to the far end of the
pen, looking back over their shoulders in alarm, as if to see a
group of humans once again going mad.

Success of course is the result of persistence. With outstretched arms and whispering noises the three made another
push, though Frosty and Zanzi easily outflanked them and
leaped off to free ground. With another advance, they managed to herd Zanzi into the shed, and again the shaggy, dung-
encrusted Frosty threw himself at his counterpart, spitting like
a cobra, with Erika, Josh, and Verna holding on. But this time
Erika managed to get a syringe into him. They let go, and off
the two llamas went again. All caught their breath while the
sedative took effect. Soon Zanzi's head was drooping, and he
wobbled like a drunk with each step.

Erika had seen enough of Frosty to know that he too would need a sedative. Another chase began, and another, with feints and leaps, until Josh tackled Frosty and wrapped his arms around him and Erika floated up from behind and unloaded a dose in his rear. They again relaxed and waited. Erika gathered up her tools.

From then on, the work was as straightforward as any doctor's visit. Three people held on to, and seemed to be holding up, the woozy llamas while Erika injected the vaccines. She did the manicures too, lifting their legs and coolly snipping their hoofs with the clippers and cutters. It was smooth work for her, and pleasant too, with the fresh air on the winter day and the views from the little hill long and spectacular. She left Frosty and Zanzi standing apart and drooping, but soon to return to llamatude.

Back in the warm house, Erika prepared the bill. Not a bad price for a farm call and all that work, not to mention the danger—$145 for shots, clipping, and restraints. "They got off good on that one," she said on the way out. Again she stopped at the paved road to turn the hubs back into place and shift into two-wheel drive.

"That went well," she said. Her cheeks were flushed. "I feel really good about that one."

It made you consider the meaning of "well." She meant of course that it had gone as she had hoped, that she had successfully held the animals and gotten the shots in. But how difficult it had been—the image remained of Erika with her arms around the lower part of the neck of the big llama, her face pressed to him, so determined, while he thrashed and tried to jump away and she tried to reach for a syringe.

Compared with most other vets, Erika had significant experience with llamas now. She was becoming a mixed-practice vet with a llama expertise. There happened to be a lot of llamas in these towns. She could do business on that experience. They sure were fun to watch, for their curiosity and physical grace, those woolly highfliers with the ponderous eyes.

On the return to Walpole, Erika talked about a new approach she was taking to being a vet. She said there had been a change after her sixth-month review with Chuck. She had hoped he would say, You're a great vet, but he hadn't. "Which was good," Erika said, "because I came away realizing that I had to think differently about the work."

For inspiration, her thoughts turned to athletics. She remembered when she had been running track and training for the hurdles, trying to get the right three-step stride between them. "My coach told me I had to attack the hurdles and see them as a challenge. I eventually gave up hurdling and switched to the quarter mile, but in the quarter I used the same idea, that you should attack the hurdles, except I attacked the distance."

Now she had taken the advice further and was thinking along the lines of the hurdles she faced daily.

"I've been trying hard to take what have been feelings of dread and turn them into feelings of challenge. I've tried to see something I have feared as something I want to succeed with. When I saw it in those terms, I began to feel a little better."

Erika still wasn't sleeping well, waking at four most mornings. She cried in the shower almost daily before going into work. She knew that she might lose it and break down at the clinic again, but she wasn't going to castigate herself if she did. "I'm beating myself up about enough already."

She did think that she had a useful new approach, a workable metaphor. "Running track taught me that you can be very tired and in pain, and still do so much more."

Attack the hurdles—even when they run away from you.

11

SPRING ARRIVALS

1.

A fifteen-year-old Siamese cat appeared at the clinic, and got roaming privileges too. She soon found her own place in a closet next to the storeroom that Hobbs called his own. Darcie placed a litter box there. The Siamese had kidney problems and needed subcutaneous fluids daily. The owner wasn't able to give fluids subcutaneously, so Chuck told her that the cat could stay at the clinic, at least for a while, and the owner could visit her.

Aside from the kidney problem, this slender cat was in good shape, and with fluids she soon looked even better. She moved with that long-legged feline lope, and seemed to attract attention whenever she crossed the treatment-room floor. Her name was Sandy, but Darcie elaborated the name to Sandy Sue Shaw, which made her more of a, well, possibility. When Chuck was asked if Sandy Sue was now a clinic pet, he hesitated to answer. Chuck had recently said at a staff meeting that no more stray animals were to be taken in without his permission, that they were boarding enough already, and they weren't a humane society. But he said of Sandy Sue, "Yeah, we're keeping her. I'll tell you, she rules Hobbs. He is a much better behaved cat now."

"She's a great cat," Darcie said.

"She's got a lot of personality," Erika said.

"The best thing is she's whipped Hobbs into shape."

Still, it was hard to tell who was winning that battle. One morning, there had been a howl, and when Carol went into the treatment room, she found Hobbs with fur in his mouth. Yet there were also times when Sandy Sue loped across the room, Hobbs barreled up to her and stopped short, and she gave him her cross-eyed look and batted at him without backing off. This was something Chuck loved to see.

One incident proved what Sandy Sue was really made of. A dog came in for treatment for a minor skin condition and was left temporarily in the staff room. Hobbs charged at him and jumped on the dog's back, which set off a howling. But while Hobbs was in motion, so was Sandy Sue, and she jumped on Hobbs's back. When Darcie ran into the room, she found the three of them stacked up, the dog howling, Hobbs howling, and Sandy Sue riding high.

There were other changes under way. Hobbs had been slimming down, thanks to a stricter diet and a bout of constipation severe enough to cause Chuck to call in from a trip away to check up on him. Many who knew Hobbs mentioned his new look to him, and he seemed to blink proudly and lift his head at the compliment. When a photographer specializing in pet portraiture asked to place a display in the reception room, a deal was struck. Before long a photo appeared—in the treatment room of course, where it could be properly appreciated—of Hobbs stretched out on blue satin with a blue background, his body long, his belly flat, his face serene and sincere.

"He the man!" Darcie said.

2.

As spring approached, Roger began doing ultrasound checks with horses. Many foals would be arriving soon within the reach of Roger's practice. Erika began doing more dairy work. Chuck said that Erika had come a long way, and she was almost over the hump if not already there. He thought she was ready to preg check the big herds. "She can take some of the pressure off me now," Chuck said.

They had been increasingly busy since January, especially at the dairies, where DAs were running high. Chuck thought the cause was the warm and wet weather they'd been having. When rain got into the corn silage and made it heavier, the proportions of grain tended to be increased during the mixing process. This resulted in hotter feed, high in protein and low in fiber, which put the cows into a condition where they were more likely to develop ketosis and turn up the abomasum after calving. And low fuel prices and high milk prices had made the farmers more likely to treat for DAs.

Soon Erika would have to take over for Chuck completely. He needed to have some surgery. Recently, while lifting something, Chuck had felt a tear in his abdomen, and he immediately knew it was a hernia. His doctor said he should stay out of work for two weeks because the suture could tear. But Chuck knew how to time such things, and figured—surgery on Monday, forty-eight hours for the swelling, four days until the tissue healed around the sutures, and eight days until he could be back at Boggy Meadow for the Tuesday check.

Meanwhile, for at least those eight days, Erika would do all herd checks and dairy calls. Help would be available from Roger if needed. And so came the time Erika had been anticipating.

At the weekly herd check at Westminster Farms, while Erika was washing her boots in the milk storage room, Mike Perry greeted her with, "Where's the great one? He said he was the Iron Man. I'm gonna have to give Charlie Shaw some shit about this."

"You'll probably see him next week," Erika said, "though he probably shouldn't come."

They went out to the barn, Mike with his clipboard, Erika with her tray of vials, box of sleeves, and jug of Lubrivet. They had just begun when Mike looked off, saw a machine starting, and said he had to tend to a downed cow. He set the clipboard on the floor and trotted off. Erika watched the bucket of a front-end loader rise, with a cow in it. She thought she'd examine her later, in the sick bay, but they left the cow in the bucket and parked the loader by a manure pile. Then the truck from the slaughterhouse rattled in, and the driver waved to Mike. Erika said, "That's sad."

"That's how it is at a dairy farm," Mike said. "That's where the money is. When she can no longer produce milk, that's what you have to do. She'll bring maybe $650 for beef, and that money will go toward a replacement for her."

He added, "But replacement cows are hard to find. They're in demand. The other day, one of the helpers put a heifer on the truck with the bull calves by mistake, and she brought $450 at the auction. That was for a week-old heifer. An average cow will bring $2,500, and a scraggly one can bring $1,500. Some of the cows in this herd, the ones making 150 pounds per day, one of those could bring as much as $5,000.

"That's life on the farm," Mike said, and studied his clipboard.

Erika started working down the line. The temperature was in the 40s, but she was in short sleeves and the green coveralls. Erika was letting her hair grow out because she wanted hair that looked good in a wedding dress. She kept tossing it back as she worked. Sometimes it seemed that all the help on the farms came out to talk to Erika while she checked the cows. At the clinic, one client had told her he liked her manner, and also liked her face. She had said, "I'm glad you like my face, but I want you to like me because I'm your vet."

Now she looked at the floor and pondered, the coppery hair falling over her eyes.

"Follicle on the right, small CL on the left," she said, "so we'll go ahead and Lutalyse her."

"Got it," Mike said, and made the notation.

Inside another she said, "FARO, flat active right ovary."

Mike knew the language and the response. "In other words, she ain't bred, so let's move on."

A flock of birds, riding the spring breeze, swept through an east window, drifted over the rafters, and swept out the opposing west window, leaving a chattering on their way.

Erika held two fingers close together and said, "Her ovary is literally this big. She's got a tiny ovary on the right side."

"We'll breed her," Mike said.

Except where Erika and Mike worked, where the mood was tense, the cows lowered their heads and ate from the mounds of silage, with its rank, fermented smell, its look of powders and grains. They chewed, and their breath pulsed like organ pipes.

Erika found a pregnancy and again held two fingers close together. She smiled and tossed her hair. "There's a calf in there about an inch big," she said.

"Six weeks old," Mike answered. "They stay that way for a long time, and then they really grow."

Another cow had not become pregnant after several attempts at artificial insemination. "How long are you going to keep her?" Erika asked.

"Until she doesn't breed."

"How long might that be?"

"I don't know. I've got a short fuse. She'll probably end up with John Henry soon."

"She's got a small CL on her left ovary. I'd Lutalyse her and breed her in three days."

Some were puzzlers, especially the cows that Mike called "alley rats," meaning the young heifers that preferred lying in the muck to lying in a stall on sawdust. On one of these, Erika pushed in, backed off, probed again. She dropped her head lower until her chin was to her chest.

After watching for a while, Mike said, "You praying in there or what?"

"It's hard to tell. She's so small."

"I'm just kidding you. We can recheck any one you want. You want to recheck this one?"

"Let's do that. Thanks, Mike."

An hour passed, then another as they picked their way through the first of sixty-five cows, then moved to the other row and made their way back to the starting point. Pregnancies, CLs, flat ovaries, rechecks.

On another puzzler, Erika squinted, thought hard.

"No one home?" Mike asked.

"No one home at all, nothing."

Clearly Erika was more confident now, more capable and at ease. She was not as sure or quick as Chuck, of course, but she was not so far behind him anymore.

A free-roaming cow edged up, sniffed at her and then at

her tray. When the cow began nosing and pushing at the box of gloves, Erika yelled, "Stop messing with my stuff!" It came out as a kind of laugh.

"They all have a personality," Mike said.

The herd check lasted nearly three hours, and before it was done, Erika's arm was very tired, though she didn't mention it to Mike. She arrived back at the clinic as Chuck was about to begin a staff meeting. He took a look at her face, red from working in the cold, and knew that she was happy to be doing the big herds.

Chuck began the meeting by saying that profits were up so far this year. "The gross for the entire practice for February was up by ten percent. Dog business is up. Cat business is up. Cows are up fifty percent. Horses are double."

He announced that as of March, the clinic would be incorporated. He laughed a little at the sound of that. He said he wanted to establish a profit-sharing system, if possible. He wanted to have an incentive system based on a sense of ownership among the employees. "I want everyone to take an interest in the place. Look at the front entrance. If you see anything there, clean it up. Cobwebs out there, clean them up. If we have tests to do, do them the same day. Ask the kids to clean up the dog shit when they walk the dogs. There's way too much out there." That part could be a hard sell—last week a couple of the kids went out on a stool-gathering expedition but came back in gagging.

He said they would keep defining the system. Clearly the prospects of sharing pleased him. He finished the meeting by saying, "It's all about teamwork."

A few nights later Erika was on call, and she got called out to Bascom's dairy at 6 a.m. for a calving. She stopped off at Roger's house along the way to pick up a calf-pulling tool—a noose on a handle—that Roger's father had made for him. But when Erika got to Bascom's, things were very far along and the cow was closing down again. The calf was dead. Erika couldn't reach the head, even with the help of Roger's tool. She tried for a while, then turned to the obstetrical wire, cutting off a leg before she called Roger. He came out, and they couldn't get the body out. The cow was done.

"If they had called at two or three instead of six," Erika said later, "I might have been able to do something more." That seemed a significant step, not automatically blaming herself or feeling incompetent, but placing responsibility where it belonged.

Later that morning, Erika went to Windyhurst Farm, with plans to meet Roger in the afternoon to watch him do a C-section.

The Windyhurst check was a much-anticipated one, both for Erika and for Chuck. She had been told that it would be the most difficult place to work because Roger Adams was the most demanding of dairy farmers. He was willing to go to the limit, she was told, but unwilling to accept shortcomings. This was the farm where Roger Osinchuk had lost a cow after a DA and was not allowed to return for months.

Another day in the low 40s. Erika left the clinic in short sleeves again, wearing surgical scrubs under her coveralls and no jacket. "She's warm-blooded," Darcie said as she was leaving.

At Windyhurst, Erika scrubbed up, washed her boots, and went into the barn, but no one was there. Chuck had told Erika that it was important to be on time here, and she noted that Roger Adams wasn't on time. "I won't tell him that right off," Erika said. "I'll wait until he says something."

The herdsman, Jeremy Benoit, came after a few minutes. He began the check with Erika. The dialogue came fast and was technical. A first Holstein had "an oldish corpus luteum on the left ovary," Erika said, and a follicle coming up on the right. Jeremy said she was 160 days in milk and they should probably give her Lutalyse.

"So do I do that?" Erika said. Jeremy said yes, give her the injection.

The next was a fifty-three-day pregnancy, a recheck. Erika said the cow was still pregnant.

Roger Adams stepped into the doorway then. His cheeks were red, his eyes twinkling. He looked about, taking things in. Erika was deep into a big Holstein.

"To be accepted here, you have to say they're pregnant," he said.

"I thought to be accepted here, you had to be on time," Erika replied.

He looked away, smiled, and said, "Oh yeah, that helps too."

Another recheck, an easy call. "Pregnant," Erika said.

"We're being kind to you today," Adams said. They were giving her easy cows, he meant.

"Yeah, you're being kind to me today," Erika said.

"I don't think we have a cow named Erika. How many letters? We'll have to name one Erika."

"Wait until I come to a calving and give you a live calf," she said. "Then you can call it Erika."

Adams took the clipboard from Jeremy and looked at the notations, which had grown increasingly complicated since Adams began farming years ago. "Dr. Shaw is always confusing me, saying FARO, or CARO, or whatever."

"This one's pregnant," Erika said.

"Oh, Erika. You're going to have to come again."

They released that cow and pushed another into the chute. Erika pulled out the manure and reached in. Her expression turned inward. "What she is now, she's got a corpus luteum on the right, and a flat active ovary on the left." A healthy uterus.

"Maybe we'll give her Lutalyse," Adams said. "Let's do that. Getting too much manure for you there, Erika?" She was about ankle-deep in what she had retrieved.

"Getting a little slidey," she said.

"We'll get the bulldozer in there soon."

Jeremy left to round up another group of cows. During the interval, Adams led Erika to a heifer pen, where she checked eight heifers that had been bred at fifteen months. She worked her way down the line, and all eight were pregnant.

"Erika," Adams said slyly, "you're better than Dr. Shaw."

Back at the chute, Adams pointed out an older cow lying in a pen nearby. She was white, mostly, with speckles. Her name was Ruthie, and she had been a great producer not only of milk but also of other Ruthies on this farm. Lately, though, she had been having difficulties with her feet, and was milking slowly.

"Jeremy and my son Stuart don't like it when they're slow," Adams said.

"We want them out of here," Jeremy said, tossing a thumb.

"They want me to get rid of her. I will, I know I have to get rid of her, but I'd like to hang on. She's been a good cow for us."

Erika didn't pause, though she was listening. "FALO, FARO [flat active right and left ovaries]. You have two options, one ovary or the other."

"I'll put her on the program tomorrow," Adams said, meaning injections for timed ovulation. "There will be four on the program tomorrow, four getting shots, and that will be all. No more than four program cows in any one day."

This wasn't as long and laborious a check as the one at

Westminster Farms, but for Erika it was just as satisfying. There was a lot of talk from Roger Adams about how well Erika was doing. It helped that all but eight of the cows she checked were pregnant. Erika was feeling so enthusiastic that when the check was done, she asked if they had any calves that needed dehorning, and then burned the horn buds on five of them. "Better now than later on," she told one wide-eyed calf.

As she washed her boots, Erika said to me, "This was the easiest herd check I've had. All that talk about how hard it would be! There were so many definable structures. They said, 'You should come back again.' I had nothing to do with it, and was just a bearer of good news, but it makes you feel good."

She said, "Now I feel like a real vet." She thrust her arms overhead and yelled, "I'm ready to preg-check the world!"

3.

Erika ate a sandwich on the doorstep of the house she and Gary rented in Westmoreland, while nearby a crew gathered buckets of maple sap from the trees and carried them to a holding tank. The pleasure of the check stayed with her as she drove about a mile down the road to the small sheep farm where Roger was waiting.

He would be showing Erika the surgery he liked the most, the one in which the vet opened up an animal and pulled out babies that might not have made it otherwise. It was the procedure that had inspired Roger to become a vet.

The owner of the farm, Laurie Goodrich, kept a valuable breed of sheep called Oxfords, large-sized, with thick coats of wool. This ewe had been trying to go into labor, but her cervix was not opening. After Erika arrived, Roger flipped the ewe on her back and restrained her by tying her legs crosswise.

"You restrain them with ropes," he said, "not chemically, so she can get up and nurse afterward." Erika nodded. She crouched down next to Roger and the ewe.

He gave the ewe a local anesthetic on her abdomen, making a series of injections on either side where he would make the incision. "You make the incision just off the midline, about the length of your hand," he said. Quickly he made several cuts, saying, "You've got to be real careful with sheep. They don't have thick skins like a cow. On sheep there's not much skin and not much body wall."

He told Erika how to open the uterus. "On a cow you make the cut in the middle of the uterus. But on a sheep you make the incision at the back leg of the lamb, wherever that might be."

Roger reached into the ewe with gloved hands, felt around, and then pulled the uterus out of her body and laid it on her stomach. It was huge and wobbling, and inside you could see legs. Quickly Roger made an incision, reached inside, and pulled the lamb out. It was still in the amniotic sac, so Roger cut through that. He cleaned the lamb off and handed it to Laurie.

She held the lamb by the back legs, walked a few feet away, and gave the little creature a big swing to clear its lungs and start it breathing. Then she toweled it off. "Better not be a ram," she said, but she soon saw he was, and she smiled. "Actually, I'll get a lot of money for this ram," she said. He was trembling but breathing when she laid him on some hay in a stall near the ewe.

By then Roger had reached into the uterus again and pulled out a twin. Again he cut it from the amniotic sac and gave it to Laurie, but this one was bloody, so she went outside to swing him. He took his first breath, and she set him next to his brother, who was already testing out his front feet.

The uterus was pulsing like a heartbeat on the ewe's belly. Roger began trimming placental lobules from it. "Same thing as with a calf," he said. "Cut out all the crap that's handy, and leave the rest alone. Finish up as fast as you can."

He reached for a needle and threaded it. "You have to sew the uterus up fast because of contractions," he said. It was true—with each pulse, it seemed, the uterus had grown smaller. Where the two lambs had been only minutes ago, a twelve-inch bag the size of a football remained now.

"Four sets of stitches," he said, "in the uterus, the body wall, the subcutaneous layer, and the skin." He began stitching. "I sew it up like a tractor tire. You know how a tractor tire is, with the cross treads? I sew it like that. The Utrecht pattern, or whatever it's called."

With only a local anesthetic, the ewe had been conscious through all of this, though she couldn't see what was going on, because she was on her back with her legs tied. Roger fed the uterus back inside and began closing her up. Erika sat on her heels, watching him work.

Roger turned toward Laurie and asked, "How are the babies?"

"Ready to get up," she said.

When he had sewn up the skin, Roger untied the ewe. She quickly rolled over, and when she stood up, Laurie led her into the pen with the lambs. She sniffed them and almost immediately moved to protect them, putting her body between them and the onlookers. This was a wonder. Watching her as she stood over the lambs while they struggled to get up and make contact with her, it was easy to see why Roger had such high regard for this surgery, easy to see how it made him feel like a magician, like a wonder himself.

"You'll be ready to do it next time," he said to Erika.

Roger remained at the farm to finish up. He would go on

another call while Erika returned to the clinic for appointments.

"Now I know how to do that one," she said as she drove. "That's one more thing I know."

Maybe someday she would know how to do it all, I said, to see how she'd answer.

"No, I will always gladly accept more learning. I wish I had more, that I wasn't alone so much. I wish I had more mentoring."

She said, "Some get none at all. I've got a friend in Maine who has a terrible boss. She doesn't get shown anything, and she's not supposed to call during off-hours. She's expected to be on her own, to wing it at all times.

"In vet school it was all learning, too much of it. Hours and hours of note-taking. They call it trying to take a drink from the fire hose. Then the fire hose is turned off, and you're sucking at the end of it, trying to get the last two drops of water."

This was not the case now. Looking off down the road, she thought about the past few hours, what had transpired at Windyhurst, and what she had just seen at the sheep farm.

"It's been a great day," Erika said.

One of Roger's mares, Holly, was very close to term, and he had been watching her closely. Roger considered Holly a superb broodmare, and he thought she might produce Shawne's eventual replacement. Roger had installed a small video camera above Holly's stall and connected it to the television in his living room. He had been sleeping on the couch, leaving the TV on, which was preferable to running to the barn repeatedly to check on the mare.

Late one night he awoke, glanced at the screen, saw Holly lying down in the stall, and knew she was foaling. He hustled down to the barn and saw the tip of a leg sticking out of her, a tiny hoof. He lay down on the floor, reached into Holly, and pulled. It was over in ten minutes. Two hours later the little colt was up and had found his mom's teats. Roger wiped him down, to prevent the colt's ears from freezing at the tips.

Such a leggy animal! Such long back legs, and so shapely— a son of Shawne too, with Shawne's white socks. Long legs, a little belly and tiny ribs, and a narrow face. He was going to be a looker, Roger said, and would bring top dollar. In fact, within a few weeks Roger would sell "Pistol" for $5,000 dollars.

Pistol was the first of the foals Roger produced as part of his breeding business, though many would follow. The next morning, Roger was the proud father as he ran his hands over the little colt. Eventually Pistol wanted to lie down and rest, but couldn't manage his awkwardly long legs. He tried to lower himself, but kept wobbling backward and bumping up against the wall. Finally he got into the middle of the stall and bent his stilty front legs forward. They trembled and shook before he dropped to the floor, rolled over on the hay, and slept.

4.

A month later, in May, in the prime of the busy season, Chuck finally got to go on a fishing trip to the Connecticut Lakes, at the source of the Connecticut River, in northernmost New Hampshire. Roger and Erika were on their own again.

Roger's good fortune with his horses had continued. Another of his mares, a Thoroughbred, had foaled out, and he had sold that colt too. He had traded a future Shawne foal for a broodmare soon to arrive from Thunder Bay, Ontario. During May he had begun collecting Shawne again and shipping his semen. By the end of the season he would make thirty shipments. Shawne's son, the colt who had arrived from Alberta with him and whom Roger had traded to a trainer in South Carolina, would certainly be a champion, he had been told, and so was providing an advertisement for Shawne's bloodline.

Erika did not have such an easy time of it during the week Chuck was gone. Strangely enough, just as she seemed to be coming into her own as a veterinarian, she also seemed to experience her greatest level of self-doubt. Two days of difficult office visits didn't help.

There was the appointment with the German shepherd who wasn't well trained. "She was growling and getting grumpy, and I said we had to put a muzzle on her. But can you blame her for getting grumpy? I smell, I'm weird, and I'm gonna poke her with things. The owner was upset about the muzzle and kept saying, 'Can we take the muzzle off now?' I said, 'No, I'm going to spray something up her nose!' She said, 'She'll never trust me again. She won't want to come back again.' And I wanted to say, Can't you see she's dangerous! You have to do your part! She won't even sit down!

"Another owner kept talking to her fox terrier about me when I was trying to give a shot. She said, 'She's just practicing. She needs more practice,' and I wanted to say, I'm not practicing! I've given hundreds of shots! Another client had me cut her dog's nails. One of them bled, and she got panicky and said, 'Will they stop bleeding?' I wanted to say, Yes! They will stop bleeding! They will grow back to where they are now in two weeks. You don't even need to do this!

"And another dog was leaping all around when I was trying to get blood, and the owner said, 'Boy, you're like one of those ladies at the hospital who have to poke me all over to get blood.' I wanted to say, I hope you don't wiggle so much!'"

On it went, routine but difficult visits, fueled by doubt that compounded until Erika was wondering whether she should have even become a veterinarian. This compounded into dismay. She felt she had to talk about it, so on the afternoon of the second day of difficult appointments, Erika pulled Roger aside and told him how she was feeling. She talked about the clueless clients, the frustrations of dealing with them, and the growing feeling she had been having that she was out on the edge by herself. She said that Chuck had not told her she was doing a good job, and at the sound of the absurdity of that, she broke down.

Roger tried to reassure her. He told her that one way Chuck had of saying she was doing a good job was by writing that check every week. It was a good-sized check, Roger said. Chuck had bought her a truck too. Roger said that the next time she was feeling this way, if she thought she was close to the breaking point, she should say she had to do some research on the Internet and go into the office. "Lock the door and let it out, and don't let the staff see you," he said.

Chuck wouldn't know about any of this.

Something was wrong, Erika knew, but she wasn't sure what exactly. She had to do something to change her feelings. One thing she did was to make a phone call to a vet in Massachusetts who had called her a few weeks before about an associate he was interviewing, someone Erika had gone to school with. He had invited Erika to come down and spend a day on the road with him. He too had a bovine practice. She wasn't thinking of applying for the job, only that it would do her some good, possibly, to spend a day at another practice.

The day before Chuck was due back, Erika went to Barrett's to do a DA.

"Things are well now, but I've just been through a bad patch," she said. "I've wanted Chuck to be a mentor, but mostly I just wanted Chuck to tell me I'm doing a good job. But he hasn't been. And I thought, Why should I worry about that? Why should I care? It's been six months since Chuck said anything critical to me, since the truck spun out. I figured, if that's the case, then things are going good. If he can go away fishing and leave me to do the herd checks, that must mean he trusts me. I just wish he'd tell me." But she didn't seem to be able to talk to Chuck about it, and the gap between them widened.

A cool breeze was blowing at the Barrett farm. The grass around the barns had turned a deep green, and dandelions had bloomed a yellow so bright it almost hurt to look at them. Erika had been at the farm to do a DA the day before. They had a fairly high rate of DAs at Barrett's. Though they refused to use bovine growth hormones, they did push the cows nutritionally.

Erika had become quite experienced in the DA procedure. She said she had lost count of how many DAs she had done now. "Thirty to forty, I guess. More than I've done dog spays."

Inside the barn, it was milking time. The cows were huddled before the entrance to the milking parlor, a head poking up here and there to check on how things were going on up ahead. As Erika walked along the alleyway past them, she stopped at the sick pens and pointed at one of the three cows inside. "That's the DA I did yesterday," she said. The incision was neatly stitched in an interlocking pattern, just the way Roger did it.

One of the help tied today's patient into a stanchion. Erika prepped—the sedative, the shaving, the washing, the line block of lidocaine, and the initial cut with the large-gauge needle. Mike Barrett joined Erika. He was wearing his usual shorts, running shoes, and T-shirt, as well as the metal-rimmed glasses that gave him the look of his Cornell engineering training. As he often did, Mike talked about numbers. Mike had 240 cows in the high group now, and many were producing 120-pound daily averages. A few were giving 160. His cows averaged 22,000 pounds per entire lactation period. "We don't milk three times a day yet," Mike said, "but when we get to three times a day, in the high group, just the high group, we should go up to 26,000 pounds per lactation."

Nearby, while Erika began her surgery, a crew was building a new milking parlor for the specific purpose of milking three times a day—at 4 p.m., midnight, and 8 a.m. Mike said he had purchased the secondhand milking equipment from a company in Wisconsin, for a cost of $100,000.

As he talked enthusiastically about the parlor, Erika interrupted. "What would really make me happy would be if you'd build a room with bedded pack, a Club Med–type area for transition cows to go into once we treat them." A soft bed, with soft footing, she meant.

Here was another significant step, it seemed, in Erika the doctor, advocating for a recovery room for her patients. A year ago she had been hoping to someday be able to make these kinds of recommendations, and now she could say such things with some force. Mike smiled, said the parlor had to come first, said the problem was that they'd have to pay for it, that it takes time, but then he said, "Five or six years, we'll have it."

In a thoughtful way, Erika gave Mike a pink sleeve to wear on his arm when he held up the cow's tail to keep her from kicking. Mike lifted the tail and leaned forward. With it hanging above his head, he mentioned that he had worked twenty hours yesterday. A milker had called in sick.

A bell began to ring, causing the cows to start moving forward toward the parlor. They looked like a crowd of commuters at a train station. The bell had once been a signal to the cows that a steel gate would begin pushing them toward the parlor, and the bell had also indicated that an electrical current would be running through that gate. But the electricity and the gate were no longer part of the process, and the bell was now enough to make the cows push forward along the parlor runway. It seemed to work efficiently, though Mike had his doubts. The bell got the cows excited, he said, which caused a release of adrenaline, which in turn inhibited the release of a hormone called oxytocin that let the milk down. A good trick, the bell, but it was hard to know if the reduced labor was worth the possible loss in production.

Erika rolled her short sleeves up over her shoulders and scrubbed her arms with Betadine and water. She put on latex surgical gloves. She pulled out strands of suture and cut them to length, then threaded the needles. "I want to have everything ready for when I open her up," she said. "The longer she's opened up, the more susceptible she is to infection."

She made the incision easily and was soon reaching, then probing, then in contact with the inflated abomasum. During the deflation period, she looked off over the cow's back almost pensively, as if thinking about the spring day. She may have had some difficulty in the office a few days ago, but she was relaxed here.

She knew a trick too, that if you got the farmer talking, he might not think about the time passing. "What do you think of the quota system?" Erika was shoulder-deep then, her face against the cow's side.

The new federal milk-pricing system was the talk of the farms. This program would replace the New England Dairy Compact, which had worked wonderfully for the dairies in keeping up prices. It had been subsidized by producers but opposed by competitors outside of New England. The federal program would be subsidized by taxpayers and would cost millions, Mike said. There would also be limits on the subsidies, intended to discourage production. "I guess I'm just against a government program that tells me what I have to do," Mike said.

Erika let go of the abomasum and began fishing for and pulling up the omentum, the layers of fat. "All right," she said, and began to sew.

Before Erika closed the outer layer of the incision, Mike got a cylinder of penicillin and doused the exposed flesh thoroughly with the milky fluid. "You gonna pump her?" he asked. She said she would. Mike left to get the buckets and water.

As with palpation, Erika was at 80 percent of capability, as Chuck had predicted. Forty minutes for a DA, not all that much longer than the time Chuck would take.

On her way to another farm, she was thinking about cows. She said it seemed strange now to look back at vet school and remember that she had thought farming was, as she put it, "an evil human way to use animals. Then I got interested in bovine, and my feelings changed."

Her thinking had advanced, but she was still skeptical of the treatment of cows, and she wanted more of the Club Med–type treatment she had talked about with Mike. "They go from dormant lactation to giving all this milk, way beyond what they would produce normally. From zero to sixty in nothing flat. I've come to think it's not the nutrition that gives them problems, but the stress factor. The farmers like to focus on the nutrition because it's numbers you can crunch. But nobody can quantify how comfortable cows are, because you can't ask them. You can't measure that. Still, if you accept the idea, you can go about alleviating stress, and that's good for the cows."

5.

Chuck had been in pursuit of landlocked salmon at the Connecticut Lakes, but hadn't caught anything because their prey, the smelts, weren't running yet. That didn't matter, though. Chuck had a great time. He stood in 45° water in the small rivers between the lakes, and cast flies for hours. The wind blew so hard that he hadn't been able to wear a hat, but even the strength of the wind felt good.

"Four hours, smoke a cigar, take a nap, eat a Snickers bar, and do it again," Chuck said at Putnam's after his return. He was looking lean and fit in his coveralls.

"I'm looking forward to when we have four vets," Chuck said. "With four vets I could take a whole week off. So much of fishing is timing. If I could have stayed a week, I might have caught something."

He had been able to relax because he felt comfortable about leaving the clinic, he said. "Especially when I saw things this morning." Cases, records, tests, everything was in order. Calls had been made, crises averted and solved.

"Erika worked through the weekend. She was on call and worked right through. A year ago she would have been a babbling idiot doing that. But she was fine. She handled it well.

"She got to check the big herds, which she likes. The farmers, they like her, and have been easy on her. They will knock off a quarter to a third of the cows if they know Erika is coming. And they won't give her 35-day cows. They give her 45 days or more, usually."

So—was Erika over the hump?

"No, it's too soon. You can't master it in a year. It takes two years. Everything is exciting in the first year. The second year is payback for the first. That's when the vet starts to make money for the clinic. Two years to get over the hump.

"It takes two years to build up your arm for doing herd checks. You can get really tired in there. The herdsman can see it when you sigh, when you look at your watch or at the list to see how many are left. They get tense if the vet is in there too long. Scott gets anxious when he hears, 'How many days in milk?' because it means she's probably not pregnant."

He turned to Scott Kemp, who was studying his clipboard, and said, "How many days in milk?" Scott's lips tightened, and his head bobbed a bit.

"I always say they should stay for at least two years. If they don't, then something is wrong. But I'm really happy about the time I was gone. She never could have done that a year ago."

12

THE REVIEW

1.

Ginny Prince, the relief vet who had worked for Chuck on Fridays and filled in for him on days off and during vacations before Erika joined the practice, admired his approach. She liked the way he thought hard about cases and the way he could alter his treatment, bare-bones or progressive, according to the needs of the client. One thing that had struck her was how deeply and thoroughly he engaged in diagnostic thinking and, at the same time, how little the client knew of this process. She had observed that what an animal owner might perceive as quietness or even aloofness was actually the process of working out the diagnosis, of solving its mystery—which sometimes took incredible mental effort, she knew, from twenty years of her own experience dealing with patients who couldn't talk and owners who could. Over the years, she had come to think that the veterinarian himself or herself was the most important diagnostic tool.

If the practice of this method of thinking is an art, as some claim, it is acquired by way of sustained experience, by way of becoming. And if the becoming is essential, so sometimes is change, especially in the early years of practice.

To frame it differently, if artful diagnostic thinking is evident in thoughtful consideration gained from years of experience, then in its opposite, inexperience, lie anxiety and self-doubt, or their corollary and line of defense, egotism. Within that frame, change may be compulsory.

Though the AVMA does not keep statistics on the attrition or longevity of first-year associates, it's safe to say that departures are common. One veterinarian—writing on the Web site Veterinary Information Network about the difficulties of being a first-year associate—claimed that 90 percent of new graduates working in private practice leave after their first year, an excessive figure certainly, but perhaps 40 or 50 percent is closer to reality. Of the Tufts graduates Erika had kept in touch with, four of five would leave their practices after one year. As a dean of students at Tufts explained, graduates move around a lot until they find the right fit. Certainly Chuck's experience bore that out. Of the ten associates he had employed, four left after a year, another four after two years.

Does the blame lie within the structure of a profession that requires the majority of graduates to go directly into private practice after four years of education? Or does it lie in an educational process that can't possibly fully prepare its students—that even creates self-doubt, as one veterinarian claims, by showing them all that they don't know in a system of rapidly advancing medical knowledge? Does blame lie with the practice owner who hires a new vet and, expecting fair value within a business structure, throws that associate into situations he or she isn't ready for? If so, what is the alternative? A graduate may have unrealistic expectations, wanting the guidance and counseling of an internship rather than the full responsibility of a doctor's position. Is it a system that by nature causes frictional relationships? Is blame even relevant?

In Chuck's case, he certainly understood that associates joined his practice to gain experience while deciding what to do for the long term.

At the beginning of June, Chuck met separately with Erika and Roger for their yearly reviews. This was a formal written review, using a rating system and a discussion of those ratings. Two weeks after the reviews, Chuck and Ellie made a trip to Kansas to visit Chuck's son in Lawrence. They left on the day of Erika's anniversary of joining the practice. Chuck called her from the airport to congratulate her. Erika was on call that weekend, and she said she would wait to celebrate.

One morning soon after Chuck returned, Erika said she had to talk with him. He asked how soon. That day, she said. They met following the afternoon appointments. When Erika told Chuck what she had to say, he said merely, "That's too bad," and he asked when.

The three vets met at Murray's the next morning. They discussed patients and cases and business matters as usual. Chuck didn't say anything at breakfast about Erika's plans. But outside on the street after Erika had left for the clinic, Chuck handed Roger a slip of paper and said, "That's our ad for the new vet." The new third vet, he meant.

"That was his way of telling me," Roger said later. "It was probably the review."

Disappointment set in all around. When Erika told Chuck she was leaving, he had considered letting her go that very day. But he decided not to make a "command decision," as he put it, and he discussed it with Roger and Darcie. They wanted her to stay on until the end of July, to make the transition easier, for "stress relief." Roger's vacation was coming up, another trip to Alberta, so Chuck decided to keep Erika on, to get as much use out of her as he could, even though he had seen in the past that an associate who had given notice "can become a lame-duck associate very fast." They tended to stop caring about the practice, no longer identified with it, and refused to take on some cases. And he was right to a degree with Erika. Soon after she told Chuck she was interviewing elsewhere, she got out of her truck just as she was about to go on a series of calls one day, including a call to treat a sick pig, and went back inside, saying, "I don't know anything about pigs." She told Chuck she wouldn't take that call.

2.

"Chuck didn't seem surprised at all when I told him I was leaving," Erika said on the day she turned down the chance to work on a pig. She seemed surprised by his response. There was uncertainty in her reasoning, perhaps even evidence that she had wanted someone to change her mind. On the day before she talked to Chuck, she had left a folder with a résumé and application letter in the exam room, and though Chuck hadn't seen it, Darcie had. Later, when Chuck learned about it, he thought there had to be some element of unconscious behavior at work. Maybe this slip was just a way of starting the conversation. When Erika realized that she had left the folder behind, she decided she had to tell Chuck immediately.

She said that although things had come about very quickly, the decision had been a long time in developing. When Chuck was away, she had passed through a bad patch. She had read her journals and found them full of doubt, even about having become a veterinarian. She had visited the mixed-

practice veterinarian in Massachusetts and done some palpation with him. That day, free of the normal pressures, she
had reflected on her situation, and returned thinking primarily that there was more than one way to practice veterinary medicine. By the time of her review, Erika was already
considering looking into other positions.

"When I had the review with Chuck," Erika said, "he
didn't tell me I was doing a good job, and I needed to hear I
was doing a good job. I told him how hard it had been that
year, and that it would have been great if he told me I was doing a good job once in a while, and all he said was, 'Yup.' " A
day later she picked up a copy of the *AVMA Journal* and
looked at the employment ads. She found several openings in
Vermont, all within a two-hour drive of Walpole. She made
calls and sent letters. A week later she visited a clinic in Montpelier, and the owner asked her when she could start. She had
another appointment soon in Middlebury and another later in
the month in Shaftsbury.

"I'm not blaming Chuck," she said. "I have no ill will
against him. He is an honorable and decent person. But I
want something that Chuck calls hand-holding and that I call
mentoring, and Chuck was unable to give it. He was unable
to explain it, because he goes by instinct and doesn't explain."

She hadn't told Chuck or Roger one important detail: she
was applying at small-animal clinics.

"With the way I was feeling, I was questioning whether I
wanted to be a veterinarian. I kept asking myself, had I made
a mistake? That was too much to accept, too far-reaching a
conclusion after all I had invested. But I could say I wanted to
work with small animals, to leave the large-animal work behind.

"I can't be good at everything, so I have to do one or the
other, and I like working with people and pets. I like the rela-

tionship people have with their pets. I don't know when it changed, but suddenly I wasn't interested in palpating anymore. What used to be an interesting treasure hunt was suddenly just another butt to stick your arm up. And I don't like going into appointments smelling like cow shit."

You had to say that Chuck predicted that part of it.

"It would have been nice if I had known when I graduated that I wanted mentoring. Then I could have looked for it. I don't feel I was mistreated. But it's in the mentoring thing, and in the you're-doing-a-good-job thing. Sometimes we didn't talk to each other at all during a week."

She said, "I just want a change." And then, somewhat uneasily, "I only have twenty days left to work here."

Erika did a herd check at Echo Moon Farm that morning. Echo Moon was a sixty-cow dairy run meticulously by Tom and Sharleen Beaudry with some help from their children. Tom Beaudry had a graduate degree in herd management from Virginia Tech, and Sharleen kept watch over their cows the way some people watched over their pets. Their Holsteins all had names, oddball names like Eggs, Salad, or Baureen. Despite Chuck's concerns about Erika becoming a lame duck, the fact that he had sent her here was proof of his confidence in her.

Tom gathered the cows one by one and herded them to the parlor, where Sharleen took notes and worked with Erika.

"Do you want advice?" Erika asked.

"Sure," Sharleen said with a smile. "We can always use good advice."

"The uterus is enlarged, and there seems to be a follicle on the left ovary, but I'm not sure if she's coming in or going out of heat. We better check her again."

An hour of palpation, preg checks on half a dozen heifers, a wrestling match in the dehorning of a calf, and down the road on a day of calls—minus the pig.

3.

As Chuck stated it, not all breakups are pretty. Roger wasn't pleased that he had to learn of Erika's decision from Chuck. He had been to dinner at Erika's house during the week Chuck was away, and she hadn't said anything about leaving. In fact, she had talked about wanting to have three weeks off in the fall when she and Gary got married.

Erika also was beset with conflicting emotions. She felt that she was letting both Roger and Chuck down. But she also felt she had to defend herself. When she called Roger, four days after telling Chuck, Roger didn't hesitate to say he was disappointed. He said she had made him promise he would stay, and now she was leaving. He told her he had tried to help her out and show her things. In the heat of the moment Erika said that he hadn't shown her very much.

"That hurt," Roger later said, and he had called several friends to ease the pain and vent the anger. Roger soon told Chuck, with apologies, that he intended to stay away from the clinic and to avoid Erika as much as possible during the next month. Chuck said he was going to avoid her too, so as not to have a confrontation and say things he might regret.

Otherwise, things were going quite well for Roger. His breeding season had been more successful than the year before. He had collected Shawne nearly thirty times, and he had used the proceeds to buy land in Vermont a few miles north of Bellows Falls. He already had extensive plans for the site. The house would sit on a rise not far from the road, with pastures for his horses and good views into New Hampshire. Beyond the pastures lay a mature stand of oaks that he would have milled for the beams in his house, selling some of the wood to

pay for other materials. He had traded one of Shawne's foals
for the digging of a well. Shawne would be at the heart of the
business Roger would run there, and he had devised a name
for the enterprise—Cross Border Performance Horses. He
wouldn't be doing this alone. During the trip he was about to
make to Alberta, he would take along an engagement ring and
propose on horseback to Danelle Philbrook.

"Just fine for a Vermont horse farm," Roger said late one
afternoon, beer in hand, as he leaned against his truck at the
edge of the pasture. "We'll have lots of babies here."

He described his plans, and the light changed, and the day
lengthened, and the pasture seemed to fill with grazing animals. But dreams give pause, and Roger also mulled over
Erika's departure and what he thought it represented.

"You know, women vets are the big thing now," he said.
"It's someone like Erika, Phi Beta Kappa, the good grades—
that gets into vet school. And then decides that she may have
made a mistake.

"I have never questioned becoming a vet. Not once. Never
questioned a day of work, never not wanted to go in. I knew I
wanted to be a vet from the time I was a kid, but almost
didn't get into vet school. I was turned down twice. I was on
the alternate list and then got called in at the beginning of the
term. Then I graduated at the top of my class, in the top ten,
once I figured out how to play the game. Because of people
like her, some poor bastard like me, some dumb farm boy
wanted to be a vet his whole life, couldn't get into vet school.

"All this business I have, the equine practice, I had to work
for it. The truth is, you don't get something from nothing.
You have to go out and get it. You just don't get something
from nothing. It doesn't happen.

"I showed her how to do surgeries. I showed her how to

amputate a dog's leg just last week. I was going to show her how to castrate a horse just a few days ago, but she took so long getting there, I had to do it without her."

Then came the cases and exchanges that lifted the spirits. A man named Ed Fielders arrived at the clinic to pay a bill, and asked to see Roger. Fielders was one of Roger's favorite clients—an ex-con and a preacher, he had a pet wild turkey that Roger had worked on and a motley collection of other animals. One time Fielders had brought an old orphaned dog in for an exam, telling Roger, "I didn't need him, but the good Lord decided that he needed me."

In the reception room, Fielders told Roger that he had two new quarter horses. One was a mare, the other a gelding. "That gelding wants to go everywhere with me," Fielders exclaimed. "He will even leap over the fence to get beside me. You should come out and see him, Roger. Bring your saddle and ride him."

"I'll bring my saddle, and you can ride him," Roger said with a laugh.

"That gelding marched in the Peach Blossom parade, with Clint Eastwood on him. I didn't believe it until his last owner showed me a photo of Clint Eastwood sitting on that horse. And that mare, she must have been a barrel racer, because she's so agile."

"How's Loretta?" Roger asked. Loretta was the name of the pet turkey.

"She's doing fine," Fielders said, turning to me. "I rescued her. When she came to me, she was nearly plucked clean. I took care of her, fed her, and brought her back to health. She follows me around wherever I go. If I work on the car, I'll look up and she will be right there sitting and looking at me. She talks to me. I got kind of attached to her, so when the horse stepped on her leg, I had to do something about it. I couldn't just put her down. Roger did the surgery."

There was a photo in one of the albums in the reception room of Roger doing this surgery. Wearing a bonnet, he stood beside a turkey laid out on the table, the feathers plucked from her leg. Roger had put a pin in Loretta's leg.

"She calls in the wild ones, brings them right into the yard. She had twelve of them in there the other day. I keep quiet about it, though. Don't want people to know. Someone like Roger might come in and shoot her. He'll get a load of buckshot in his ass he does that." Roger laughed again.

Fielders said he had written a book about his life, and that it had come to him whole, over a period of three days. It was titled *The Death and Life of Eddie Bananas*—his pseudonym in his life of crime. His was a story of confinement, conversion, and resurrection. "It's been to prisons everywhere," he said of his book. "It's about what I learned in those forty-foot walls, about what I used to be. When I was in there, we had a conversation, and I know He's there. How is it that I can lay my hands down and heal an ankle in five minutes?"

He had needed Roger to heal Loretta, though.

"Roger and I both treat animals. The only difference between him and me is that he's got money and I don't."

Fielders paid his bill and headed out to his beat-up car, where an old dog was waiting in the backseat. He said, "Animals can tell when you've got the spirit."

4.

Chuck was on call the weekend after Erika gave notice. On Saturday he put to sleep a dog named Bo Kelly. Bo Kelly was well known in his neighborhood. He made his rounds, visiting houses and getting treats, which had been at the root of a weight problem, Chuck said.

Bo had returned the many kindnesses. During one of his visits he came upon an elderly neighbor who had fallen in his garden and couldn't get up. The neighbor told Bo to go home and get his owner, and Bo did as he was told, found Jim Kelly in the yard, and began barking at him. Finally Jim said, "What's the problem?" and followed Bo to the neighbor, who said, "What took you so long? I sent Bo off a half hour ago." When the neighbor later became bedridden, Bo had visited regularly, climbing up on the bed and taking naps with him.

Chuck joined Jim and Jane Kelly for Bo's final hour, made the house call that made the Kellys grateful, was there when Kelly said, "Good-bye, my friend."

On Friday night a severe HBC came in. Chuck was about to have dinner when he got paged. Two dogs had run into the road in front of a truck. One had died. The other, a young golden retriever, had gotten his jaw crushed and mangled underneath the tire. It was an exposed fracture, with one part of the jaw draped below the other. His name was Merlin, and he was going to need some magic. Chuck spent from 9:30 to 11 p.m. getting Merlin stabilized. Then he went home and had dinner with Ellie.

After Saturday's appointments, Chuck repaired Merlin's jaw, piecing it back together with wires. Chuck told the owner the tire had to have gone right over Merlin's nose. But though the dog's right canine tooth was gone and his blackened tongue would always hang out of the gap, making him look a little goofy, he would be okay. When Chuck finished the surgery, Merlin, from the depths of the anesthesia, expressed his appreciation by peeing all over him, so Chuck had to go home and clean up.

On Sunday, Merlin's owners came to visit. Chuck told the kennel worker to take them all into the back room so that Merlin could have a bath, and he careened along beside them, game but wobbly. A half hour later, bathed and dried, Merlin would have to be dragged back into his cage by his owner, and he whined terribly for a while after they left. He stopped when Tony, the high school girl, climbed into the cage and fed him by hand.

Chuck said, "Could you imagine one of us getting up and walking around two days after getting mangled by a car?"

"We're bags of jelly, aren't we?" I said.

"Precisely."

Later, sitting on his porch, Chuck talked about the reviews he'd given Erika and Roger.

"I told her I would be taking a hard line, and focus on areas where she could improve. Should I have given her more strokes? I don't know. I'm not particularly known for giving strokes. I tend to be harsh."

The categories consisted of Personal and General Skills, Communication, Surgical Skills, Record Keeping, Examinations, and Management and Marketing.

For Erika, most of Chuck's criticisms were for time management and confidence issues. "I told her that she was slow on surgeries. It took her a whole morning to do a spay and castration the other day. She disagreed and said there was no reason to go any faster. I told her she should be taking on more surgeries, that a first-year vet should do surgeries until they're blue in the face.

"I also told her that she takes too much time writing records. She goes by the SOAPS method, which means you organize information in four sections—subjective, then objective, an assessment, and a plan. When I said it takes too long to read her reports, she said to just go to the assessment, that she did this and this and this. My response was to let it go, to not bug her about it any further."

Because Chuck hadn't known of the feelings Erika brought to the review, his perspective was far different from hers. He thought they would be negotiating a salary increase, while she was waiting for praise.

"I thought she was going to ask for a raise, but she didn't. We talked about percentages, and about how Roger gets ten percent of everything he brings in over $10,000 a month. My goal is to have an associate earning her own money on a commission basis as an incentive in the second year. Erika grossed $128,000 for services last year, but that's not really accurate, because she started on June 14. The fiscal year starts on June 1, so Erika's year was two weeks short. I told her that Roger and I grossed about $175,000 each last year. I told her that, and I told her not to worry about it. But she was very upset about that part of it."

Chuck said that Erika had scored higher than Roger in several categories. Roger scored higher in surgical skills and time management, but she outranked him in communication skills and client interactions during exams. "Erika is a team player," Chuck said. "Roger has no interest in buying into the practice."

Chuck pointed out that Roger had responded to the review quite differently. He had tossed the review on the table after they were done and said, "Whatever. Let's talk about the money," which Chuck found amusing.

In Chuck's mind, Erika's decision to leave had seemed irrational, but the experience had been useful. "It has shown me that we can run this as a three-vet practice. I took a hit financially last year, but it was worth it because Ellie and I could do things together. My mental health has never been better than this last year. What this has done is to make me determined to replace her, even if it is hard to find replacements."

5.

Before Erika had even been hired, Chuck had predicted that she might grow tired of cow work and smelling like manure, and might leave. Ann Bruner's prediction for her daughter had also come true—that after a slow climb and a long self-doubt phase, something would fall into place, like getting up and walking. And it had been a feeling thing, as Ann said, largely an intuitive thing.

Erika took a job in Montpelier, at the Onion River Animal Hospital. The practice was owned by Colleen Bloom, a veterinarian with eighteen years of experience. Bloom had two associates, both women, each with eight years' experience. "Four doctors there," Erika said, now including herself.

"The level of communication is high. There will be lots of good mentoring. There are always two doctors at the clinic at all times, so I'll always be with another doctor. On Fridays they have doctors' rounds, when they meet to discuss cases. I sat in on them when I went there, and I was grinning from ear to ear the whole time. Nothing is perfect, but I think this will be a much better fit."

Onion River fell into the category of a high-end small-animal clinic, with lengthy thirty-minute appointments that suited Erika's approach. She would get a salary increase there, while her work hours would decrease. With four doctors, she would be on call one night during the week and every fourth weekend.

But it would be only small animals, all cats and dogs— wouldn't she miss working with large animals, and with cows?

"Right now I don't know if I'm going to miss it. I suppose I could always go back to it if I did. But I'm tired of going out and not knowing what I'm doing. Tired of faking it. I don't know any more about cow diseases than I did a year ago. It's always just pneumonia or a DA, milk fever or a few other things. Cows have just as many diseases as we do, but the economics don't allow us to go any further. You can't go and look up the diseases of cows, read the research, because it's not there. I feel like I've just been throwing steroids and antibiotics at them.

"Now it will be much more about the animals and less about herd health. I felt I had to make a choice, large or small, and get good at one. I didn't want to give up dogs or cats. There are differences in the feelings you get between seeing clients with cats and dogs and palpating cows all day. There's not much satisfaction in palpation. I lost interest in it once I got good at it. At Onion River I will have more of a chance to do more interesting diagnostics."

Though it was generally observed that Erika became more cheerful and relaxed after she decided to leave and found a job, the three vets kept their distance during her last days. Their interactions tended to be formal, sometimes with undercurrents of resentment. Once, when Erika was treating a dog for a uterine infection, she asked Chuck what he thought she should do, and he told her. Not liking or agreeing with what Chuck said, she turned to Roger and asked the same question. Roger had overheard what Chuck said, and he repeated the recommendation word for word. During her last on-call weekend she called Chuck several times to tell him of cases she couldn't or wouldn't handle.

On her last day, Chuck and Roger met at Murray's, but Erika wasn't there and hadn't been for the past several weeks.

She did the full range of work that day, however, starting with surgeries, moving on to appointments, and finishing with calls. Her first surgery of the day was to remove a small growth from the eyelid of a poodle and then another golf ball–size growth from his rear leg. She proceeded without hesitation, assisted by Darcie.

"The light is at the end of the tunnel," Erika said, "but the tunnel isn't ending. I can't wait until it's over."

Hobbs was wandering around, feeling restless it seemed. He appeared at the door and caught Erika's eye. "Ah, it's great to be king," she said. Hobbs was having a difficult day too. He'd bitten Carol, so she had put him in the staff room and closed the door. When someone let him out, he went out front again at the start of office hours, and when Carol saw a little girl starting to get interested in Hobbs, she brought him back again and told the others to keep him out of there.

When Erika was suturing up the poodle, Carol came back and said that a client would be coming in with a dog for euthanasia. Erika said they should put a muzzle on the dog. There was some discussion about the size of the muzzle that should be used. Carol called the owner, who said that if he didn't have the right size muzzle, he would duct-tape the dog's mouth.

"He must be having a hard time," Erika said.

Soon the owner arrived. He was a dairy worker at one of the farms Chuck serviced. The dog was a tawny-colored cur, short-haired, with a wrinkled face. She was muzzled and leashed, and she was terrified. The owner said, "She had her first heat at age three and has been aggressive ever since. She bit me last night, grabbed onto the back of my leg. She had twelve puppies last month. I've got other dogs, and she just can't fit in."

He held her while Erika prepared a sedative. "This will calm her down," she said.

"Okay," the owner said. Erika gave the injection, and then asked him to put her into a cage. The dog didn't want to go, but he pushed her in.

"This will take a few minutes," she said.

The owner said okay again, but he'd had enough, and he left.

"They're hunting dogs," Darcie said of the cur. "The owner said this one killed a raccoon at eight months. They hunt bears too. We had one that came in a while ago, a nice dog. His ears were in shreds, and there were claw marks on his side. The owner said, 'Don't worry about that.' "

Erika went to the cage door and opened it, crouched down and started talking softly. She patted the dog and ran her hand along her side. The cur looked about as worried as a dog could be. But Erika kept talking to her for several minutes while the sedative took effect.

Chuck came in wearing shorts, an old T-shirt, and rubber boots. He was about to leave for a herd check. He walked up to Erika and said, "Are you going to leave the keys to the truck?"

"Yeah," Erika replied, keeping her eyes on the dog.

"What about the keys to the building?"

"I'll leave it all tonight."

"Okay, see you later." He turned and left.

Erika kept stroking the cur. "I'm ready," she said, and led her out to the open floor. "She's not wanting to settle down." The dog looked frantic, thoroughly anxious.

"Darcie, do you want to help?"

Darcie crouched over the dog and held off the vein in her foreleg. Erika inserted the needle, pulled back some blood, and pushed.

Darcie did something very thoughtful then. She laid the dog's chin on the floor, as if she were sleeping. It gave the poor worried cur some dignity. It certainly made it easier to look at her.

Erika got up and washed her hands. She recorded the euthanasia solution in the ledger. Carol announced that the first appointment was in, and Erika was ready. Soon she came out of the exam room with a little black-and-white cat and gave her some shots. Darcie helped with this too.

"Little ball of kitty," Erika said.

"Kittens are the best," Darcie said.

Myra J. Perkins Cray was this kitten's name.

"That's a lot of name for such a little girl," Darcie said as she held her.

The next appointment was with a golden retriever owned by a woman who found him at the Humane Society. Erika was typically thorough. She looked his skin over and his ears, which were stinky. She brought him out back to have his ears cleaned. She told the owner he had skin problems, and she recommended a shampoo. She said they would do a heartworm test. She said she would put him on steroids and antibiotics. She explained the problems with the skin and the ears. "The ears are just an extension of the skin," she said. And she would take a scraping for mites.

After the appointments and before she went out on calls, there was a going-away party for Erika. Carol had made a cake. It was a "girl's party," as Darcie called it, with Carol, Lynn, Darcie, and Ellie present. They talked about Erika's wedding, coming up in three months. There was a card with several signatures, all girls too. Ellie had signed, "Thanks for giving us a year, and good luck." They said good luck to Erika as she sat in front of the cake and read the card.

Erika worked on sheep that afternoon and vaccinated calves at two dairy farms.

"I gave up early and stopped talking about everything," she

said on the way to the first call. "That happened months before the review. Gary said to me, 'You have to talk to him,' but I gave up because I was afraid of what Chuck would say. It went back to September, right after September 11, when I went into the clinic. I told Chuck that I was really stressed out, that I wanted to stay home, that I didn't care, that I was feeling overwhelmed. He blew up at me and said I wasn't the only one who had problems and that I had to buck up. I know that I can in no way understand how he felt, that there are things he went through in the war that made him feel especially affected by September 11. I know I shouldn't have taken it personally, but I did take it personally. I couldn't go to him and tell him my feelings after that."

You could wonder whether gender differences played into this communication impasse. If you viewed it in the terms that Carin Smith outlined during the AVMA convention and subsequently in the *Journal*, women tend to undervalue themselves, while men tend to overvalue. Under that scenario, one party was asking for support in the form of praise, while the other party was offering support in the form of "don't worry, you'll be all right." One was perhaps undervaluing herself and looking for a boost. The other party was perhaps refusing to undervalue and offering reassurance in the form of outcome. Definition asked for, result given.

Or perhaps it had nothing to do with gender or any other generalities. Maybe it was just a matter of individual personalities or of differing backgrounds not fitting precisely. Or self-reliance, self-confidence, and maturity—issues in the process of becoming.

Erika drove through the center of Charlestown and then east into the hills. She went along a back road to a place with a small farmhouse behind a grove of lilacs. Across the road from the house was a paddock with two hefty white Charolais cows. Behind the house, spreading up a hillside, were a set of pastures, some barns and pens, and about two hundred sheep.

The place was owned by a Mrs. Lord, who soon came out and began talking with Erika about the farming operation she and her husband were developing—wool and meat, on land that had been used to raise sheep two centuries ago, as it happened. She said they were worried about the economics of their endeavor, and that the bank was worried too.

First Erika vaccinated half a dozen sheep, holding them wriggling between her knees while she gave the injections. These sheep would go with Mrs. Lord's children to the summer fairs and take part in 4-H competitions. Then Erika followed her to the lower pasture to vaccinate a ram—the younger ram, who would soon be siring the next generation. The woolly and venerable fellow stood nearby, round as a barrel, under a pocked apple tree.

There was much discussion between Mrs. Lord and Erika about sheep diseases and precautions to be taken. The discussion continued as Erika gave shots to the family's three dogs and a cat. The first to come under attention was an old adopted dog who had been abused, Mrs. Lord said, a stunted husky cross who howled from the moment they touched her. Erika next tended to a slender Rottweiler, another rescue case, who was playmate to the third dog, a border collie getting his first rabies shot. This dog would be a sheepdog, Mrs. Lord hoped, because she was tired of herding sheep by herself.

Erika explained about the perils of distemper, heartworm, and rabies, and of letting dogs wander, since they were more likely to contract ailments and get into trouble. Then Mrs. Lord's daughter ran inside the house to get her Siamese kitten. She brought out the little wide-eyed gray-and-brown cat and held her while Erika listened with her stethoscope. The girl was tall, about five ten, and athletic-looking, with the gait and firm shoulders of a basketball player. She hadn't given the cat a name yet. Erika said, "Don't you have something you call her, like Cabbagehead or something?"

The girl thought for a moment. "Gingerbread," she said.

"That's a good name. You hold Gingerbread while I give her this injection."

Erika talked to the girl and Mrs. Lord about the increased incidence of distemper among wandering cats, and the importance of an early spay in averting mammary tumors, and other matters, adding, "If you have any questions, don't hesitate to ask."

While Erika talked, something seemed to happen to the girl. She looked Erika up and down, looked at the coveralls with the yellow symbol on them, at the stethoscope draped over her neck, at the face with the reddish hair swept back, at the silver earrings. The girl's eyes widened, and her mouth went slack as she stared at Erika, stared at her as if she were the most fascinating thing she had ever seen.

Like she was something to be.

On the way to her last call, to vaccinate calves, Erika remembered two cases that she considered milestones. One was a cat named Lucky who'd had conjunctivitis. The owner had been willing to pursue treatments. Erika had finally referred him to Rowley Hospital in Massachusetts. "I did a lot of research. The opthalmologist at Rowley said he thought I was doing a bang-up job. The owner was happy with the treatment. He took the cat to Rowley once a month for three months. I got to see her again a month ago, and she was happy, with good eyes."

The other case involved a rectal prolapse in a dairy cow. "I was told only that there was something sticking out of the butt. I didn't know at first if the problem was in the vulva or the anal area. But I read up on it, went out, scrubbed her up, and sewed her up, to a good outcome. It was a case where I was faking it, and it worked out all right.

"I don't think there's anything wrong with winging it. I'm willing to wing it more than some. You just have to be aware of how far you go, that you don't become unethical."

At Barrett's, Erika vaccinated about twenty calves against several viruses. Peter Barrett came by while she was working and said to her, "I hear you're leaving us. It's been good to have you coming around. Good luck in your next job."

"Thanks," Erika said.

She worked down the line, injecting the calves, clamping on ear tags, and giving tattoos. When she reached the end of the line, she said, "This might be the last cow I ever vaccinate."

This reminded her of her last track meet in college, she said. Suddenly she wasn't ready to be done. "I like cows. I really like cows. I like farmers too. It's been a real macho thing, to say you were a cow vet."

When she returned to the clinic, she encountered Chuck, just back from his herd check and about to do appointments. Erika asked him if he needed to have anything done. "I'm right on schedule," Chuck said, and disappeared into the exam room.

As the day ended, Erika drove to the car wash in Westminster, about a mile away, and washed the truck.

"Then I said good-bye to it," she reported later. "I said I hoped the next person to drive it took good care of it. It looked great. Hadn't been washed since I got it. I took it home, back to the clinic. Chuck was working on an Irish setter, owned by one of Lynn's friends. I said 'Good-bye, I hope you find someone good.' And then I left."

EPILOGUE

1.

With Erika's departure, the Walpole Veterinary Hospital returned to being a two-vet practice, for the time being. Chuck took his vacation after Erika left, and Roger ran the practice solo for ten days. Ginny Prince had not yet resumed her Fridays at the clinic.

Another ad appeared in the *AVMA Journal*, but responses were few. The first was from a woman who had been working as a large-animal vet, primarily with horses, in northern New Hampshire. Roger spent a day with her and was impressed with her abilities. He had decided he would be easily impressed. The fact that she was breathing was enough for him, he said. Chuck was more skeptical. Though she said she could refresh her small-animal skills with some applied study, he decided not to hire her. He said he just wasn't ready to begin a training period of that kind.

Following another successful breeding season, Roger and Shawne entered various horse shows. He and Danelle took Shawne to the New England Quarter Horse Show, held in

Keene. Shawne was quite an attention-getter, with his English tack, his color, and his stature, and he would have placed high in the hunter-and-jumper category had he not let loose with a mighty kick while showing for the judge. And Roger, a western-saddle rider all his life, had under Danelle's influence made the transition to English style. He wore the jodhpurs and helmet, and he had begun taking lessons in dressage and jumping at a stable in Massachusetts. They were a pair, those two, and a striking sight to anyone who beheld them.

But at the end of that summer, tragedy struck.

Roger saw Shawne lie down in his stall. The horse seemed to be in abdominal pain. Roger took Shawne out and walked him, but he was still uncomfortable. After Roger put Shawne on a lunge line and trotted him in a circle, Shawne collapsed, rolling on his back and kicking at the air. Roger knew things were bad then. He called Chuck to come and help, and he also called Ted Johnson, another equine veterinarian who lived in Walpole. They did what they could, but Shawne worsened, and his pain increased. Really worried now, Roger decided to take him to the emergency equine clinic in Manchester, Vermont, where there was a vet who specialized in equine surgery. They pushed Shawne into a trailer, and Roger rushed off, with Danelle's father, Jeff Philbrook, at the wheel. Chuck watched them go. He felt sure that Shawne wouldn't make it.

Roger knew too. He had seen horses in this condition more times than he could remember, but he had never seen a colic as severe as Shawne's. As the surgeon in Manchester was about to put Shawne under anesthesia, he died. The surgeon opened him up anyway, and when Roger saw how black his guts were, he knew how bad the pain must have been. He could watch for only a few minutes. He cut Shawne's tail off, as a keepsake, and left.

He didn't sleep at all that night, but he went into work the next morning, with red-rimmed eyes, saying it would do him no good to sit home and think about it. He went out on calls, with Dexter curled up next to him in the truck, as always.

"Shawne brought me so much," Roger said. "He was responsible for my reputation, for everything I've got going with horses. He got me the land and the house. He brought me more than any person has. Shawne always came through for me. Whatever I asked him to do, he always came through. I can't believe he's gone."

Roger had so often reassured and consoled. Now an outpouring of condolences came from the clients. At one stable a client threw her arms around him. Just a year before, Roger had put down a beloved Connemara pony for her and then helped bury the horse on a hillside behind the barn. Calls came in to the clinic throughout the day. Jane Fitzwilliam called, crying, when she heard, and later she came by and dropped off a gift, a dandelion-scented candle—for spring, she said.

Spring seemed to be the best mantra. It was important to consider spring. Roger had four broodmares successfully inseminated by Shawne. "I think I'll keep all the babies," Roger said. "Maybe one will be a black one."

In March came a little colt named Rascal, born to Holly, the bay who had already produced two Shawne colts. In April came a very long-legged colt named Legacy—Legs for short—and that summer he proved to be quite the athlete, jumping stumps in his pasture during the race for the grain pail. Legs might be the best bet for a replacement, and Roger thought that at the least he would send him back to Alberta for his brother Duncan to stud. In May, Danelle's mare produced a colt, and in June the mare from Thunder Bay produced a filly. Though Roger no longer had Shawne, by midsummer he had a wealth of horses—six of Shawne's foals, ten horses in all.

Horses bring love, and they bring heartbreak. Jane Fitz-william's mare foaled a Shawne baby that spring, a beautiful and affectionate little filly, but the mare collicked and died when the foal was six weeks old. Mother to the end, she kept trying to get up to nurse her daughter, Jane said. She called Roger, of course, and after several hours of tending to the mare, he put her down, talking Jane all the way through it. Too heartbroken to keep the filly, and also concerned that she would panic in the stall where her mother had been, Jane asked Roger to take the filly home and pair her with her year-old half sister. Within a day they were inseparable. It was decided that at least for the next year, the two would stay together. Jane's opinion of Roger soared now. "That man has wings," she said. "Don't take this the wrong way, but men don't always understand pain. That man understands."

Chuck put it a little differently. "That man can do all the horse work he wants now." He spoke true. In the coming year, Roger's horse practice would double. In Shawne's last season, twenty-one mares were successfully inseminated, and twenty-one live foals were born the following spring. There were places around Walpole now where you could occasionally hear a whinny quite similar to the magnificent one that used to rise at Roger's place.

In the meantime, Roger and Danelle were married in Wal-pole in August, holding the service in a church on the town common, with the reception in the town hall across the way. Danelle arrived at the church with her wedding party in a wagon pulled by Jen Schreiter's draft horses. Many of the big farms were represented, not only because of Roger's work, but because Danelle was the granddaughter of a dairy farmer who had once been the manager of Boggy Meadow. There was also a healthy contingent of owners of Shawne's sons and daugh-ters, and a delegation from the ranch country of Alberta, of course. Among the last of the photos taken on the common, after others had left for the reception, was a shot of the bride in her white wedding dress, surrounded by three men—the groom, his father, and his brother—wearing black tuxedos and black cowboy hats.

Roger and Danelle honeymooned in the Canadian Rockies, visited the Osinchuk ranch, and then moved into their new house in Vermont, with the new oak beams and the view of the pastures. Roger entered his fifth year with the practice, the longest tenure of any of Chuck's associates. He felt that he could sustain the two-vet rotation for the time being. But he knew that once he had children, it would be impossible to continue with the brisk demands of a mixed practice without relief.

2.

In Montpelier, Erika and Gary moved into a house that was painted, strangely enough, fuchsia and blue. After two months she and Gary returned to Walpole to have their wedding, and they also held their reception, as well as the ceremony, in the town hall. Erika looked stunning in her white dress, with her hair up. Gary's family made wine in the Portuguese tradition—Rocha wine, they called it—and there was a bottle on every table. Several young vets were in attendance, and many friends, with lots of dancing and, for Erika, a surprising feeling of ease. She said it was the happiest day of her life.

As for her job, she seemed indeed to have found the right practice.

Not long after beginning at Onion River, she came in and was told by one of the other vets that she would be doing a spay that morning. As she walked away, she heard one of them say in jest, "and it's a gastroplexy"—a procedure somewhat similar to a DA. Erika merely said, "Okay," and continued toward the surgery. They told her they were kidding and said, "Erika, you're unflappable!" Erika replied, "It must be the large-animal thing." Later she reported, "I thought it was funny that they would say that I'm unflappable, when Chuck and Roger probably think the opposite."

The clinic at Onion River was in a converted barn attached to a farmhouse. Though you wouldn't describe the treatment areas and surgery as cramped, space was limited. There was an office in a corner of the X-ray room. On one particular day several people were working there—two veterinarians, a veterinary student performing a castration, two veterinary technicians, and a receptionist coming and going—but the mood was relaxed and cooperative.

Erika said that she had found the kind of mentoring she wanted. "There's lots of talk about cases here. It's not an in-your-face type of mentorship. It's just that I always feel I can talk to them. They have a philosophy of shared cases. It's not just me wanting help. Everybody wants help from other people. And I'm never alone, because of the structure of the practice. I don't have to get into a situation where I don't know what I'm doing."

But she acknowledged that her experience in Walpole had made her stronger. "I gained confidence there because I had to do stuff on my own and be on my own a lot of the time. Sometimes it was so crazy, though, when the beeper would go off and the message would be something like, 'One dead cow at the Graves's, another on the ground, come quick.'

"When I got to Onion River, they said one time, 'Okay, we're gonna leave you alone for a day, is that okay?' I said, 'Sure, I can handle that.' Now, when I'm the only one here, when there are those times, I can usually handle it."

One weekend when Erika was on call, a dog came in, bleeding at both ends. She asked the owner questions—had the dog done this or that—while she examined him and wondered what to do. She had begun to put a catheter in when, "bing, a light went on, and I thought, Hemorrhagic gastroenteritis. I suddenly knew what it was. I knew I had to replace fluids and to move blood. He was dehydrated. By the next morning he was feeling great."

The interesting thing about it, Erika said, was that she was already doing what she needed to be doing—putting a catheter in—before she had worked out the diagnosis. She had learned about the condition at school, and then suddenly remembered it and could look up the treatment for it.

A good example of diagnostic thinking, you could say.

On another case, her mixed-practice experience came into good use. Though Onion River was a small-animal clinic, someone brought in a sick lamb and asked that it be treated. Erika was there, and she thought, Here's something I might know that nobody else does. She quickly saw that the lamb was dehydrated and chilled and that it needed a jugular catheter. She administered it, and soon the lamb was better.

In her second year of practice, Erika had begun to do more advanced surgeries. She had removed the ball joint from a dog's hip in preparation for a hip replacement. She had done an enucleation, the removal of an eyeball.

"I'm happy here, in large part," she said. "I still have issues over confidence stuff. The amount of time it takes to be a good practitioner is huge. I'm still trying to balance work and the rest of my life. I'm trying to keep up with the profession through continuing education courses. That helps build confidence too.

"What I liked about mixed practice was that salt-of-the-earth thing, that Herriot thing. I still miss that. I miss seeing the cows. I wanted to be everything for everybody, but you can't do everything. With mixed practice, I think it would be better if the practice were divided into specialties, with each person keeping up with a particular specialty. The profession has changed. Thirty or forty years ago a vet was pretty well prepared when graduating from vet school. Now you aren't. You know how to look things up."

She was about to have her first annual review. "When we had the one at six months, we ate Thai food in my boss's living room and she told me what I should do to improve. Such as, be a better manager out back, do a better job out there. That was hard in the beginning, but now it's getting easier. You get to be more confident. It's difficult for a first-year vet because you're not confident and you don't want to pretend. It's starting to seem a little less improbable that I can do this, and do a good job."

3.

Hobbs continued to amaze. One day when Chuck was trying to put down a very elderly Labrador retriever who had low blood pressure and fragile veins, a vein tore, and Chuck left momentarily to prepare another injection. Darcie and Lynn remained crouched down with the dog on the treatment-room floor.

Hobbs had been watching. Suddenly he ran up, pushed his head under Lynn's arm, and pressed his nose to the nose of the Lab. He remained like that for a moment, nose to nose with the old dog, before turning and running off.

"Was that weird?" Darcie asked.

"That was weird," Lynn said.

4.

When Erika joined the practice, Chuck had followed through on his intention to join the local school board. He enjoyed the intellectual challenge of thinking through problems of education and school funding. It posed another form of diagnostic thinking. When Erika's departure threw him back into the two-vet rotation, he didn't resign from the board. In fact, he was elected chairman.

As spring approached, Chuck interviewed two students about to graduate from Tufts. One was very green, Chuck thought, and he told her not to consider taking the job unless she could promise to stay for two years. The other candidate seemed like a good fit. He had grown up in New Hampshire and had worked at a neighbor's dairy farm throughout his youth. But his fiancée didn't want to move from the coastal region to rural Walpole, so he took a position elsewhere.

Then Chuck learned that a vet whom he had interviewed before Erika was hired—the student who wanted more bovine work and moved to northern Vermont—had lasted a year before moving to a small-animal clinic twenty miles from Walpole. Normally, Chuck would not have contacted someone already employed at another practice, but here he felt entitled, since the man had interviewed with him before. This didn't work out either. The vet had bought a house, and his wife, with two young children, had little enthusiasm for living under the demands of a mixed-practice schedule.

A year passed, and the ad remained in the *Journal*. Communications with veterinary schools also brought no results. Finally, as another season approached, Chuck decided to advertise for a small-animal position. Roger urged him on. They worked out a plan for handling the large-animal calls themselves while sharing the small-animal work with the new person in a three-vet rotation. The new ad mentioned the possibility of a share in ownership of the practice.

Chuck eventually hired one of his former associates, Laura Ladds. She had recently left a small-animal practice in Keene. Ladds had preceded Roger at Walpole Veterinary Hospital, and for four years handled the on-call work bravely until it wore her down. She was very interested in returning to the practice to do just small-animal medicine. She also liked the prospect of working for Chuck again. "What you get with him is honesty," she said after she began. "You get someone who tells it like it is. I've come to appreciate that."

One weekend a nine-month-old golden retriever was brought in for euthanasia. He was an energetic, playful, and perpetually grateful dog with no health or behavioral problems, but his owner had recently had a baby, and as Chuck put it, "She didn't know what to do with the dog anymore. But we won't kill him." Two weeks later they adopted him out.

Another case that weekend was a sixteen-year-old cat named Alpha Richards that had come in for treatment of a kidney problem. A tiger tabby, Alpha had the bleary-eyed look of a kidney cat. Chuck gave her subcutaneous fluids in an attempt to keep her going. He wanted to keep her going. Chuck had an affection for Alpha, born of many years of treating her.

Alpha had been spayed when she was six months old, and she'd been given the usual rounds of rabies shots, feline leukemia shots, and boosters. Over the years she had been treated for coughing, bleeding from her ears, and various wounds. For quite an extensive period in her middle years she had been treated for abscesses and skin lesions, with biopsies taken and consultations made for a chronic inability to heal her wounds. After two years, however, her health had changed, and she had improved substantially, and the sore that wouldn't heal suddenly did. Later she entered another chronic period and was treated for weight loss, anorexia, and chronic vomiting. She passed through this too, and her coat became shiny again. Late in life as an elderly cat, her teeth were cleaned and a tooth was extracted. Finally Alpha went into kidney failure.

Chuck suspected that Alpha was near the end, and sure enough, a few days later her owners would come in to be present for her euthanasia.

But this weekend, Chuck was just treating Alpha, hoping to keep her alive a little longer. Nothing fancy, just fluids and antibiotics and attentive care. Making a note on the card in her thick file, which ran to more than thirty pages, Chuck gave a terse take on their relationship.

"I owe this cat a lot," he said.

What you owed, how you paid, these were important things.

ACKNOWLEDGMENTS

First and foremost I would like to thank Chuck Shaw for giving me access to his clinic and for allowing me to tell the story in the way I thought best. He spoke his mind and made no demands. My thanks to Ellie Shaw as well, for her stories about the clinic and her role as veterinarian's wife.

Roger Osinchuk went out of his way to give me many opportunities to observe him at work, and he talked openly about his professional life and aspirations. It was a pleasure to watch Roger interact with animals, especially with horses.

When I began going to the clinic, I didn't know that Erika Bruner would arrive at some point, but when she did, she gave this book greater dimension. Articulate, knowledgeable, and expressive, she let me know what was going on inside, right from the tender first day. It's not easy to have someone next to you, carrying a notebook, during the beginning days of a career, but Erika seemed happy for the company. I hope I listened well enough.

Many thanks to Darcie Sprague, Laurel Gibbs, Lynn Hayes, Carol Zachary, Susan Armstrong, Jennifer Schreiter, Deb Dupell, Nicole Reinhart, Nicole Guerriere, Jennifer Wilson, Ben Chaffee, Kat McClenning, Tony Firenze, Carolyne LaCerte, Marrie Macri, Amelia Bacigalupo, Jessica Foreman, Karen Smith, and Laura Ladds. Thanks also to Shirley and Richard Osinchuk, and to Ann Bruner, for their comments and information.

I would like to thank the many dairy farmers, animal owners, and clients who talked with me and provided many stories, more than I could possibly use.

Dr. Frank Krohn told me about his work and provided articles about veterinary medicine. Dr. Julio Malnati talked about his early years in the profession working in the field of bovine uterine palpation when that skill was first being taught in the vet schools. Gail McManus of the New Hampshire Department of Agriculture provided useful information about dairy farming in New Hampshire. Kate Murphy spent time retrieving various articles on veterinary education and other subjects. Barbara Berman, at Tufts University, offered information about veterinary students and their careers. Dr. Carin Smith sent me a draft of her article about the role of women in the veterinary profession that later appeared in the *AVMA Journal*. Dr. Phyllis Larsen of the Association for Women Veterinarians provided information and a copy of their history, *Women in Veterinary Medicine*.

This book probably would not have come to be if it hadn't been for my friendship with Bob Graves, and I'll thank him here for allowing me for two winters to feed his oxen when I lived near his family's dairy farm. Titan, Presidente, Te Amo, and Bauza will long live in my memory (though Bob called both pairs Duke and Dime, easy names for working pairs). When Bob had to be away for two weeks, I also had the chance to feed the calves at Great Brook Farm, going to the milk parlor each morning to get a bucket of milk for them and giving some of that milk to the barn cats. It was during one of those trips to the parlor that Peter Graves asked me if I wanted to help pull a calf. I agreed and spent one of the most startling hours of my life, reaching inside a cow and hauling a slick and very large—though dead—bull calf from his mother. Afterward, when I stood catching my breath, Chuck Shaw appeared in the doorway, saying, "I probably could have saved him, Peter, if you had waited." That set me to wondering about Chuck Shaw and led to the idea for this book.

My thanks to Dr. Virginia Prince, who read drafts of the manuscript and made many helpful comments, including about how veterinarians think. Two decades ago Ginny had experiences similar to Erika's, though in a time when there were far fewer women veterinarians, and Ginny has her own story to tell. I also thank Tracy Kidder for his comments on this book, given with his characteristic acute insight.

My thanks as well to the School of the Arts at Emerson College for providing assistance during the research of this book.

With pleasure I express my gratitude to my agent, Ike Williams, who gave his support immediately and enthusiastically. Thanks also to Hope Denekamp for her efforts, and to Alexis Rizzuto for hers.

I'm fortunate to have worked with a compatible and skilled editor, Becky Saletan. My thanks to Becky for her diligent work, and to Jonathan Galassi for his continued encouragement.

Thanks also to Isha Whynott and Elizabeth Whynott, both good listeners and readers. And to Kathy Olsen, whom I can't really thank adequately, other than to say that she was involved in every aspect, including visits to the clinic, where she had a special affinity for the cat named Hobbs.

I must thank Hobbs too, and the many other animals who inspired the days.